INTERNATIONAL STUDIES OF NATIONAL SPEECH EDUCATION SYSTEMS:

Volume I, Current Reports on Twelve Countries

Australia
Austria
Canada
Finland
Germany
Greece
Japan
Korea
Lebanon
New Zealand
Philippines
Sweden

Edited by

FRED CASMIR

L. S. HARMS

Published in cooperation with the
PACIFIC SPEECH ASSOCIATION

Burgess Publishing Company

426 South Sixth Street • Minneapolis, Minn. 55415

FOREWORD

I find this volume of great interest. It helped me to answer two challenging questions: "What has been happening in speech education?" and "What changes will shape the future study and teaching of speech-communication?"

If the reader is a teacher of speech he will find that reading this book will reinforce his "world view," his realization that speech education is a global enterprise and that what happens in any culture impinges significantly upon related projects in all other places. Truly, we are together in the crusade to help people solve their problems of spoken interaction. These essays treating speech-education systems of twelve countries make abundantly clear that modern mass media and jet travel have ended the era of isolated problems in education. We are all part of the main, and we are diminished by inept management of speech education wherever it occurs, just as we benefit from fruitful innovation, no matter how remote. Consequently, we can be thoughtful about "where we are" and "where we are going" only when we are informed about relevant events outside the boundaries of our immediate cultural milieu.

The study of others typically informs us about ourselves. The reader will find himself comparing practices abroad with those in his own and other familiar communities. In 1965, I made a "round-the-world" survey study of speech-communication between American businessmen overseas and the host nationals with whom they worked. I expected to discover critical cultural differences affecting their communication which would be exotic and unique to the remote places. The differences emerged, but instead of being indigenous, they resembled difficulties in communication in organizations scattered about Mainland, U.S.A. Other remote cultural patterns that generated communication problems differed from local domestic contrasts in degree rather than in kind. As a result, an unanticipated by-product of the overseas study was new insight into interpersonal business communication at home. Similarly, the directions and emphases of speech education in foreign countries relate meaningfully to change and lack of change elsewhere. Any teacher of speech is certain to experience *déjà vu* more than once as he reads the following descriptions of speech instruction abroad.

Summarizing the status quo of speech education outside the United States from a sampling of a dozen countries is risky business, but I think it can be done. I will venture some generalizations that seem to me to be relevant and representative. Then I will speculate concerning what appear to be the major forces causing change, and finally, I will attempt to predict some consequences of the impact of the agents of change upon the status quo, the probable new directions of speech education.

Characteristics of Speech Education Outside the U.S.A.

I will remind the reader that my generalizations are normative, and that such sweeping statements must not be expected to apply to the single, individual instance. Consequently, exceptions will not be hard to find.

The major conclusion concerning the nature of other-than-U.S.A. speech education is phrased succinctly in this quotation from one of the essays: "Speech is not a subject of detailed study in New Zealand." Where speech per se is taught, the teachers often do not admit teaching it. Instruction in spoken communication is interwoven with the teaching of other subjects, rather than being conducted separately. Hence, departments of speech or other academic units with improvement of speech as a central educational objective are rare. But, apparently increased attention is being given to the spoken dimension of more traditional subjects in the curriculum.

The speech taught outside the United States is predominantly linguistic and/or artistic. The popular label "the speech arts" is significant, as is the emphasis upon voice and diction. Goals of speech training tend to resemble those of elocution, with correctness and stylistic qualities topping the list of performance-oriented criteria. English as a second language is mixed up with the concept of speech around the world. Often "speech training" means direction and practice in the speaking of English as a foreign language. Stress on matters like pronunciation, intonation, and grammar tends to result in speech for display rather than speech as a functional tool of communication.

Two specialized varieties of speech education, namely vocationally oriented training in speaking for adults and school extracurricular speech activities, tend to outstrip speech taught in the curriculum. Again, both of these substantial efforts tend to focus upon the learning and speaking of English as an other-than-native language.

By and large, those engaged in instructing nonpathological speakers abroad have had minimal training in the teaching of speech.

Little public speaking is taught, and where found it tends to be associated with law and theology. Speech and hearing therapy is usually separate from other speech studies. Oral interpretation is a major part of the speech curriculum, by contrast. Theater seems to be fairly firmly connected to other training in speech, but in many places it has gone its own way, and, at least in the academic scene, it may be said to be in limbo. Nevertheless, a large share of speech education around the world is accomplished in theater-related activities.

The ways of speech education in the United States have had major influence in some countries, negligible influence in others. Where American methods have modified national practices, there is disturbing evidence that we are exporting a product not always suited to the recipient culture. Instead of developing something from the local values and customs that will meet local needs, we seem to be saying more often than not, "Do it the way we do in the United States." Japan, in particular, seems to be struggling in its effort to assimilate Western rhetorical theory. Modern communication theory, with its emphasis upon functional interaction, cannot be exported unchanged to a country with fundamentally different patterns of social interaction. Hence, the progress of other countries in adopting our models and theories of interpersonal and organizational speech-communication is slight.

To the extent that the above summary statements are valid, they can serve as a starting point to predict the future. Now let us inventory some current forces that opt for changes in speech education in the United States and in other countries of the world.

Forces for Change in Speech Education

The importance of speech as a method of getting things done is more generally recognized today than ever before. John Kenneth Galbraith, in a convocation address at the University of Minnesota in April, 1968, said, "It is only by a kind of face-to-face communication that one can retrieve and test information." Governmental, educational, and business organizations are relying upon the spoken word to an unprecedented extent. They are doing so in the belief that principles and techniques of eyeball-to-eyeball communication can be studied, analyzed, and consciously applied. They turn to education for guidance and help in accomplishing those objectives.

But the pressure of our organized groups is only one aspect of the public demand that forces expansion and refinement of training in speech. Effectiveness in a free society is now seen to be proportionate to how well one understands the process of speech-communication and how skillful one is in its use. Speech education thus becomes relevant to an on-going dynamic cultural context in both philosophical and utilitarian dimensions. Changing labels dramatize this evolution with their connotations: "Oral English" yielded to "speech," which now is being replaced by "speech-communication."

Speech-communication connotes interaction rather than display. "Task-oriented" speaking is an emerging concept, and social action has become the predominant objective of the speaker. Defining speaking as interaction forces us to conceptualize speech as an interdisciplinary discipline. Psycholinguistics, sociology, anthropology, political science, psychology, philosophy, literature, and a dozen other academic ventures are busily studying speech as social action. If our separate efforts are to be cumulative, we must cooperate with them. By coordinating the resources of academe, speech-communication may well attain the status of the dominant applied liberal art.

A final pressure and opportunity for speech education is the crisis of intercultural communication. Our inability to exchange ideas with contrasting ethnic groups at home and with representatives of foreign cultures is recognized as the cause of catastrophic misunderstandings. The need to improve intercultural speech-communication calls for substantial changes in all systems of speech education, with urgency.

The forces for change mentioned here might well have included internal needs to modify the long-established speech-education functions, e.g., rhetoric and public address, oral interpretation, drama, and broadcasting. However, these seem to be dependent upon the above-mentioned pressures from outside, and, as established functions, will be modified by them. Each of the traditional speech areas can contribute substantially to meeting society's needs, but only if it retains a flexible willingness to change with the times, and systematically collects feedback to aid in implementing change.

Directions of Global Speech Education

To me, the way of the future for speech education around the world is suggested in a recommendation from the essay on the Philippines: "The concept of speech as communication should be emphasized more in curriculum change and development." The authors of the essay on Japan make the same point when they criticize speech education there because it stresses "...the art of saying the appropriate thing at the appropriate time rather than the art of persuasion." Both observations imply the necessity of teaching speech as a means of effecting contemporary social action.

The values and customs of a society will be accepted as the frame of reference and the limits of speech education in that society. Ways of communicating with members of other cultures will become a significant part of speech education. Cultures will maintain the uniqueness of their communication patterns and procedures and teach respect for contrasting patterns of other groups.

The common ground that will link nations, races and ethnic groups is the understanding that the quality of human relations everywhere is a function of the ways people talk with one another. Humane considerations will triumph, in any culture, only when people are able to communicate accurately and to interact with openness and good will. Speech education can exert direct influence on the means by which human beings relate to other human beings more than can any other discipline. To be effective in preparing people to participate in humane formal and informal task-oriented interactions is the central responsibility of world-wide speech education.

January, 1970   *William S. Howell*
Minneapolis

CONTENTS

ix

INTERNATIONAL STUDIES
OF SPEECH EDUCATION:

AN INTRODUCTION

During the past several years, The Speech Association of America (SAA) has engaged in activities designed to broaden the outlook and deepen the understanding of its members regarding the international and intercultural aspects of the field.[1] Perhaps as many as 10 per cent of the 8,000 SAA members would today express a strong interest in some international and intercultural aspect of our field. Several milestones bear noting.

The 1968 New Orleans "Preservation Hall" Conference—jointly sponsored by the SAA and the U.S. Office of Education—has released a conference report: *Conceptual Frontiers in Speech-Communication.* Several of the recommendations contained in that report relate directly to international and intercultural matters. In particular, that report expresses concern with research and instruction on those speech-communication "problems that agitate our society at individual, community, national and international levels."[2]

In early 1968, SAA joined with The East-West Center, The Pacific Speech Association (PSA) and The Department of Speech-Communication at the University of Hawaii to host a conference in Honolulu on Speech-Communication and World Development.[3]

Most recently, the SAA has decided to devote its 1970 annual convention to the theme: Intercultural Speech-Communication, Domestic and International. The convention will be held at New Orleans. Plans are underway to encourage participation by persons from as many countries as possible.[4]

In August of 1968, The German Speech Association and SAA cosponsored at Heidelberg The First International Conference of the Speech-Communication Arts and Sciences.[5] This conference was followed by a second in Tokyo under the joint sponsorship of The Japan Speech Society, PSA and SAA.[6] It is hoped other joint conferences can be arranged in the future.

For several years, The Committee for Cooperation with Foreign Universities (CCFU) of SAA has been active in international speech education. Both editors are members of that Committee. In April, 1967, the Committee met in Memphis, Tennessee under SAA sponsorship to discuss its future course of action. Initial plans were sketched at that meeting for the present volume of *Studies* and were further developed by the editors later during additional meetings.

There are several reasons for publishing this volume. In the absence of easily available information, an individual scholar in any country may conclude that significant work in his field has not been undertaken in other countries. Only a relatively few scholars in the speech-communication field have established and maintained relationships with scholars in other countries. Of particular urgency at this time is the necessity of building the cooperative framework from which might evolve a soundly based approach to intercultural speech-communication.

These *Studies* provide a descriptive reference source for the reader which would help him to understand, first, the framework in which speech education in a particular country exists and, second, the specific programs that have been developed in that country. The names of individual scholars, the names of institutions and organizations, as well as the titles of some major publications provided in the following pages perhaps will make it easier for any scholar to take the important first steps to establish contact and to discover existing avenues and resources for future research projects or programs of international cooperation.

In recent years, a much greater feeling of interdependence and need for international cooperation has developed in many academic disciplines. Whether one speaks of a "global village" or considers the intricacies of "intercultural communication," whether one reads McLuhan or Toynbee, in many cases one discovers that Man is becoming more aware of his counterparts in the other countries of the world. For instance, our own historic relationship to England and its rhetorical and educational traditions has influenced the pattern of speech education developed in America. Until recently, it was relatively easy for an American to assume that his was the most logical, most "natural" approach. More than a few speech-communication scholars have been disturbed by the fact that scholars in other parts of the world organized the field differently. So, as new nations develop and old nations change, the speech-communication scholar should renew his understanding and expand it to meet the demands of a field with vital world-wide obligations.

Each nation has developed its own educational system in agreement with its own national goals and trends. In the pages of this volume, some clues will be found to the world-view of each country as a result of the place it has assigned to speech education. One may in this way begin to learn about the goals and trends of other nations and to learn about the influence such goals and trends have had and will come to have on intercultural speech-communication. From that base of national understanding, it would then seem possible to develop guidelines which could result in a mutually beneficial exchange concerning the nature and function of cross-national or intercultural speech-communication.

Speech-communication scholars will be much more likely to understand each other if they have adequate information about existing situations which both resemble and differ from their own. Scholars are invited to read the pages of this book to discover the important similarities and the potentially creative differences identified in the programs of speech education in the several countries. Whether or not we will be able to sufficiently project ourselves as scholars into existing situations different from our own without becoming ready converts to a new vogue of "internationalism" must yet be discovered. We feel fortunate to have found authors who are able to write authoritatively about speech education in a specific country. Undoubtedly, some prejudices and incorrect perceptions have found their way into this book. Where this has happened, we hope the reader will help to correct the record.

What the authors of the studies in this collection have done is to present an outline of the historical background and current status of the speech-communication arts and sciences in the twelve countries. In fairness to the authors it must be noted that they accepted assignments under demanding deadlines. As a result, hurried trips, long-distance calls, and air-mail special-delivery correspondence were necessary to meet those deadlines. On the other hand, most of the authors collected far more information than could reasonably be included in a chapter. It is hoped that these authors will be encouraged by others to undertake the full book-length studies that the nature of the material requires.

To the authors of the *Studies* in the present volume, the editors extend their warmest *Aloha* on behalf of themselves and their colleagues.

We must finally thank the Pacific Speech Association, its Board of Directors, and particularly Dr. Donald Klopf, editor of *Pacific Speech*, for making the publication of this volume possible.

December, 1969   *The Editors*
Los Angeles   *Fred Casmir*
Honolulu   *L.S. Harms*

FOOTNOTES

[1]Dr. William Work, Executive Secretary, Speech Association of America, Statler Hilton Hotel, New York, N.Y. 10001, U.S.A., has been instrumental in moving the Association toward a world-view of Speech-Communication.

[2]*Conceptual Frontiers in Speech-Communication,* ed. R. S. Kibler and L. Barker (New York: Speech Association of America, 1969), pp. 1-224.

[3]*Speech-Communication and World Development,* ed. H. E. Ellingsworth (Honolulu: Pacific Speech Association, 1970.)

[4]Dr. William S. Howell (author of the preface to this volume), Department of Speech-Communication, University of Minnesota, Minneapolis, Minnesota 55406, will plan the 1970 SAA Convention program.

[5]*Proceedings of the First International Conference of the Speech-Communication Arts and Sciences* at Heidelberg, Germany, ed. L. S. Harms (Honolulu: Department of Speech-Communication and Pacific Speech Association, 1969), pp. 1-110.

[6]*Proceedings* will be published.

DIRECTORY OF EUROPEAN
SPEECH-COMMUNICATION SCHOLARS

Prepared by
Fred Casmir

AUSTRIA

Frank, Friedrich (M.D., director of the voice, speech, and pedo-audiological department of the Ear, Nose, and Throat University Clinic); Ear, Nose, and Throat Clinic, University of Vienna, Spitalgasse 23, A 1090, Vienna 9, Austria; German, English.

Giese, Alexander Max (Ph.D., program director for the Third Program—Austrian radio); Wohllebengasse 10, Vienna, Austria; adult education, radio play, broadcast lectures; German, English.

Rossel-Majdan, Karl (Ph.D., also Dr. jur., Dr. rer. pol., head of department for broadcasting research, Oesterreichischer Rundfunk, GmbH, head of department for performing arts of the Wiener Kunstschule); 1070 Siebensterngasse 27, Vienna 7, Austria; sociology, rhetoric, problems of speech and creative speech formation; German, English.

Trojan, Felix (Ph.D., university professor and former director of the station for speech and voice disorders at the Ear, Nose, and Throat Clinic of the University of Vienna; president of the International Biophonetic Association); III Wassergasse 5, Vienna, Austria; vocal qualifiers, therapy of stuttering and voice disorders; German, English.

BELGIUM

Hermans, Hubert J. (program director of school broadcasts, Belgium Institute for Radio and Television); Ruggeveldlaan 651, Deurne (Antwerp), Belgium; television for schools, general problems of radio and television; English.

Wajskop, Max (Ph.D., director of the Institute of Phonetics at University of Bruxelles); A. Huysmans 78, Bruxelles 5, Belgium; experimental phonetics, general linguistics, language teaching; French, English.

BULGARIA

Minkov, Michael A. (chief—research department, Bulgarian radio and television); 6, Brest, Sofia, Bulgaria; information and political journalism in radio and television, character and structure of radio and television programs; English.

CZECHOSLOVAKIA

Hala, Bohuslav (Ph.D., doctor of science, professor); 16 Na Valech, Praha/ Prague, Czechoslovakia; phonetics, speech technique, oratory, recitation; French, English.

Romportl, Milan (Ph.D., associate professor of phonetics, Charles University, Prague); Hevlovska, Praha 6-Dejvice, CSSR/Czechoslovakia; phonetics and phonemics, linguistics, Slavic philology; German, English.

DENMARK

Abrahams, Henrik N. (Ph.D., director of a National Clinic for Speech Pathology in Aarhus, Denmark, lecturer of general phonetics in University of Aarhus); Statens Institut for Talelidende, Tjorneveg 6, Risskov, Denmark; phonetics, language disorders; English.

Arnholtz, Arthur (Ph.D., professor of rhetoric, recitation, and metrics; professor of University of Copenhagen); Jernbanevej 19, Lyngby (Ly. 1887), Denmark; recitation, drama, rhetoric; English.

Epstein, Abraham Gerson (M.A., speech pathologist, instructor at State Institute for the Handicapped of Speech at Aarhus); Tamperdalsvej 11, Aarhus, Jylland, Denmark; articulation testing, childhood aphasia, phonetics, language disorders; English.

FINLAND

Miettunen, Helge L. (Ph.D., head of programs); Sateenkaar, C13, Tapiola, Finland; mass communication, radio, television; English.

FRANCE

Faure, Georges M. (Ph.D., professor of phonetics); 181 rue Bretenil, Marseilles 6, France; phonetics, phonemics, speech correction; French, English.

Flacelie͂re, Robert (Dr., professor); la Sorbonne, rue de la Sorbonne, Paris 5c, France; rhetoric; French, English.

Fourgon, Fernard C. (honorary inspector of Institute for Deaf and Dumb Boys); 19, boulevard Taine, Annecy (Haute-Savoie), France; phonetics, teaching language to deaf and dumb; French.

Leon, Pierre R. (Ph.D., director of language laboratory, professor of phonetics); 30 rue Megevand Besancon, Doubs, France; phonetics, applied linguistics, language laboratory; French, English.

Tomatis, Alfred (Dr., director of the Centre du Language); 10, rue Lyautey, Paris 16, France; audio-psycho-phonology; laterality; re-education of hearing and language, integration of foreign languages; French.

GERMANY

Aderhold, Egon (lecturer at University, certified speech teacher); Esplanade 6, Berlin-Pankow, East Germany; speech education for actors, oral interpretation; German, English.

Dill, Richard (Dr., head Eurovision Office of ARD); Lamontstrasse 11, Munich 27, West Germany; mass media, language teaching by television, education and television; English.

Faber, Karl (Ph.D., university lecturer in speech education and lecturer in public speaking); Graf-Adolf-Str. 50, Schwerte (Ruhr), East Germany; public speaking, speech education, teaching German; German, English.

Fährmann, Rudolf (Ph.D., lecturer in speech); 74 Tübingen, Burgholzweg 74, Württemberg, West Germany; psychology and sociology of speech, voice and speech diagnostics; German, English.

Fiukowski, Heinz G. (university lecturer, head of Department of Speech of Leipzig University); Helgoländer Weg 9, Leipzig N 22, Leipzig, East Germany; German speech science, interpretation of poetry; German, English.

Fror, Kurt (Ph.D., professor of practical theology, pedagogics, and Christian education); Membacherweg 45, Erlangen, West Germany; homiletics, child psychology, Christian education; German, English.

Geissner, Hellmut K. (Ph.D., university lecturer in speech and speech-education, chief of the Seminary of Speech and Speech-education at University of Saarbrücken, chairman of German Association of Speech and Speech-education); Pfaffenkopfstrasse 20, Dudweiler, Saarland, West Germany; theory of speech, poetry reading, rhetoric; French, English.

Gunther, Rudolf (teaching appointment for speech education at the Studien-seminar Offenbach); Morfelder Ldstr. 198, 6 Frankfurt/Main, West Germany; public speaking, rhetoric; German, English.

Harth, Karl-Ludwig (Ph.D., director of speech science at Pädagogische Hoch-schule, Potsdam, university lecturer); Br. Burgestrasse 76, Potsdam–Babelsberg, West Germany; speech education, rhetoric, oral interpretation, speech correction; German, English.

Heese, Gerhard (Dr., professor); Bismarckstr. 2, Hannover, West Germany; phonetics, speech pathology; German, English.

Hoffe, Wilhelm Lucian (Ph.D., professor of German language and speech); Rheinlanddamm 203, Dortmund, West Germany; German speech, speech education, phonetics, rhetoric; German, English.

Kabel, Rainer (Ph.D., head of Science Department of Saarländischer Rundfunk, Saarbrücken, Postfach 1050); Zweibrücker Str. 20, 66 Saarbrücken 3, Saarland, West Germany; broadcasting law, cultural and science programs; German, English.

Kaumeyer, Barbara (actress and licensed speech teacher, teaching appointment at the Dolmetscher Institut of the University of Heidelberg); Wiesenbacher-strasse 98, 6903 Neckargemund/bei Heidelberg, West Germany; public speaking; German, English.

Kempkes, Wolfgang (assistant to the department head, Department of Compara-tive Education, University of Hamburg); 2081 Ellerbeck, Pinneberg, Muhlenau 3, West Germany; press, radio and television in education, audio-visual materials; English.

Kliem, Richard W. (Ph.D., lecturer); Albertus Magnus Akademie der Dominik-aner, 5301 Walberberg, West Germany; phonetics, rhetoric, homiletics; German, English.

Kuhlmann, Walter (Ph.D.); Buss-Strasse 7, Freiburg i. Br., Baden-Württemberg, West Germany; oral interpretation, voice training, speech correction; German, English.

Kurka, Eduard (Ph.D., university lecturer, director of Institute for Speech Education and Phonetic Collection of Martin Luther University); Klement-Gottwald-Str. 3 Halle/S., East Germany; phonetics, rhetoric, psychology of speech, speech correction; German, English.

Lange, Gerhard (Ph.D., university teacher for German language, University of Bonn; university teacher for speech on University of Cologne staff); Arndstr. 2, 53 Bonn, West Germany; German language and literature, speech education, theater; German, English.

Lerg, Winfried B. (Ph.D., teaching assistant); Domplatz 23, 44 Muenster/ Westfalia, West Germany; communication theory, research methods, history of radio and television; German, English.

Lockemann, Fritz (Ph.D., professor and lecturer in speech and German literature); Am Judensand 45, Mainz, Rheinland-Pfalz, West Germany; oral interpretation, science of literature, phonetics, rhetoric; German.

Lotzmann, Geert (Ph.D., licensed speech teacher, university lecturer in speech and speech education); Zur Forstquelle 3, Heidelberg-Boxberg, West Germany; German speech science, phonetics, oral interpretation, rhetoric, speech therapy; English.

Magnus, Uwe (Ph.D., teaching appointment for radio and television at the University of Hamburg, editor of the quarterly "Rundfunk und Fernsehen"); Heimhuderstrasse 21, Hamburg, West Germany; research in communication, press, radio, television; German, English.

Mangold, Max (Ph.D., university professor, University of the Saarland); Department of Philosophy, University of the Saarland, 66 Saarbrücken 15, West Germany; phonetics, phonemics, normative phonetics, ear training, transcription language; English.

Meingold, Gottfried (Ph.D.); Grosse Steinstrasse 19, Halle (Saale), East Germany; phonetics, logopedics, history of German speech; German, English.

Ross, Dieter (Ph.D., teaching appointment at the University of Hamburg); Heimhuderstrasse 21, Hamburg 13, West Germany; communication research, radio and television; German, English.

Schennemann, Klaus L. (radio editor); 20 Niersteinerstrasse, Frankfurt/Main, West Germany; mass media; English.

Schmid, Gerhard (teaching appointment at the Institute for Speech, University of Munich, in the area of speech correction); Genterstrasse 17, Munich 23, West Germany; German.

Schmidts, Ludwig (Ph.D., university professor, Abteilung für Erziehungswissenschaft, Justus-Liebig University); Nelkenweg 74, D 63 Giessen, West Germany; phonetics, audio-visual training and programming; German, French.

Schmidt-Linnemann, Rena (licensed speech teacher at the Teachers' Institute of Freiburg i.Br.); Beethovenstrasse 25, 78 Freiburg, West Germany; public speaking; German.

Schubert, Kaete (Ph.D., head of department of speech education); Schubertstrasse 7, Karl-Marx-Stadt, East Germany; speech defects of teachers, the voice of the teacher; German, English.

Schulz, Werner (Dipl.-Ing., teaching appointment at the Institute for Speech, University of Munich, in the area of the use of the microphone); Schraudolphstrasse 9, Munich 13, West Germany; German.

Stelzig, Helmut (Ph.D., director of Department of Speech Science, University of Greifswald); Goethe-Strasse 8, Greifswald, East Germany; German phonetics and phonology, public speaking, speech therapy; German, English.

Stötzer, Ursula (Ph.D., scientific collaborator); Zeppelinstrasse 38, Halle/Saale, East Germany; German pronunciation, history of rhetoric; German, English.

Straub, Erna (licensed speech teacher at the Teachers' Institute of Freiburg i.br.) Dreikönigstrasse 27, 78 Freiburg, West Germany; public speaking; German.

Trenschel, Walter (director of Department of Speech, university lecturer, University of Rostock); August-Bebel-Str. 43, East Germany; speech training and therapy, phonetics; German, English.

Ulbrich, Horst (Ph.D., lecturer for speech education, Humboldt University); Köpenicker Landstrasse 54, Berlin-Treptow, East Germany; speech education, phonetics, linguistics, logopedics; German.

von Essen, Otto (Ph.D., professor, director of phonetic laboratory); 3 Alsterglacis, Hamburg 36, West Germany; phonetics, linguistics, logopedics; German.

Wachtershäuser, Gabriele F. (licensed speech teacher); Keplerstr. 85, 69 Heidelberg, Baden Württemberg, West Germany; general speech, voice, diction, discussion; English.

Wangler, Hans-Heinrich (Ph.D., professor), Alsterglacis 3, 2 Hamburg 36, Hamburg, West Germany; phonetics, linguistics, speech education, speech psychology; German, English.

Weithase, Irmgard (Ph.D., university professor, director of the Institute for Speech at the Ludwig-Maximilians-University, Munich); Winzererstrasse 31, Munich 13, West Germany; history of the German spoken language, German and applied phonetics, German poetry and its development; German, English.

Winkler, Christian (professor doctor, lecturer in German speech); Zeppelinstr. 7, 355 Marburg/Lahn, West Germany; speech, speech education, speech science, psychology; German, English.

Wittsack, Walter (Ph.D., professor); Institut für Deutsche Sprechkunde der Universität Frankfurt/Main, Senkenberganlage 27, Frankfurt/Main, West Germany; speech education; German.

Wolf, Edith C. (speech lecturer); Bornhövedstr. 19, Schwerin, East Germany; speech training of actors; German, English.

Zehetmeier, Winfried J. (Ph.D., lecturer in speech, rhetoric, and public speaking); Sonnenblumenstrasse 1-8, Munich 55, West Germany; phonetics of German language, rhetoric; German, English.

GREECE

Carter, George (producer at Hellenic National Broadcasting Institute in Athens); Al. Manoutiou 9/18, Athens (603), Ambelokipi, Greece; production; Italian, English.

ITALY

Meriggi, Piero (Ph.D., professor of linguistics); Facolta, Lettere, University Pavia, Italy; phonetics as part of linguistics; German, English.

NETHERLANDS

Hofstede, Peter (Ph.D., head of the Studies and Research Department, Netherlands Radio and Television, lecturer, School of Journalism); 12 Couperusweg, Hilversum, Netherlands; sociology of broadcasting, pretesting of TV and radio programs; English.

Moolenaar-Bijl, Annie (speech pathologist and therapist, head of university department of logopedics); University Hospital, Groningen, Netherlands; cleft palate, retarded speech development, esophageal voice; English.

Rösener, Rudolf K.H. (Ph.D., lecturer at Groningen University); 100 Hora Siccamasingel, Groningen, Netherlands; phonetics, speech education, theater; German.

Schaafsma, Henk (director at Television Academy); Karel Doormanlaan, 205 Utrecht, Netherlands; educational, political, and cultural use of radio auditor; English.

Van den Berg, Janwillem (professor in medical physics, doctor in physics, director of Laboratory of Medical Physics); Bloemsingel 1, Groningen, Netherlands; physics of voice production, medical physics; English.

NORWAY

Jensen, Martin K. (Ph.D., university professor, University of Bergen, head of Department of Phonetics); HF-bygget, Nygard-shyden, Bergen, Norway; phonetics, speech therapy, language teaching; English.

Vanvik, Arne J. (Ph.D., university lecturer in phonetics, acting head of phonetics department); Phonetics Department, University of Oslo, Norway; phonetics; English.

POLAND

Sivert, Tadeusz (university professor, University of Warsaw, also Polish Institute of Arts, Theater Section); 6, Dantyszka, Warsaw, Poland; theory and history of the theater, history of drama; music problems in the theater; French, German.

Stopa, Roman (Ph.D., professor of linguistics and African languages); 52/36 Mogilska, Krakow, Poland; general linguistics, Indoeuropean languages, African languages, general phonetics; English.

PORTUGAL

Bivar, Antonio (head of External Relations Division); Rua do Salitre, 84 Lisboa, Portugal; radio-television; English.

SPAIN

de Aguilera, Joaquin G. (head instructor, Staff Training Department, Television Española, Madrid, Spain); Argensola, 17, Madrid 4, Spain; television direction, production, and educational television; Spanish, English.

Llosá, Vincente S. (head of Outside Broadcasting Division of T.V.E. and script writer); M. Concepcionistas 18, Madrid 6, Spain; direction, script-writing, management, outside broadcasting; Spanish, English.

SWEDEN

Hammarstrom, Goran (Ph.D., head of phonetic studies of the university); Fonetiska Institutionen, Thunbergsvagen 3, Uppsala, Sweden; general phonetics; French, English.

Hanson, Gote K. (Ph.D., associate professor of psychology); Tiundagatan 39, Uppsala, Sweden; phonetics, psychology, hearing disorders; English.

Karlgren, Hans A. (university lecturer); Styrmansg 17, Stockholm C, Sweden; computer methods in linguistics, research in speech; English.

Lindgren, Olle (leader of Internal Training Department of Swedish Broadcasting Corporation); Sveavagen 91, Stockholm, Sweden; communication, psychology, sociology; English.

Rende, Gundel (instructor of speech, part-time at Stockholm University, instructor of phonetics; also teacher's college); Gubbkarrsvagen 29-13, Bromma, Sweden; public speaking, public speaking in secondary schools, discussion; English.

Weiss, Mary (Ph.D., university teacher of phonetics); Tiundagatan 41, Uppsala, Sweden; phonetics, auditory training, speech and voice disorders; English.

Witting, Claes R. (Ph.D., associate professor, university lecturer); Murargat 26 D, Uppsala, Sweden; phonetics; English.

SWITZERLAND

Brunner, Rudolf (Ph.D., lecturer in phonetics at University of Zürich); 116, Seestrasse, 8706 Feldmeilen, Switzerland; general phonetics, phonetics of Swiss German dialects; German, English.

Frei, Guido (Ph.D., director of television for German Language Service, Switzerland; teacher in speech at University of Zürich); Lindenstrasse 6, 8125 Zollikerberg, Switzerland; sociological impact of television, educational programming; German, English.

von Eckardt, Milena (lecturer for speech); Marschalkenstrasse 725, Basel, Switzerland; drama, preaching, discussion; German, English.

UNITED KINGDOM

Brandt, George (senior lecturer in radio, film and television studies, Department of Drama, University of Bristol); 20 Park Row, Bristol 1, England; practical film making; sound recording techniques, film history, mass media; English.

Bruce, David J. (Ph.D., lecturer in psychology at Cambridge University, Department of Education); Department of Education, Cambridge University, 17 Brookside, Cambridge, England; speech perception, verbal classification, bilingualism, and linguistic behavior of children; English.

Hunt, Hugh (M.A., professor of drama); Department of Drama, University of Manchester, Oxford Road, Manchester 14, Lancs., England; drama; English.

Gordon, Neil (consultant neurologist to the Royal Manchester Children's Hospital and Booth Hall Children's Hospital, Manchester; honorary lecturer to the Department of Child Health, Manchester University); 15 Hill Top Avenue, Wilmslow, Cheshire, England; disorders of language development, epilepsy, metabolic disorders causing brain damage; English.

Wohl, Maud T. (speech pathologist, Southern General Hospital, Glasgow; lecturer in speech pathology, Jordanhill College of Education, Glasgow); 13 Neward Dr., Glasgow, S.I., Scotland; stammering, speech re-education; English.

YUGOSLAVIA

Guberina, Peter (Ph.D., university professor), Trg Zrtava fasizma 3, Zagreb, Yugoslavia; linguistics, experimental phonetics, audiology, teaching foreign languages; French, English.

Mitrovic, Melita (doctor, assistant of medical faculty); Savska cesta 3, Zagreb, Yugoslavia; stuttering, dysphonia, esophageal speech; French, English.

AUTHOR BIOGRAPHIES

DR. NOBLEZA ASUNCION-LANDE received her Ph.D. from Michigan State University and is presently serving as an assistant professor of speech-communication at the University of Kansas in Lawrence. Her experience includes teaching positions at the University of Hawaii, Yale University, the State University of New York at Paltz, Michigan State University, and the Peace Corps Training Center of San Jose State College in California. She has taught in the city high schools in Manila. Philippine linguistics and political communication in the Philippines have been among her major academic areas of interest.

DR. EUGENE BAHN is director of interpretative reading, Department of Speech, Wayne State University, Detroit, Michigan. He has been dean of Anatolia College in Thessaloniki, Greece, and has also served with the U.S. High Commission and the U.S. Department of State in Germany, where he was university advisor for the universities of Marburg and Giessen. He was chief theater officer for the U.S. Zone of Occupation after World War II. He has published numerous articles and is the author of *A History of Oral Interpretation* and coauthor of the *Communicative Act of Oral Interpretation* and *Literature for Listening.* Dr. Bahn received his Ph.D. from the University of Wisconsin.

HELEN E. BEHL has a B.A. degree from Heidelberg College, 1933. She was YWCA secretary in Tonawanda, New York from 1937 to 1941, and directed the USO in Montgomery, Alabama from 1942 to 1945.

DR. WILLIAM A. BEHL holds the Ph.D. from Northwestern University, Evanston, Illinois. He is currently professor of speech and deputy chairman for graduate studies at Brooklyn College of the University of the City of New York. He has written many articles concerning speech education in the Netherlands, Denmark, and East Germany for professional journals. His publications include a book, *Discussion and Debate.*

DR. JOHN CAMBUS received his Ph.D. degree in speech from Wayne State University. He is currently an associate professor of speech and drama at California State College in Hayward. He serves as coordinator for educational television at California State College, and has received a number of awards in the area of educational broadcasting. He has also served as vice president of the

Western Speech Association. He studied in Greece during 1958, while completing his dissertation dealing with the study of public address in that country.

DR. P. READ CAMPBELL is one of the foremost speech educators in Canada. She initiated and directs the only graduate speech education program in Canada. She is an associate professor, Faculty of Education, University of British Columbia, and serves as the chairman of the speech department. Dr. Campbell completed her doctoral work in speech at the University of Wisconsin. She serves as associate editor of the *Canadian Speech-Communication Journal.*

TAI SI CHUNG is executive secretary of the Korean Teachers Federation, numbering over 750,000 teachers, and Secretary-General of the Korean Federation of Education Associations. He has also served for several years as a member of the Executive Committee of the World Conference of Organizations of the Teaching Profession.

DR. JOHN COLLINS received his B.A. and M.A. (in English) at Akron University in 1957 and 1959, then took his Ph.D. in dramatic arts at the University of Iowa in 1963. He taught rhetoric and dramatic literature at Edinboro State College, Pennsylvania from 1963 to 1967, then moved to the American University of Beirut to become coordinator of the communication skills program.

WILLIAM JAMES CROCKER is currently head of the Department of English and Speech at Armidale Teachers' College, New South Wales, Australia. He received his B.A. degree from the University of Sydney, his M.A. from Pennsylvania State University, and the Litt. B. from New England College.

DR. NABIL DAJANI is a Palestinian citizen who was raised in Lebanon, where he received his B.A. and M.A. degrees in sociology at the American University of Beirut. He earned a doctorate in mass communication from the University of Iowa in 1968, and his fields of interest are communication theory and research and international communication. He is presently director of information and lecturer in journalism at the American University of Beirut.

DR. JOHN DEETHARDT, JR. received his Ph.D. degree from Northwestern University and is currently serving as an associate professor of speech and secondary education at Texas Technological University in Lubbock, Texas. Among his major areas of interest are German speech education, speech education, classical rhetoric, and public address. He has also taught in public schools on the secondary level.

DR. WILLIAM HOWELL, professor of speech-communication at the University of Minnesota, is an authority on persuasion and on conference methods. He directs graduate research and teaches courses in speech, persuasion, intercultural communication, and discussion. He serves as consultant on communication, conference methods, human relations, and public speaking. Dr. Howell is listed in *Who's Who in America.* In the spring and summer of 1965, Dr. Howell completed a round-the-world study trip, investigating cross-cultural communication problems encountered by American corporations with bases in foreign lands. In 1966, his research into intercultural communication in business and education placed teams of investigators in Tokyo, Beirut, and Bogota. He is vice president of the Speech Association of America.

MISS IRJA INNOLA has earned an M.A. degree from the University of Helsinki and an American M.A. in speech education from Northwestern University, where she studied in 1965-66 as a Fulbright student. Her degree is the first American degree in Finland in the field of speech. She is teaching Finnish and speech in the evening school of Tampere.

TAKEHIDE KAWASHIMA is associate professor of speech and English at Nihon University, and was lecturer in speech at Aoyama Gakuin University in 1955. He has studied at Los Angeles City College, University of California, Los Angeles, the University of Southern California, Columbia University, California State College at Long Beach, and University College, London. Several of his articles on speech, linguistics, and phonetics have been published in scholarly journals in Japan.

MRS. INKERI LAMPI is teaching speech at Helsingin Normaalilysea, a secondary school where student teachers are trained. In addition, she teaches at Ebeneser, a kindergarten-teacher college.

DR. ROBERT T. OLIVER is a research professor of international speech at Pennsylvania State University. Author of some thirty books in speech and history, including five books about Korea, he has devoted many years to becoming acquainted with Korea. His area of specialization is the psychology of persuasion, particularly as applied to intercultural and international relations. In 1964, Dr. Oliver served as president of the Speech Association of America, and in 1946, as president of the Speech Association of the Eastern States.

DR. WAYNE H. OXFORD is assistant professor of speech-communication at the University of Hawaii. The son of educational missionaries, he spent his first sixteen years in Japan. He has frequently returned to that country—his latest visit having been made during the summer of 1969. His doctoral dissertation is on the speeches of Fukuzawa Yukichi, the nineteenth century "father of speech education in Japan."

MISS CAROL S. RAMSEY received her B.A. in speech from California State College, Hayward, in June, 1968, while she was also enrolled in the University of

Uppsala in Sweden through the California State Colleges International Programs. She is pursuing graduate study in speech at California State College.

MISS LAHJA SALONEN has her M.A. degree from the University of Helsinki, and has graduated from the Finnish Speech Institute. Miss Salonen is teaching at the Teachers' Training College in Helsinki and temporarily at the Speech Institute.

DR. IRWIN R. SHAW received his doctorate in speech and speech pedagogy from Wayne State University. He is currently an assistant professor of speech in the Faculty of Education, The University of British Columbia, Canada. He serves as editor of the *Canadian Speech-Communication Journal.*

JOHN N. THOMSON is currently a teacher of speech and drama in Auckland, New Zealand. He has received his diploma in dramatic art from the University of London and his diploma of the Central School of Speech and Drama, London. He is founder member, fellow, and past president of the New Zealand Association of Teachers of Speech and Drama.

EDITOR BIOGRAPHIES

DR. FRED L. CASMIR received his Ph.D. from the Ohio State University. He has a number of publications in various areas of political speaking, mass communication, and radio-television, which have been published both in English and German. He is currently serving as an associate professor of speech at Pepperdine College in Los Angeles, California, and also serves on the part-time faculty of San Fernando Valley State College. He was coorganizer and director of the First International Conference in the Speech-Communication Arts and Sciences in Heidelberg, Germany during August of 1968, a cooperative effort of the Speech Association of America and the German Speech Association.

DR. L. S. HARMS received his Ph.D. from the Ohio State University. He has published a number of articles on social dialects, programed learning, and speech-communication systems. He worked on an international curriculum project at the University of Kansas, spent a year as a senior specialist at the East-West Center, and is currently associate professor of speech-communication at the University of Hawaii. He is chairman of the Committee for Cooperation with Foreign Universities of the Speech Association of America. He is author of *Phonetic Transcription: A Programed Introduction; Intercultural Speech-Communication Theory* (forthcoming), and with others, *A Speech-Communication Learning System.*

SPEECH EDUCATION IN AUSTRALIA

William J. Crocker

INTRODUCTION

Just 181 years ago, in 1788, the first European settlement in Australia was established at Sydney. Around this little town the colony of New South Wales was developed. Five other colonies were founded in different parts of the continent: Tasmania (1825), Western Australia (1829), South Australia (1836), Victoria (1839), and Queensland (1859). After 1855, these colonies achieved a great measure of independence. In 1901, they federated, becoming states in a new nation, the Commonwealth of Australia. The Commonwealth today has a population of approximately twelve million.

One of the functions specifically reserved to the states under the federal constitution was education. The federal government assumed responsibility for the sparsely settled Northern Territory and for Australian territories in New Guinea, but did not interfere in any way with the development of the state education systems. In 1942, however, under the stress of a critical wartime situation, the states gave up nearly all of their taxing powers to the Commonwealth. They are now largely dependent for revenue on disbursements from the federal government, which has shown an increasing tendency to influence educational policies. This "states' rights" issue is being fought fiercely at the present time.

Although each of the six states has developed its own education system there is considerable uniformity over the whole country. Schooling is compulsory for all children up to the age of either fifteen or sixteen, according to the state. Each state has a highly centralized system of primary and secondary schools which caters to about 75 per cent of the children. The remaining 25 per cent of the children are educated in private (predominantly Roman Catholic) schools which, however, must be inspected and certificated by the state education departments.

1

The primary school stage begins at age five or six and is generally seven years in length. Children then transfer to a secondary or high school, offering a five- or six-year course. Approximately 20 per cent of the children complete the high school course.

A number of different kinds of institutions offer tertiary education of various kinds. First in prestige are the universities, the only institutions with the power to confer academic degrees. Then there are the teachers colleges, most of which are controlled by the state departments of education, offering courses of three or four years duration. Recently the Commonwealth government has allocated substantial sums for the establishment of colleges of advanced education. The exact function of these colleges is yet to be determined, but they will offer such courses as liberal arts, business administration, education, librarianship, and forestry. There are also institutes of technology, technical colleges, and specialized institutions such as agricultural colleges and theological seminaries.

HISTORY OF SPEECH EDUCATION

It is helpful to an understanding of the present situation to examine briefly some of the influences on speech education in this country in the past. Certainly reference can be found to speech in the curriculum in the very early days of the colony. The *Sydney Monitor* for January 23, 1833, contains an advertisement for the "Australian College and Clari-montes Academy" (near Campbelltown) run by Mr. Hammond:

> III. The Classical Department comprising elementary tuition in the Latin and Greek languages, with daily expositions of the philosophy of speech. . .by the Rev. Henry Carmichael.

Then there is a report on "The State Sydney College, 1839" which includes this item:

> Our Elocution Lessons are taken from Enfield, Barker's Reader and some of my own selections, besides reading from the Bible on Monday and Saturday.

The principal concepts of speech education, however, were adopted from the United Kingdom at the end of the last century.

The Legacy from Britain

When compulsory education was introduced in Britain, speech training was given an important place in the work of the school.

Some children were actually unintelligible outside the small local area in which they lived. Many more children (the majority of the population, oddly enough) suffered social and economic handicaps for the lack of an "acceptable" manner of speaking. In order to minimize these disadvantages and to increase social mobility, teachers set out to modify the accent of their pupils. An artificial southern standard English accent was established by the speech experts and became the recognized goal of students' endeavors in most of England. More advanced work in speech was devoted to the mastery of the voice as a medium of artistic expression, which led to the almost invariable association of drama with speech training. Many teachers also taught their pupils to arrange material logically and to present it effectively in oral reports, debates, and so on. The dominant aim of speech activities in the school, however, was to inculcate "correct" pronunciation, inflection, and grammar.

Speech Training in Australia

Not only was this concept of speech training generally accepted in Australia, but the English standard of "correctness" came with it. In an address to the teachers' conference of December, 1926, S. H. Smith, then director of education in New South Wales, said:

> Why should there be any distinctive Australian speech? Why cannot we share with other parts of the British Empire a common language— pure and untainted by crudities of pronunciation?[1]

He went on to urge teachers to struggle to eradicate the Australian accent "by means of definite drill which, preceded by simple breathing exercises, should occur daily."[2]

Many teachers struggled conscientiously to have their pupils say *dānce* instead of *dance,* or *Saturdi* instead of *Saturday* because (even though the teachers themselves normally used the latter pronunciation) the former were regarded as correct. Children meticulously asked ridiculous questions of imaginary brown cows in the hope of modifying their production of the diphthong to that which was thought to be the pronunciation of the "best people" in England. The speech training lesson rarely had any relationship to the realities of life in Bendigo, Bondi, or Broome.

It is not surprising that speech training of this sort fell into disrepute and was largely neglected in our schools. Some private schools employed specialist teachers but speech was rarely taught in state secondary schools. Clive Sansom, who was until recently supervisor of speech in the Department of Education in Tasmania, summed up the position in 1958 thus:

> Until recently, Speech Education in Australia meant elocution and the preparation of concert items. These were usually left to the private teachers after school hours.
>
> Classroom education has been book-centred, a disproportionate amount of time being given to the written word.[3]

Mr. Sansom suggests that one of the main reasons for the scant attention to speech is the importance attached to preparation for public examinations in which oral expression played no part. He adds:

> The result is that the average Australian child spends most of his "English" time in reading and writing and the skills associated with them. His teachers, effectively trained to deal with these aspects of language, have seldom received training in the spoken language—either in the use of their own voices as teaching instruments, or in the oral development of their pupils. Consequently, speech activities have been neglected.[4]

After a visit to Australia in 1957, Dr. Robert T. Oliver, of the Pennsylvania State University, wrote an article which supports Sansom's judgment. Oliver says:

> The schools are dominated to a large extent by a tradition of external written examinations, which has the effect of placing emphasis primarily upon a rather narrow corpus of learning (chiefly literature, writing, arithmetic, history, etc.) which can be readily tested in written form.[5]

Oliver wrote that, where speech was taught in the schools,

> To too great an extent speech is being judged as "correct or incorrect" rather than as "effective or ineffective." This emphasis on correctness leads to overmuch formality and tends to inhibit rather than encourage free, full and communicative expression of ideas.[6]

Similar conclusions were drawn at the time by Dr. Alan L. McLeod of Lock Haven, Pennsylvania, who had had considerable experience as a teacher in Australia. He wrote that "speech implies voice and diction, declamation, choral speaking, and speech therapy." He added that, even in this limited sense, speech was seldom taught in the state secondary schools, and that "the feeling that speech and drama are still considered educational frills persists."[7]

The three writers cited accurately depicted the situation ten years ago. Most of the problems described then still persist. There have, however, been considerable changes in the last decade. A growing interest in speech education is clearly discernible. The departments of education in all the states have been making efforts to give the teaching of speech more emphasis, especially in the secondary schools. New attitudes toward speech education have emerged as a result of influences arising inside Australia and coming from abroad.

Toward Australian Speech Education

In the period since World War II, there has been an upsurge of national feeling in Australia. This sense of national identity is reflected in the considerable interest shown, at both the popular and scientific levels, in descriptions of the Australian form of English.[8] Attitudes toward speech education have been influenced by these studies of Australian English, especially by the work of Dr. A. G. Mitchell, vice-chancellor of Macquarie University. It is worth considering his contribution in some detail.

When, on the advice of its own Inspectors' Institute, the New South Wales Department of Education established a Standing Advisory Speech Committee in 1949, Dr. Mitchell became the first chairman. Through this committee, but more widely through his books, articles, and radio talks, Mitchell had tremendous influence on Australian teachers of speech. He argued against the practice of training children to conform to a standard of "correctness" in speech. He wrote:

> We must accept variety of speech as we must accept the human variety it reflects. A great deal of speech education in Australia has been rendered ineffective by the myth of a standard pronunciation, and by the conviction that there is something inherently distorted, unclear and unmusical about Australian speech.[9]

Elsewhere, Mitchell stated that, though some school pupils may wish to modify their accent for social or vocational purposes "and should be helped to do so," normally

> it is sufficient if his (the student's) speech is clear, pleasant, free from mispronunciations, and appropriate to the occasion and the setting. He is not to be required to rise to the higher ranges of artistic expression through his speech. The artistic is the highest level and every teacher will always have pupils who wish to attain proficiency in it and have aptitude for it. Every pupil should, perhaps, have some acquaintance with the art of speech so that he may become a good listener even if he never becomes a practitioner.[10]

Mitchell's attitude toward speech education was succinctly stated (and most widely distributed) in an article in *The Australian Women's Weekly*. He is quoted as saying:

> I feel that if teachers can eliminate the crudities and errors of speech, can give children even a little appreciation of the aesthetic values of drama and poetry, can encourage children to be articulate human beings who can speak clearly, effectively and pleasantly, then they will give them what I regard as a good speech education.[11]

Mitchell dealt a mortal blow to the already discredited procedure of slavishly imitating southern standard English. But he unintentionally established another "standard" in its place. In his book, *The Pronunciation of English in Australia*, he distinguished two types of Australian pronunciation which he named educated Australian and broad Australian. Mitchell was describing Australian speech as he found it. Many teachers, however, adopted educated Australian as the new standard of correctness which, as even the brief quotations cited above illustrate, was not Mitchell's intention.

Shortly before his resignation from the Chair of English in the University of Sydney, Professor Mitchell, with Professor Arthur Delbridge, completed a new survey of Australian speech. This study reaffirms Mitchell's opinions, and those of other phoneticians, that there is "no reason, at the phonological level, for speaking of dialects in Australian English."[12] The authors, however, did distinguish three linguistic communities—those speaking broad Australian (about 34 per cent of the total population), those speaking general Australian (about 55 per cent), and those speaking cultivated Australian (about 11 per cent). They warned that "these communities are more apparent than real, since they have no geographical or even cultural boundaries firmly drawn, and members of all three might be found in the same city or town, the same school, the same family."[13] It seems likely that the publication of this report will further weaken the belief that accent modification is the primary aim of speech education.

The old belief is still expressed, however. For example, Mr. J. Brunton Gibb, a well-known speech teacher and examiner, told a Sydney Rotary Club meeting in 1966:

> The Australian accent is a product of laziness. . . .Australians fail to use their mouth, lips, jaw and tongue correctly in pronunciation. . . .I am a bit ashamed of the Australian accent.[14]

Ideas from Abroad

The point of view presented by Mitchell and advocated by others at the same time has gained widespread acceptance among Australian teachers of speech. Attitudes have also been influenced by somewhat different ideas coming from abroad, chiefly from the United States.

In 1957, Dr. Robert T. Oliver was invited by the Commonwealth Office of Education and the directors-general of education in five of the states to visit Australia as a consultant in speech. On this tour Oliver urged Australian teachers to be less concerned with eliminating errors of speech and more interested in helping their pupils to develop skills which would increase their effectiveness in any speaking situation. He pointed out that an understanding of the functions, processes, and effects of oral communication can help an individual to become a more effective speaker and a more critical and discriminating listener. He also stressed the ethical responsibilities associated with speech. Partly as a result of the interest aroused by Oliver's visit, more American speech texts began to be read.

Some of the ideas presented by Dr. Oliver had been put forward in England also. M. M. Lewis, for example, had urged that teachers should be concerned to help children to develop what he calls "the manipulative functions of language,"[15] that is, the ability to use language to elicit a desired social response. The Norwood Committee pointed out that "it happens too often that little stress is laid upon oral expression as a means of developing ease in social relationships."[16] More recently writers such as J. L. M. Trim[17] and Andrew Wilkinson[18] have presented a much broader concept of speech education than the traditional English or Australian one. Their ideas have not gone unnoticed in Australia.

SPEECH EDUCATION TODAY

The ferment of ideas about the responsibility of the schools for developing the speech competence of their pupils has aroused interest in speech education among teachers and administrators throughout Australia. Many inspectors of schools and principals are now supporting the teaching of speaking and listening with an enthusiasm which was rare ten years ago. Although budgets for the encouragement of speech work in the schools are still very small, departments of education are spending far more in this way now than ever before.

From among the many opinions expressed about the objectives of speech education it is possible to distinguish three major points of view.

1. Speech education should help students to acquire a cultivated Australian accent because of its social, economic and aesthetic advantages. Students should develop control of the vocal mechanism and of physical delivery so that they may be able to achieve an artistic standard of oral expression. This point of view might be called the art-of-speech approach.

2. Speech education should help students to speak confidently, clearly, and pleasantly. It should eliminate crudities and errors from speech without necessarily modifying accent. It should develop an appreciation for the speech arts. This attitude generally produces a technique-centered approach.

3. Speech education should help students to master the principles and methods of effective oral communication so that they become more skillful in eliciting a desired response and more critical and discriminating in listening. This point of view regards speech as an expression of the total personality. It is, by and large, a process-centered approach.

There is, of course, a good deal of overlapping among these attitudes. They seem, however, to represent real differences in kind rather than in degree of emphasis. Many members of the general community tend to think of speech education as implying an art-of-speech approach because this is the traditional one. Unfortunately, this approach is still sometimes associated with the elocutionary extremism of a few teachers. Support for it has declined in educational circles. The second viewpoint now has by far the widest acceptance in Australia, especially in the state schools. The third attitude seems to be gaining more support. Each of these points of view has its supporters in all the various groups of speech teachers— those in the schools, those in private practice, and those teaching at the tertiary level.

In the Schools

It is difficult to present briefly an accurate account of speech education in Australian schools. Conditions vary from state to state and from school to school. One interesting variation is in the name given to that section of the curriculum which covers speech. These names include oral English, spoken English, the speaking of English, oral composition, and art of speech, as well as speech education. It is possible, however, to make some reasonably accurate generalizations about the present situation.

The most consistent attention is given to the teaching of speech in the early years of the elementary school. Special attention is usually given at this level to pupils' articulation, voice production, and rhythm of speech. Increasingly a wide diversity of speech activities is being included in the language arts programs. These activities include discussions, reports, story telling, oral reading, verse speaking, drama and, with new emphasis, listening.

Generally speaking, the further a child progresses through the school, the less attention his speech receives. Although syllabuses have usually contained some reference to the responsibilities of English teachers for the speech development of their pupils, these responsibilities have been widely neglected in the past. Most state secondary schools, however, have encouraged debate and drama as extracurricular activities. Debating competitions for high schools are conducted annually in all the major cities and in many smaller centers. Some sort of annual presentation of plays is a feature of most high school calendars. These activities may be directed by teachers from any department of a school (though usually from the English department) and do not carry any extra compensation for the teacher, either in money or in reduction of teaching load. In schools where there is a keen and able teacher, these extracurricular activities provide valuable experience for the small number of talented pupils who participate in them.

Speech activities are given more prominence in non-state schools than in state schools. Most of the independent schools offer courses in the art of speech, usually as an extra for which an additional fee is charged. These courses are generally taught by private teachers of speech who come into the school for one or two days a week. In some independent schools a specialist teacher of speech is a full-time member of the staff.

Although art-of-speech courses have been offered in private schools, and extracurricular speech activities have existed in both state and private schools since their inception, it is apparent that speech education is now being given a more important place than ever before in the secondary-school curriculum. It has now become an important strand in the English syllabus for virtually all pupils. Many schools set aside one period a week specifically for speech work for everyone. In some states high schools offer optional courses in speech. From 1969 it will be assessed in some way for the public examinations in all states under a variety of titles. It is a comment on education in Australia that teachers of speech should consider recognition in the public examinations of such importance to the status of their subject.

Special advisers are employed by the departments of education in all the states except South Australia to foster the teaching of speech. In Tasmania (the smallest of the Australian states, with a population of only 350,000) an excellent speech education center was founded by Clive Sansom. A speech education program for schools conducted by Sansom is presented on national radio by the Australian Broadcasting Commission. The present supervisor, Miss A. K. Caughly (Speech Education Centre, 73 Brisbane Street, Hobart, Tasmania 7000) coordinates the work of about fourteen specialist teachers of speech, acting as advisers. In the other states, however, the supervisors face their tremendous tasks with dishearteningly small resources. In New South Wales, for example, Mr. Dan Dempsey (Department of Education, Box 33, G.P.O., Sydney, New South Wales 2001) makes a Herculean attempt, with the aid of one colleague, to provide an advisory service for all the schools serving a population of 4,500,000 people.

In a few private schools the art-of-speech approach described above still persists. Overwhelmingly, however, Australian schools have adopted a technique-centered approach. New South Wales, which has recently introduced new syllabuses in both primary and secondary schools, may be taken as an example.

In 1962, a new six-year curriculum was introduced into New South Wales secondary schools. The previous English syllabus had given a brief paragraph to "Oral Composition." The new one made "The Speaking of English" the first of a five-part division of the syllabus. This was certainly a major change of emphasis. It is stated that "the aim of speech education is effective communication." There is no attempt to define effective communication, but it is described in this way:

> Effectiveness is a compound of many things; of having something to say, of willingness to speak, of clarity, ease, pleasantness, fluency and sincerity.[19]

The 1967 syllabus for primary schools also gave much greater prominence than earlier syllabuses to speech education, this time under the title of "Spoken English." The aim is expressed thus:

The general aim of the Spoken English program is the development of the child's powers of effective oral communication. It is concerned with the child's ability to make his sounds clearly, correctly and pleasantly and with his ability to give variety and interest to what he says by the appropriate use of pitch, rate, stress and phrasing.[20]

Encouraging progress has been made recently throughout Australia in the treatment of speech defects. Well-qualified speech therapists are now being trained in small but increasing numbers at the Universities of Queensland, Sydney, and Melbourne. These students are attached during training to faculties of medicine. On graduation most accept employment with a state department of health and work in para-medical clinics. Some therapists visit the schools. In Victoria (Miss Doris Irwin, Supervisor of Music and Speech, 224 Queensberry Street, Carlton, Victoria 3053) and Western Australia (Mr. John Bottomley, Senior Advisory Teacher of Speech and Drama, c/o Department of Education, Perth, Western Australia 6000), there are specially trained teachers working as speech correctionists who refer serious cases to speech therapy clinics.

Private Teachers of Speech

There are probably several thousand teachers of speech in private practice throughout Australia. They work with individual students and small groups and offer courses in oral interpretation, public speaking, theater, radio and television, and English as a foreign language. Many are employed as part-time teachers in private schools where their chief concern is to help their pupils to improve voice and diction, to develop poise and self-confidence, and to develop socially acceptable pronunciations. The most frequently employed activities are articulation drills, recitations, and drama.

Many of the pupils of the private teachers present themselves to the Australian Music Examinations Board for examination in speech and drama. (Mr. Robert Jacques, Federal Secretary, University Conservatorium of Music, Parkville, Victoria 3052.) Others may be examined by Trinity College, London. Each of these bodies appoints itinerant examiners and awards certificates through a series of grades leading to a diploma. Candidates submit themselves for both practical and theoretical examinations. The diploma examination of the AMEB consists of the recitation of a poem, a solo dramatic performance, an interpretative reading (usually of prose), and oral questions on interpretation. Candidates "must demonstrate their ability to use correct pronunciation as consistently in answering oral questions as in their prepared performance." The written test is made up of questions on the physiology of voice, phonetics, and set literary texts. The requirements of Trinity are similar. In 1967, however, Trinity College offered an alternative to its examinations in speech and drama. The new *Effective Speaking Syllabus* "has been designed to meet the needs of all—whether children or adults—who want to express themselves clearly and articulately in ordinary day to day situations."[21] This syllabus gives less emphasis to oral interpretation and is mainly concerned with public speaking.

No qualification or registration is necessary for a private teacher of speech. Anyone may put a brass plate on the door and charge what the traffic will allow. In several of the states, however, there are associations which are trying to raise standards and to provide some sort of registration.

One of the oldest of these organizations is the Speech Teachers' Association of Queensland, which at present has about one hundred dues-paying members, mostly in Brisbane. The objects of this association are (1) to promote and encourage the cultivation of spoken English; (2) to unite in closer relationship all those who are engaged professionally in teaching the art of speech and all those who are interested in and working for the advancement of spoken English. Members of the Association meet monthly, March through November. Meetings usually consist of ten minutes of poetry reading from two members, followed by a paper from a guest speaker. The members present an annual poetry recital, profits going toward two prizes awarded to students gaining top marks in the annual speech examinations. Leaders of the association include Miss Marcia McCallum (447 Logan Road, Stone's Corner, Queensland 4120), Miss Therese D'Arcy (Gowrie House, Wickham Tce., Queensland 4000), and Miss Rhoda Felgate (85 O'Connell Street, Kangaroo Point, Queensland 4169).

The Speech Association of New South Wales is an active organization with nearly 150 members. Its stated aims are almost identical with those of the Queensland Association. Members meet bi-monthly for talks ("Method Acting," "Throat Disorders," "Auditory Aspects of James Joyce," "Australian Bush Ballads," etc.) and discussion. A register of qualified teachers of speech is kept, qualification being granted for possession of a speech diploma or for evidence of successful teaching experience. A scale of minimum fees has been accepted by the members. A small journal, *The Voice,* is issued three times a year. The president is Noel Cislowski (Department of Education, Box 33 G.P.O., Sydney 2001).

The Victorian Speech Association, founded in 1940, also meets bi-monthly and has up to fifty people at its meetings. The members present an annual Shakespeare Festival and other recitals. The secretary is Mrs. Daphne Powell (41 Warnes Rd., Mitcham, Victoria 3132). There is also a Victorian Drama Association with particular interests in fostering the teaching of theater. Its secretary is Mrs. Loys Caudwell (46 Bundy St., Mentone, Victoria 3194).

The Tasmanian Association of Teachers of Speech and Drama was founded in 1964. It is a small organization with branches in Hobart and Launceston. It publishes an occasional newsletter. The founder and mentor is Mr. Clive Sansom (31 Gordon Avenue, Lenah Valley, Tasmania 7008).

The Western Australian Speech Association seems to have been dormant for some time, in spite of the efforts of the secretary, Mrs. Anita Le Tessier ("San Marie," Hall Road, Rolystone, W.A. 6111).

There is no speech association in South Australia. The doyen of speech teachers there, however, is Mr. A. Musgrave Horner, of the Adelaide Teachers College.

Although the suggestion has been made from time to time, especially following the important UNESCO Conference on Drama in Education held in Sydney in 1958, no serious attempt has been made to form a national association of private teachers of speech. There is, in fact, little contact between the state associations. However, this is an interesting possibility for the future.

Speech in Tertiary Education

In Australian universities, until recently, the only courses usually associated with the field of speech were phonetics, in departments of English, and speech therapy, in some association with faculties of medicine. Now the University of New South Wales is offering a diploma in human communications, under the direction of Professor Broadbent. Candidates for the diploma must be university graduates and must successfully follow the prescribed two-year curriculum. Courses to be taken are:

1. Linguistics and Written and Spoken Communication
2. Basic Information Theory I and II. (Measurement of information flow. Capacity of a channel. Bandwidth and power considerations. Statistical descriptions of signals and noise. Feedback in the human nervous system. Redundancy, etc.)

3. Sound and Light. (Acoustics. Signal Fidelity. Geometric optics of film and TV, etc.)
4. Communication Body Organs. (Organs of sight, speech, hearing. Neurology and illusion, etc.)
5. Presentation of Information. (Displays. Radio, TV and film.)
6. The Person as a Transmitter and Receiver. (The process of communication. Motivation. Role. Persuasion, etc.)
7. Audio and Video Equipment.

Some of the material taught in this diploma course also would be found scattered through various departments (especially engineering) in other universities and institutes of technology. The presentation would be theoretical rather than practical.

Some universities (for example, the Australian National University at Canberra, the Faculty of Engineering in the University of Sydney, the Faculty of Agricultural Economics in the University of New England) have recently experimented with courses to help students improve their skills of speaking and writing. These have been noncredit "service" courses, taught by instructors who are not members of the faculty. The courses sometimes have been absurdly short in duration. Though there seems to be general agreement that university students need to develop their skills of communication, the kinds of tentative courses so far offered have not been highly regarded by either faculty or students.

In 1958, the University of New South Wales pioneered theater in Australian universities by sponsoring the National Institute of Dramatic Art on its campus. The purpose of the Institute is to provide training for professional actors and directors in a two-year diploma course. A third year advanced course is available for students who hold the diploma and have had some professional experience. In 1963, the University established a Department of Drama and expanded it to a full school in 1966. The school now offers courses leading to the B.A., M.A., and Ph.D. in theater. These courses are concerned with the critical and historical evaluation of the theater arts and are quite distinct from the vocational training offered by the Institute.

The University of New South Wales fosters drama in various ways. In 1966, thirteen professional productions, involving fifty-seven professional actors, were presented and several of these toured country districts. In addition, twenty-five student productions were mounted, mostly from the 243 students enrolled either in the School of Drama (Professor Robert Quentin, head) or in the Institute (Mr. Tom Brown, director).

Last year, Flinders University in South Australia commenced courses in its new Department of Drama under the guidance of Professor Wal Cherry. Other universities are known to be considering the matter.

Although the universities generally eschew the teaching of communication skills, the various professional schools are increasingly recognizing the value of developing the speech competence of their students. Theological seminaries, of course, have usually offered some work in homiletics. Now, military, naval, and business colleges are giving some attention to public speaking and discussion. The new colleges of advanced education will probably consider similar courses when designing their curricula, but this remains to be seen.

Various adult education organizations such as university extension departments, the Workers' Educational Association, and technical colleges in some states offer courses in public speaking and drama. The growth of interest in public speaking is shown by the rising number of Toastmaster, Rostrum, Penguin, and similar clubs. Amateur dramatic societies are found throughout Australia, and there are a large number of school and community play festivals.

All Australian teachers' colleges offer students some work in speech, usually through departments of English. These are sometimes taught by lecturers in English who have no special qualifications in speech. Courses are chiefly concerned with helping students to improve their own voice and diction or with methods of teaching speech in the elementary school. An increasing number of colleges are now offering the sort of basic speech course which is characteristic of so many American colleges. In some colleges the basic speech course is being absorbed into a wider skills of communication course. Most Australian colleges offer elective courses in drama and a few, e.g., Claremont and Graylands, also have optional courses in speech correction. At Adelaide Teachers College students may now major in speech and drama in their four-year course and so qualify as specialists.

Not only has Adelaide Teachers College produced the first speech major in Australia but its staff has also been responsible for the foundation of the first national speech association. This is the Australian Speech Lecturers' Association, founded in 1968. Membership is restricted to "lecturers specializing in the field of oral English in teacher education." Approximately eighty people throughout Australia are eligible for membership and of these more than sixty, representing all states, have now paid their first subscription. The first two issues of a journal, which is scheduled to appear three times a year, have now been distributed. The first convention is planned for 1969. The foundation secretary of this association is Mr. Max Wearing (Adelaide Teachers College, Kintore Avenue, Adelaide, S.A. 5000).

TRENDS FOR THE FUTURE

The formation of the Speech Lecturers' Association by Max Wearing and his colleagues could have a profound effect on speech education in Australia. It draws together a body of college teachers who are working under a variety of titles but who feel they have a strong community of interest and a special identity. The enthusiastic support for the new society is an indication of interest. It is significant that the first two issues of the *Journal* have been absorbed with defining and naming the field. The conflict is epitomized in Geoffrey Pullan's article "Oral Communication vs. Speech Training—A Title Fight." He says:

> To use the term "oral communication" instead of "speech training" may, to some specialists even, seem insignificant. To me it is of paramount importance. If we perpetuate the titles "speech education," "speech lessons," or "voice and speech" we are giving strength to the argument that speech is a frill. We are suggesting in our titles that the students' habits are our primary concern and not their communicational abilities.[22]

Not all lecturers would agree with Pullan, but there seems to be a trend toward his point of view.

Interest in speech education is high not only among lecturers in teachers' colleges but in the community as a whole. This is shown by the frequent references to the subject in the press. For example, the Governor-General, Lord Casey, in a speech opening the annual conference of the Australian Science Teachers' Association in Melbourne (Spetember 2, 1968), said it was a peculiar fault in Australia's young people not to be able to express themselves clearly in speech. "If we go on as at present," he said, "it seems to me we will end up as a nation of mumblers who will not open their mouths enough to be comprehensible."

The Governor-General's remarks brought a spate of letters to newspapers all around Australia. The most prevalent opinion was summed up in a leading article in the influential *Sydney Morning Herald* in this way:

It is time parents and teachers had their attention drawn to the need to train children in the elementary arts of communication. We say "elementary" because the days of elocution or aping English accents have passed and today the aim is effective speech which communicates clearly with the listener.[23]

The article goes on to commend the increased emphasis given to speech education in recent school syllabuses.

The current interest in speech is also seen in the increasing popularity of clubs devoted to speaking and debating in such organizations as Apexians, Lions, Junior Chamber of Commerce, YMCA, Young Liberals Club, Junior Farmers, and many others.

The present climate of opinion in Australia, therefore, seems to be very favorable for the development of speech education. Some omens concerning the direction of this development are discernible in each of the areas into which the speech profession has been arbitrarily divided in this chapter.

In the Schools

The term "effective oral communication" seems to be accepted everywhere as the aim of speech education. In a few private schools, as was pointed out above, this implies art-of-speech lessons. In the majority of schools, however, a technique-centered approach is adopted, as previously described.[24] It is gradually being realized, however, that speech is an expression of the total personality. Speech education is an expression of the total personality. Speech education is now viewed by many in a wider context than previously. Some teachers are helping their pupils to master the principles of communication in order to become more skillful in eliciting a desired response and more discriminating in listening. This rediscovery of the ancient art "of discovering in each particular case what are the available means of persuasion" seems to indicate the future direction of speech education in Australian schools. It will be a long time, however, before most teachers cease to regard voice, diction, and the elimination of errors as the primary considerations.

Whatever point of view prevails, the future of speech education in Australia is beset by a lack of trained teachers. The recent introduction of the speech and drama major at Adelaide Teachers College may alleviate the problem slightly. In some states, however, official policy is against the employment of specialist speech teachers even if they were available. The responsibility has fallen, and must continue to fall, on the general primary teacher or, in the secondary school, on the English teacher. In most cases their preparation for the task is quite inadequate.

Associations of English teachers and experts in English education in many parts of the world have pointed out that "it is obvious that no teacher can hope to handle even the general aspects of a broad program in the language arts without specific training in speech."[25] In New South Wales, however, most students preparing to teach secondary English have about twelve hours of speech work in their three- or four-year course. This work is usually done in large groups and is mainly aimed at helping the students to make better use of their own voices. A substantial percentage of students have less than twelve hours or no speech work at all.

There are at least two other aspects of speech education in our schools which require urgent attention. The first of these is the provision of some help for the huge number of children for whom English is a second language. After twenty years of an intensive imigration policy, the first tentative steps have just been taken in two states to provide some specialized teaching for these children. The second urgent need is for the provision of more speech therapists. There is great demand for the services of therapists all over the country but the supply of qualified people remains a trickle.

Private Teachers

The future looks quite bright for competent speech teachers in private practice in Australia. The present interest in debating and in amateur theater seems likely to continue. The numbers of adults who wish to modify their accent or who want instruction in public speaking is steadily increasing. A growing number of migrants to Australia are seeking help from private teachers in learning English. A relatively new but promising type of client is the business organization which sponsors courses in speech for its staff.

The trend seems likely to be toward greater specialization among private teachers. As A. Musgrave Horner wrote recently:

> That individual practitioners should claim professional specialization in both speech and drama is unrealistic. Development to a really specialist level in one can only be achieved to the detriment of the other. The corollary of this is that in "Speech and Drama" we have not yet impressively established ourselves in Oral Communication, while much that we do in Theatre is amateurish.[26]

In the eastern states, at least, the growing strength of the speech associations augurs well for the raising of professional standards and for the discouragement of unqualified practitioners who have sometimes given the profession a bad name in the past.

Tertiary Education

Speech therapy and theater have achieved the mark of academic respectability in Australia by being taught as university courses. Speech therapy is at present a diploma course only, but it seems likely to achieve full degree status in the near future. Fields related to speech, such as phonetics, psycholinguistics, and communications engineering will receive increasing attention in Australian universities. Degree courses in speech of the kind offered in the United States and elsewhere seem very unlikely in the unforeseeable future. The proposed colleges of advanced education, however, present new and unexplored fields.

The teachers' colleges will continue in their present role of synthesizing research done in various fields by universities here and overseas and relating it, with their own research, to the needs of children. Most colleges remain technique-centered and conservative. Two different trends, however, are becoming apparent in the teaching of speech in the more progressive teachers' colleges. In the first, those colleges with separate departments of speech are tending to offer specialized courses such as acting, public speaking, oral interpretation, and physiology and neurology of speech. On the other hand, some colleges which have offered speech courses through departments of English have begun to integrate courses. They are replacing speech with courses such as skills of communication, which aim to teach reading, writing, speaking, and listening. Both trends seem likely to continue to influence those colleges which at present offer only some sort of basic course in speech for all students. Optional courses in theatre or speech correction will continue to be taught as at present.

The role of the speech specialist in the teachers' colleges is already being debated by the Speech Lecturers' Association. It will be the main concern of the first convention next year. If the Association which Wearing and his colleagues have founded can grow in strength and vigor it will have a profound influence on all aspects of speech education in Australia.

CONCLUSION

Speech has always been recognized as a particular aspect of education in Australia. From the beginning of the century until World War II, the chief concern of speech training was to inculcate a standard correct accent. During the 1950s there was a revolution which made "effective oral communication" the aim of speech education. There is still no unanimity about the general approach which teachers should adopt in helping their students to communicate more effectively. Some teachers see their role as confined to improving voice, diction, pronunciation, and interpretation. The majority seek to eliminate crudities and errors of pronunciation and grammar and to teach a wide variety of useful speech techniques. A few teachers try to give their students an insight into the process of communication and to help them to apply this insight to their own individual needs.

The 1958 UNESCO seminar on drama in education did a good deal to give the Australian speech profession a sense of national identity. The growth of state associations and of a national speech association will enhance this identity. This movement is already producing discussion and some research about aims and methods.

There are other promising signs for the speech profession in Australia. There are now tertiary courses leading to specialist qualifications in speech, speech therapy, and theater. There is a small but growing number of teachers with qualifications earned in the United States or England. Some local textbooks have been produced. Above all, there is a growing recognition, among educationists and the general public, of the value of speech education.

The speech profession in Australia is growing in strength and prestige. Its future role, and even its future name, is a matter of fascinating speculation.

FOOTNOTES

[1] New South Wales Department of Education, *Education Gazette* January, 1927, p. 4.
[2] *Ibid.*
[3] Clive Sansom, "Speech Education in Australia," *The Pennsylvania Speech Annual* XV (1958); 15.
[4] *Ibid.*, p. 16.
[5] Robert T. Oliver, "Speech Teaching Around the World III: Australia," *The Speech Teacher* VII (1958); 125.
[6] *Ibid.*
[7] Alan L. McLeod, "Speech in Australia: Diagnosis and Prognosis," *The Pennsylvania Speech Annual* XV (1958); 18-19.

[8]See, for example: Sidney J. Baker, *The Australian Language* (Sydney: Angus and Robertson, 1945); G. W. Turner, *The English Language in Australia and New Zealand* (London: Longmans, Green Co., 1966).

[9]A. G. Mitchell, *Spoken English* (London: Macmillan & Co., Ltd., 1957), p. 206.

[10]A. G. Mitchell, "Speech Education: The Underlying Assumptions," *The Forum of Education* (Sydney: Sydney Teachers' College), X (1952); 97.

[11]Ronald Mackie, "Aussie Speech Sounds Sweet to Him," *Australian Women's Weekly* (Sydney), July 23, 1958, p. 19.

[12]A. G. Mitchell and Arthur Delbridge, *The Speech of Australian Adolescents* (Sydney: Angus and Robertson, 1965), p. 87.

[13]*Ibid.*

[14]The Editor, "Laziness Leaves Us Speechless," *The Voice,* 1966, p. 17.

[15]M. M. Lewis, *Language in Society* (London: Thos. Nelson and Sons, 1947), ch. 2.

[16]Norwood Committee, *Report* (London: H.M.S.O., 1943), p. 94.

[17]J. L. M. Trim, "Speech Education," in Randolph Quirk and A. H. Smith, *The Teaching of English* (London: Oxford University Press, 1964).

[18]Andrew Wilkinson, *Spoken English* (University of Birmingham, 1965).

[19]N.S.W. Department of Education, *Syllabus in English* (Sydney, 1963), p. 4.

[20]N.S.W. Department of Education, *Curriculum for Primary Schools—English* (Sydney, 1967), p. 53.

[21]Trinity College of Music, *Effective Speaking Syllabus* (London: Board of Trinity College, 1966), p. 5. Further information about Australia from the Secretary, Trinity College of Music, 310 George Street, Sydney, New South Wales, 2000.

[22]Geoffrey Pullan, "Oral Communication vs. Speech Training (A Title Fight)," *Australian Speech Lecturers' Journal,* No. 1, 1968, p. 12.

[23]"A Nation of Mumblers," *Sydney Morning Herald,* September 7, 1968, p. 2.

[24]Some of the most popular texts used are:
   1. J. R. Dyce, *Speech and Drama in the Secondary School* (Melbourne: Nelson, 1963).
   2. C. H. Hoffman, *Speech in the Australian Classroom* (Sydney: Ure Smith, 1964).
   3. New South Wales Standing Advisory Speech Committee, *Speech Education: A Handbook for Secondary Teachers* (Sydney: Department of Education, 1958).
   4. Clive Sansom, *Speech and Communication in the Primary School* (London: Black, 1965).

[25]The Commission on the English Curriculum, *The English Language Arts in the Secondary School* (New York, 1956), p. 24.

[26]A. Musgrave Horner, "Why Speech and Drama?" *Australian Speech Lecturers' Journal,* No. 1, 1968, p. 9.

SPEECH EDUCATION IN AUSTRIA

William A. Behl
Helen E. Behl

INTRODUCTION

The general education system in Austria was established in 1867. There have been two basic revisions of this system, one in 1930, and the other in 1962. Compulsory education for children from the age of six to fourteen years of age has been required since 1869. In some of the larger cities, the child may transfer to the *Hauptschule* in the fifth year. The *Hauptschule* provides a higher level of general education and includes some vocational training. Students who intend to stop at the end of the eight years or who intend to go to vocational, technical, or agricultural schools usually transfer to the *Hauptschule.* In addition, after four years in the *Volksschule,* the student may transfer to one of four secondary schools: the *Gymnasium,* the *Realgymnasium,* the *Realschule,* or the *Frauenoberschule.* Students who make the transfer to any of these secondary schools, which they attend for eight years, usually plan to attend a university:

Most of the elementary, secondary, and vocational schools are public, but a small percentage are private. In general, the federal government provides and maintains the public secondary schools, but the provinces and the cities build and maintain the elementary public schools. For the most part, the private schools are built and maintained by private organizations which, in Austria, means the Catholic Church. Until recent years, the federal government did not help the private schools in any way, but now approximately 60 per cent of the salaries of the teachers in the private schools are paid by the government. All elementary and secondary schools, whether public or private, must follow the curriculum established by the federal ministry of education. The actual supervision and inspection of all secondary schools is under the direction of the provincial ministry of education; the elementary educational system is under the direction of district boards of education, which are answerable to the provincial ministry.

Most of the elementary-school teachers are educated in one of the twenty-eight pedagogical institutes in Austria. A person may enter the pedagogical institutes after being graduated from the elementary school. One must attend the institute for five years in order to be granted a diploma to teach. The curriculum of the pedagogy institutes requires the student to take a considerable number of education courses as well as courses in his field of specialty such as mathematics, science, history, language, and so forth. After being graduated from the pedagogy institute, a student may enter the university, where he may earn a doctorate in his special field. In general, teachers on the secondary level must attend the university for their training; there they receive instruction in education courses and in their field of specialty. Many of the teachers in the secondary school system earn their doctorate in order to qualify for supervisory and administrative positions as well as to receive maximum salary.

Higher education in Austria is under the direct supervision of the Federal Ministry of Education and consists of three major universities, two minor ones, and six special schools. The major universities are at Vienna, Innsbruck, and Graz where the traditional faculties or colleges of philosophy, medicine, theology, and law are to be found. The university at Salzburg is composed of a faculty of theology and of philosophy; the university at Linz specializes in economics and social science. The special schools are concerned with engineering and agriculture. All expenses of the schools in the university complex are provided by the federal government.

THEATER, RADIO, AND TELEVISION TRAINING

At the present time, there is a distinct separation between the theoretical or academic theater training and the practical or performance instruction. The academic training is found at the University of Vienna; the practical training is found in the theater schools located in the cities of Vienna, Salzburg, and Graz.

The theater program at the University of Vienna is definitely academic. It is a separate division or department in the Faculty of Philosophy. Though students may major or minor in theater, there are no university play productions, and students do not put on plays in their classes. The nature of the theater curriculum on the academic level will become clear from the description of the admission requirement, the courses, and the dissertation requirements.[1]

The requirement for admission to the university is the satisfactory completion of the *Gymnasium,* or academic high school. Students who wish to major in theater must have Latin, and it is recommended, but not required, that they have completed some courses in Greek. In addition, they must be reasonably fluent in two modern languages other than German.

Students may either major or minor in theater. In general, those who minor in theater are not permitted to take those courses specifically prescribed for theater majors. A theater major must complete eight semesters of study, with an average of sixteen credits per semester. He may complete his study with or without a dissertation, but those who do a dissertation are usually required to complete twelve semesters of work. The theater major must have two minor areas of study, one in psychology and the other selected from art, music, German, Latin, English, Slavic language, Oriental language, classical philology, archaeology, or native folklore. When the student completes the program of studies as well as several examinations and presents a satisfactory thesis, he receives a doctorate in theater.

The description of the theater curriculum at the University of Vienna must be divided into the first two years and the second two years because the student must pass rigorous examinations at the end of the second year in order to continue as a theater major. During the first two years, the student is required to complete the following readings: the first four volumes of H. Kindermann's *The Theater History of Europe,* which begins with the history of the ancient theaters in Greece and ends with the theaters of Italy, France, and twentieth century England; Aristotle's *Poetics;* Lessing's *Hamburg Dramaturgy;* and Margaret Dietrich's *The Modern Drama. Maske and Kothurn,* a dramatic journal and Volume I of *Poetry from Austria,* an anthology of Austrian dramatic readings, are required for all students during each of the eight semesters of study. Both of these publications are edited by Dr. Margaret Dietrich, the present chairman of the department, and by H. Kindermann, the former chairman.

During each of the first four semesters, the student is expected to carry at least one principal theater course and one special theater course. The former refer to the history of the theater and the latter are concerned with such courses as The Care of the Voice and Folk Plays and Folk Songs of Austria. Because of the academic nature of the theater curriculum, introduction to library research is required during the first semester. During each of the first two semesters a proseminar in make-up, costume design, and acting is required. A proseminar in the formation or the development of the director's handbook is required during the third and fourth semesters. This proseminar is concerned with the instructions of the director to the players with regard to the interpretation of lines, the player's movement on stage, his posture, and his gestures. A course in stage design and stage scenery is required during the second, third, and fourth semesters. It is recommended that the student take one course in psychology during each of the first four semesters. In addition, the student is required to take one or more courses in his minor areas during the first two years of study.

Before the student is allowed to continue the last two years of study, he must pass a rigorous examination covering all of the theater courses taken during the first two years. In addition, he must pass examinations in Latin and in two modern languages. If he is successful in these examinations, he may continue his theater program.

The last two years of study are similar to the first two years in general pattern, but the courses are more advanced and specialized. Required reading for the third and fourth years includes Volumes 1, 6 and 7 of Kindermann's *History of Europe,* Volumes 1 and 2 of Dietrich's *European Theater Practices,* Bieber's *History of the Greek and Roman Theater,* Attinger's *Spirit of Italian Comedy,* Appollonio's *Story of the Italian Theater,* Prat's *History of the Spanish Theater,* and Rommel's *Old Vienna's Folk Comedy.* If the student's major interest is the theater of a foreign country, he is required to study the history of that country. With the permission of the Department of Theater, he may spend his junior, or third, year in the country of his special interest.

The curriculum for the last two years of study includes principal courses, special courses, courses in related areas, and seminars. Some of the more important principal courses include the following: Basic Elements of the Film; Instruction in Practical Stage Art, which includes theater management, play plans, and total workbook aids; Dramatic Practices and Criticism of Radio Speaking; Foundations of the Total Stage Picture; Practice in Theater Criticism; two semesters in the Practice of Theater Management; and Practice in

Television, Radio, and Film Production. Some of the special courses include History of Stage Costume from Antiquity to the Renaissance; Problems of Producing Shakespeare in Scandinavian Countries; Scope and Formation of Film Science; Austrian Folklore; Live Television Production; and Practice in Film Production. A main seminar is required for each of the last four semesters. Depending upon the interest of the student, these seminars are concerned with film production, theater management, history of the theater, staging of operas and ballets, television, and research for, and the writing of, the dissertation. Naturally the student is not allowed to take these advanced seminars unless he has done well in all of the principal and special courses. In addition, the student must continue to take courses in psychology and in his selected related areas.

Even though the basic concept of the theater program at the University of Vienna is largely academic, students are encouraged to participate in seminars and institutes which are concerned with the practical aspects of the theater. One of these seminars is held every summer for one week in Bregenz, Austria, the home of the professional theater for the province of Vorarlberg and the summer festival, which consists of plays and operas and is held in an open air theater with the stage in the waters of Lake Constance. Another seminar is held for one week each summer at the Mozart Theater School in Salzburg. This seminar is primarily concerned with the philosophy and the practices of Max Reinhardt, but conferences and discussions are conducted on the theater practices of other countries. Admission to both of these seminars is not limited to theater students from Austria. Actors and directors from many foreign countries are invited to, and do attend, these seminars.

In addition to the successful completion of the stringent examinations at the end of the first two years, the student must pass exacting examinations in the principal seminars which he is required to take during the last two years. A final examination is held at the end of the eighth semester or whenever the student has completed all of the course work and feels that he is ready to be tested. At least two professors test him in the theater courses; one professor tests him in the related area courses; and two professors examine him in psychology. If a student does not wish to write a dissertation, he may be granted the equivalent of the master of arts degree when he has completed the course requirements and the examinations.

In order to be granted a doctorate in theater, the student must complete all the course work, pass all examinations successfully, and write and defend his dissertation. Any time during the last two years, the student may select a major professor and have his topic or problem approved by him. Problems for the dissertations may be selected from any area of the theater: history of the theater in virtually any country in the world, stage design, costuming, theater management, dramatic film production, or dramatic production for television and radio. The final thesis must be approved by the Department of Theater. Dissertations which are especially good are published in theater journals in Austria and in foreign countries.

Courses in television, radio, film production are included in the theater curriculum. The student may not take these courses, however, without special permission from the theater department. In 1961, such courses were not offered. This is an indication that the university is determined to keep the theater curriculum up to date, but it is also an indication that there is a tendency to break away from a strictly academic course of study.

Special Theater Schools

In contrast to the academic program at the University of Vienna, there are three special theater schools which have no connection with a university but are under the Austrian Ministry of Education and are supported by the federal government. The Max Reinhardt School, the oldest one, is located in Vienna; the Mozart School is in Walserfeld, Austria, a suburb of Salzburg; the third school, established in 1961, is located in Graz, which is in southeastern Austria. From a legal point of view, these theater schools are a part of the Training Schools for Music and Related Arts. From a practical point of view, they are virtually independent institutions. Each theater school has its own director and faculty. Dr. Helmut Schwarz is director of the Max Reinhardt School; Professor Hilda Weissner is director of the Mozart School at Salzburg; and Dr. M. Terwal is director of the school at Graz.

The admission requirements for these schools are low compared with the requirements for the theater major at the University of Vienna. Girls must be at least sixteen years old and men must be seventeen, but it is not absolutely necessary for applicants to have completed high school. However, each student must pass an oral reading test consisting of the reading of scenes from a classical and a modern play. This test is designed to test the aptitude of the student with regard to interpretation and acting. The applicant is also tested on his knowledge of ancient and modern dramatic literature and on his understanding of the history of art and of music. He must pass all of these tests to become a full-time student. In general, from twelve to fifteen students are admitted to each of the three schools each year. Many of the students are from other countries. For example, approximately one-half of the students entering the Mozart School in Salzburg are from Germany or Switzerland.

In order to receive a certificate of completion, the student must spend three or four years as a full-time student. The length of time necessary to complete the training program depends upon the aptitude of the student and upon the administration of the school. The Max Reinhardt School requires four years, but the schools at Salzburg and Graz require only three years. It is possible to be a part-time student at any of the schools, especially if the student must take courses in a high school to remove some of his deficiencies in dramatic literature.

Since the Max Reinhardt School is the oldest and probably the best of the three schools, it is appropriate that it should be discussed in some detail.[2] In 1940, the state gave the Cumberland Palace, which is just across the street from the Schönbrunn Palace, to the Reinhardt School for its exclusive use. The Cumberland Palace was built in the middle of the nineteenth century for the Duke of Cumberland. The school got its name from the internationally known actor and director, Max Reinhardt, who was born and educated in Austria but became famous for his acting and directing in Berlin. In 1932, he came to the United States, where he produced the film version of *A Midsummer Night's Dream, Rosalinda,* and *The Eternal Road.* On several occasions he held seminars for actors and directors in the Schönbrunn Palace Theater. As a result of his opening speech at the seminar held on April 23, 1929, the School for Actors and Directors became an integral part of the Austrian Academy for Music and Related Arts, and was given the official name of Max Reinhardt School for Actors and Directors. From 1931 to 1938, he conducted these seminars on a private basis in the Schönbrunn Palace Theater. After 1938, his seminars became an integral part of the Max Reinhardt School for Actors and Directors.

Students at these special theater schools pursue a rigid program of study. About one-half of the curriculum is devoted to dramatic study and performance; the other half is concerned with voice, diction, gesture, and posture. The following chart gives the course of study and the hours per week for each course during the four-year program at the Max Reinhardt School.

Course of Study[3]

Subject	Hours Per Week			
	First Year	Second Year	Third Year	Fourth Year
Breathing Exercises and Voice	3	2	0	0
Speaking	2	3	2	2
Dramatic Instruction	8	10	12	4
Theater and Literature History	2	2	2	0
Ballet	3	3	3	2
Cultural History	2	0	0	0
English	2	2	0	0
Dramatic Art	2	0	0	0
Use of the Library	1	0	0	0
Costume Design	1	0	0	0
Foundations of Music	0	1	½	0
Singing	½	½	0	0
Stage Design	1	0	0	0
Theater Law	0	1	1	0
Fencing	2	2	1	0
Physical Education	1	1	0	0
Judo	2	0	0	0
Practicum in Auditions and Performance		x	x	x
Practicum in Film and Television			x	x
Practicum in Radio Drama and Use of the Microphone			x	x
Practicum in Pantomine		x	x	x
Total	32½	29½	19½	8

The hours per week for the practicum courses depends upon the number of performances and the opportunities for radio and television observations and performances.

Examinations are given at the end of each year and at the end of the training program. If a student fails the examination at the end of the year, he may appeal to the administration for a re-hearing. The decision of the administration is final. The grading system used for the yearly examinations are categorized as very good, good, average, satisfactory, and unsatisfactory. The final, or terminal, examination is graded with a pass with honors, passed, or failed. If the student is permitted to continue each year and passes the final examination, he is given his certificate of completion.

Little needs to be added concerning the theater schools at Salzburg and Graz because the Austrian Ministry of Education requires that the admission requirements, the curriculum, and the graduation requirements be the same at all three schools. Both schools are housed in very adequate buildings: the one at Graz is located in an old palace with very spacious grounds; the one at Salzburg uses about one-half of a vocational-school building which has a fine auditorium. The course of study at the school in Graz is not as complete as the ones at Vienna and Salzburg because it has been in existence for only five or six years.

All of these schools stage several productions each year. Usually two or three of the plays are open to the public. For example, the public performances at the Max Reinhardt School are presented in the beautiful little theater which is a part of the Schönbrunn Palace. It seats only about two hundred persons, but it is very ornate and is steeped in tradition as a private theater for both Austrian and foreign royalty of the past. The directors from the professional theaters in Austria as well as from other European countries come to these productions seeking new talent for their theater groups.

The Professional Theater

When the students graduate from the theater schools, they seek employment with a professional theater group or with a radio or television station. There are twelve professional theaters in Austria, and most of them are in Vienna, including an experimental theater and one which specializes in comedy. Other professional theaters are located in Linz, Salzburg, Graz, and Bregenz. About one-third of the cost of these theaters is provided by the federal, state, and local governments; the other two-thirds comes from gate receipts. Since the theaters are subsidized by the government, they are required to stage productions in towns and villages in the provinces where the central theater is located.

The theater groups in each of the professional theaters are kept very busy for at least ten months of the year. For example, the group at Bregenz Theater puts on a performance in Bregenz or at a neighboring theater in the province of Vorarlberg or in Switzerland or in Germany about every other day during each month. The production of *Urfaust*, which opened in Bregenz, went on the road to four other cities in the province and to two cities in Germany and closed with two more performances in Bregenz. A total of nineteen performances of *Urfaust* covered a period of only seventeen days. Production of *The Happy Day*, by Claude Andre Puget, was staged twelve times in eighteen days, and only two of the performances were in the home theater in Bregenz.[4]

Austria is looking forward with regard to its theater education. The course of study at the University of Vienna will probably be extended to a six-year program, especially for those who do a dissertation. In addition, the federal commission which was established to study the entire Austrian educational system has recommended that there be a closer connection between the special theater schools and the academic program at the University of Vienna. In other words, the practical is to be combined with the theoretical. But, Dr. Helmut Schwarz, the director of the Reinhardt School, said, "There are many problems to be solved before this can be achieved."[5]

SPEECH AND HEARING THERAPY

Whereas the theater education training program in Austria is developed very well, the speech and hearing therapy education programs are neither coordinated nor highly developed. In the Netherlands, for example, there is a three-year training program for speech therapists and another program for the training of hearing therapists. Both of these programs are under the jurisdiction of the Ministry of Education. Austria does not have such a training program for speech and hearing therapists.

There are actually three training programs for the speech and hearing therapists: training in the teacher training colleges, some training in the medical schools at the universities, and on-the-job training in some of the private schools. The training at the pedagogy institutes or the teacher training colleges is a very small part of a total program for the training of teachers for all handicapped children, including the disabled child, the mentally retarded child, the blind child, the child with reading difficulties, and the speech-defective child. At the Pedagogy Institute for the City of Vienna, which is probably the best teacher training college in Austria, there is only one course given each semester which deals specifically with speech therapy—Speech Defects of Children—Their Causes and Cures.[6] Mr. Franz Maschka, the director of a school for speech defectives in Vienna and the instructor for this course, said that he covered all the common speech defects of children such as sound substitutions, vowel distortions, lisping, and nasality. In addition, he said he covered some of the corrective work for stutterers, cleft-palate cases, and hard-of-hearing cases, but that most of the course dealt with the more common and less serious speech defects. He pointed out that the teacher interested in speech therapy should take several other courses offered at the Institute such as Curative Pedagogy Seminar, The Foundations of Curative Pedagogy, Medical Curative Pedagogy, Medicine for Pedagogy Students, and Actual Problems of the Psychology of Teaching.[7] The content of these courses, however, deals with all the problems of the handicapped child. The speech and hearing therapist, therefore, is given a very broad background of knowledge concerning the handicapped child but specialization in therapy per se is very limited. In addition, there were no courses in practicum where the teachers did practical work under supervision. According to Miss Maria Sommer, director of a private speech correction school in Feldkirch, Austria, the lack of therapy practice under supervision at the teacher training colleges is a serious fault.[8]

Strictly speaking, formal training for speech and hearing therapists is almost nonexistent in the medical schools in spite of the fact that probably the best speech therapy is done in the speech clinics in the hospitals. Most of the speech therapists in these speech clinics are medical doctors who have specialized in ear, nose, and throat. Not more than one or two of the courses prescribed for the medical training of these specialists is devoted to actual speech therapy work, and these courses are taken only by those who have a special interest in speech therapy. The doctors who are interested in speech therapy study European as well as American speech-correction texts.

A third source of training for the speech and hearing therapist is on-the-job training. We found this to be true at the private Speech Correction School for Children in Feldkirch, Austria, which we visited. Miss Maria Sommers, the director of the school, had received her training at the Pedagogy Institute in Vienna, but four or five of the young men and women on her staff were given on-the-job training by Miss Sommers. All of her staff were high school or gymnasium graduates, but she maintained that the basic ingredient for a good therapist was a reasonably intelligent person with a real desire to help people. She contended that if a person had those attributes, she could teach him to be a good therapist with a minimum of theory and a maximum of observation of her at work.[9]

Dr. H. Gassner, the director of a school for handicapped children in Salzburg, said that the most serious speech correction work was done in the hospitals. Even though Dr. Gassner was director of this special school for handicapped children, he did speech correction work at the general hospital in Salzburg. He discussed the various theories of stuttering but was very partial to the psychological causes of stuttering.[10]

The work in the speech clinic of the general hospital by Dr. V. Imre in Vienna, and our conferences with him and with Dr. H. Brown, tended to support our judgment that outstanding speech therapy was done in the hospitals. Both of these men are medical doctors with specialization in ear, nose, and throat. Dr. Imre does his therapy work in the office formerly occupied by Dr. E. Froeschels, who is now a recognized speech therapist in New York City. Dr. Imre showed us many old instruments used in ear, nose, and throat surgery and therapy work. One of these instruments was an accordian type audiometer, probably one of the first audiometers ever made.

Dr. Imre permitted us to observe him at work for almost two hours. During that period he worked with a university medical student from Damascus who was a stutterer, a young girl who had just returned from an extended stay in New York and who wanted to study in Russia but had difficulty making uvular or trilled *r's,* a five-year-old girl who was recovering from a cleft-lip and cleft-palate operation, a young girl who had an excessively high-pitched voice, an elderly lady who was recovering from a mild stroke, and a young man who was spastic. Dr. Imre usually had two or more patients in the office at the same time. For example, he might have the stutterer relaxing on the couch, the aphasic listening to a playback of sounds and attempting to repeat them, and the cleft-palate child in the chair where he was manually exercising the tissue and muscles of the pharynx.[11]

There is also a private Catholic School for Speech Correction in Feldkirch, Austria, a small city in the extreme western part of

Austria. Six other private schools in Austria are located at Halle, Graz, Klagenfurt, Linz, Vienna, and Salzburg. The schools, or homes, are places where most of the students live while receiving speech therapy. A serious attempt is made to provide regular school work in conjunction with the speech therapy. There were approximately fifty children between the ages of five and eleven at the school in Feldkirch. The cases ranged from simple articulation problems to hard-of-hearing, stuttering, and cleft palate.

It was rare for Miss Maria Sommers to work for more than ten minutes with a patient before she would send him out to play for a while; she would then recall him in a half hour or so for another ten minutes of therapy. It was difficult to detect any serious articulation problems with a cleft-palate patient with whom she had worked for four or five weeks.

In addition to the work done in the hospitals and in the private schools, there are in Austria eight public schools for the hard-of-hearing and the speech-defective. We talked with Mr. Franz Maschka, the director of one of these special schools in Vienna.[12] Mr. Maschka has twenty-three teachers on his staff, and any one teacher might have as many as twelve small classes each day. The classes were categorized according to defects and met for approximately one-half hour. Several of his staff were assigned to primary schools throughout the city of Vienna where they did therapy work for part of the day. There are approximately 1,200 children enrolled in these eight special schools with a combined staff of about 160 instructors. Most of the children in the special schools are between six and ten years of age.

There are some persons who do private speech therapy, but private practice does not appear prevalent in Austria. Those who do private speech therapy are usually psychologists with a doctor of philosophy degree. Dr. Imre was familiar with the training program for speech therapists, but the program would be open only to those who had completed the doctor of medicine degree with specialization in ear, nose, and throat.

PUBLIC SPEAKING

Courses in rhetoric and public speaking are hard to find in Austrian universities. There is usually a course in public speaking in the school of law and in the school of theology, and here and there one finds courses in voice, delivery, or extempore speaking. For example, in the University of Vienna bulletin the following courses are listed under a section titled, "Courses for all Faculties": Techniques of Speech, Techniques of Speech and Delivery, Lectures for Speech Technique and Oratory, The Art of Extempore Speech, and The Delivery of Extempore Speeches. Courses in ancient or medieval rhetoric were not offered.

TELEVISION AND RADIO

The radio and television industry is under the supervision of the federal government. It is basically a private enterprise with subsidies from the state when necessary. There are several radio broadcasting stations in Austria but only two television stations; both broadcast from Vienna. The television programs are relayed to the major cities in Austria where they are rebroadcasted.

There is rather extensive educational radio and television under the supervision of the Ministry of Education. Dr. Otto Kamm and Mr. Imbert Fried are directors of these programs. The yearly program is published in pamphlet form and is distributed to all schools in the country. The use of these programs is optional, and except for schools in the larger cities only the more progressive teachers make use of them.[13]

The educational television offerings are rather extensive and of reasonably good quality. Most of the showings are taped. During the 1967-1968 school year, programs were televised every Wednesday, Thursday, and Friday for one or two hours each day, beginning at ten o'clock in the morning and lasting until about one o'clock in the afternoon. Each listing in the pamphlet indicated the age level for which the program was designed. The programs ranged from highly cultural to highly practical in nature. One of the practical programs offered once or twice each month was titled, "What Can I Become?" These programs were explanations of job opportunities. For example, the showings offered during 1967-1968 explained the job of a medical technician, the profession of optometry, the work of a mechanical orthopedist, and the job opportunities as a radio and television mechanic. Some of the cultural programs offered during the year included stories for children, Austrian history, the story of Nationalist China, Austrian life and literature, American life and letters of Thornton Wilder, scenes from Shakespeare's plays, the history of Ethiopia, the atom reactor at Seibersdorf, and much church music.

The only courses offered for students interested in radio and television were offered in the theater department at the University of Vienna and in the three special theater schools. These courses were described in the theater offerings in the first part of this chapter. This appears to be the only radio and television training offered in Austria.

SUMMARY

In summary, it is fair to say that, with the exception of theater training, speech education in Austria is not very highly developed. Theater training, as well as professional theater production, is of a reasonably high quality; training for speech and hearing therapists is neither extensive nor well organized, but the therapy work done in the hospitals and in the special schools is quite respectable; training in rhetoric and public address is limited; and training for radio and television actors, announcers, and programmers is reasonably good, even though it is a part of the theater program at the University of Vienna and at the three special theater schools.

FOOTNOTES

[1] All of the information concerning the theater program comes from the following sources: *The University of Vienna Bulletin,* pp. 67-69; several mimeographed sheets of information for theater majors, which were prepared by Dr. Margaret Dietrich, chairman of the theater division; and interviews with staff members and secretaries in the theater office on March 23, 1968.

[2] Information concerning the Reinhardt School is from the following sources: *Beginnings of Theater Courses in Austria,* by Helmut Schwarz; mimeographed instructions for students at the Reinhardt School; and interviews with Dr. Helmut Schwarz, director of the school, on March 25, 1968.

[3] Academy for Music and Related Arts, Vienna 3, Lothringerstrasse 18, Division for Actors and Directors, Max Reinhardt School, p. 12.

[4] Interview with Mr. Alex Freihardt, Bregenz, Austria, on March 19, 1968.

[5] Interview with Dr. Helmut Schwarz, Vienna, on March 25, 1968.

[6] *Bulletin,* Spring Semester, 1968, Pedagogy Institute for the City of Vienna, p. 14.

[7] Interview with Mr. Franz Maschka at the Pedagogy Institute for the City of Vienna on March 25, 1968.

[8] Interview with Miss Maria Sommer, director of the Speech Correction School for Children, at Feldkirch, Austria, on March 14, 1968.

[9] *Ibid.*

[10] Interview with Dr. H. Gassner, Salzburg, Austria, on March 21, 1968.

[11] Interview with Dr. V. Imre, Vienna General Hospital, Vienna, Austria, on March 27, 1968.

[12] Interview with Mr. Franz Maschka (see Footnote 7 above).

[13] Interview with Dr. Otto Kamm and Mr. Imbert Fried, directors of educational radio and television, Oesterreichischer Rundfunk, Vienna, Austria.

SPEECH EDUCATION IN
ENGLISH-SPEAKING CANADA

P. Read Campbell
I. R. Shaw

INTRODUCTION

To understand the variant of the Anglo-Saxon tongue known as Canadian that has gradually taken form over the last several decades, it is necessary to realize that Canada has been a mixing place for two linguistic streams—one British, the other American. Indeed, it is the intermingling of the two which causes the extreme difficulty of defining Canadian English.

The influence of that country which stretches for over three thousand miles along the southern border of Canada is much stronger than an intermingling. A greater mutuality of interest exists between these two countries than between any other two nations in the world. The tradition of good will is reinforced by the ties of a common language, Canadian English being more like American English than is any other variant. Both nations were originally colonies of European nations. Ultimately, both gained complete political independence from the mother country. The history of the American Republic began with an abrupt act of separation from Europe. Canada's evolution was slow and gradual. The beginning was the French colony of the St. Lawrence which, after 1763, was shorn at one stroke of leaders and of hinterland. The various groups which, for the next century and more, penetrated into or gathered around this nucleus had little understanding of one another. The French, together with two other groups, the United Empire Loyalists and the Highland Scots, made up the bulk of the population. Although all three were under the British Crown, they could scarcely have been more unlike. They lived in different sections of the country; they spoke three different languages. Like the French, the Loyalists felt

37

isolated, but in a different sense. The author of *Foundations of Canadian Nationhood* says: "The attempt to transplant three or four generations of American traditions to a new soil in the north was an experience too grim to be forgotten."[1] The Highland Scots who brought with them their native Gaelic tongue retained for many years the traditional points of view of their mother country. Not even the most sanguine optimist would have prophesied that a nation could be welded out of such diversity.[2]

In the years that followed 1763, the English-speaking Canadian point of view lay somewhere between that of the United States and Great Britain.[3] While the most powerful influence impinging on Canadian culture came from the United States, it must be borne in mind that the various influences were imposed on an underlying foundation of British tradition. Colonial officials brought the mores, preferences, and prejudices of England and Scotland to the new land and established firm and lasting fashions in intellectual and aesthetic matters. Only in the twentieth century has Canada stepped from the shadowing of her powerful and energetic set of relatives and attained nationhood. It was in the half-century from 1900 to 1950 that a distinct Canadian language came into being. In other words, as Canada became a nation in thought as well as in constitution, as Canadians have striven to express their ideas in their own way, a distinctively Canadian way of speaking has gradually evolved. Especially surprising, when the great diversity of her beginnings are considered, is the fact that today the Canadian language is more nationally uniform than that of any other English-speaking country. The work of Canadian linguists in increasing awareness of the need for linguistic study·and involving themselves directly in such study has been invaluable. Says Scargill:

> here in Canada, among English-speaking and native-born Canadians, a study of language might prove the surest guide to the way in which we are developing. The fact that a Canadian drives a car made in Detroit does not make him think like an American. The fact that he subscribes to the *Times* does not make him think like an Englishman. But if our native-born Canadian speaks like an American, then his thoughts are probably being shaped like an American's thoughts. If he chooses to speak like an Englishman, then he is more English than he knows. But if our English-speaking and native-born Canadian prefers to develop his own habits of speech, then this must show that he is a man with ideas of his own to express—ideas that cannot be expressed in either British-English or American-English, because they are neither British nor American ideas. . .[4]

By 1815, the greater part of the English-speaking population of Canada was actually American in origin, consisting of Loyalists from the revolting American colonies. The pervasive Scots influence—a noticeable feature of Canadian life—started with settlements in the maritime province of Prince Edward Island and continued in Ontario and Manitoba. The effects of the Scots upon a country are never in simple arithmetical ratio to their numbers, hence English Canada, mainly American and Scottish by origin, although Loyalist politically, was not English in a limited sense. It was perhaps already becoming Canadian. Priestley says that the heavy immigration during the nineteenth century did nothing to change that character. If he were pressed for an explanation of the fact that there were no English-born politicians eminent in this period, he says he would surmise that:

> educated Englishmen had been associated with the official class under the old colonial regime, and were suspect from their speech, and that the uneducated English lacked the capacity of the Scot for self-education. At any rate, Canada tended to be British but by no means English; loyal but nationalist. And so she has remained.[5]

Linguists in Canada have always been aware of the value of the diversity in the Canadian way of speaking. The first volume of a series of dictionaries of Canadian English was published in 1962. Entitled *The Beginning Dictionary,* and edited by Canadian linguists Avis, Gregg, Lovell, and Scargill, it was designed to contain the kinds of information that grade 4 and grade 5 children need, and to be presented in a way that a child could understand. All three dictionaries of the Canadian series are descriptive rather than prescriptive in their approach to language. The scholar who has had the editorial responsibility for the dictionaries believes that "the descriptive nature of the good dictionary is of special importance when considering the demands of Canadian lexicography." He continues:

> . . .There has, in the past, been a tendency to make arbitrary decisions on, for example, what spellings are to be considered "correct" in Canada. Examination of educated practice in this sphere indicates two facts: first and obviously, that spelling usage is, for a great many words, divided; second, that in some words the American spelling is more frequently used, while in other words the British pattern is more common. A truly Canadian dictionary cannot automatically give its preference to either American or British usages. Surveys show, not surprisingly, that a similar situation obtains in the sphere of pronunciation.

It is common for Canadian dictionaries to be based on volumes originally published elsewhere. This is a perfectly reasonably practice provided that the adaptation is made with sufficient thoroughness and rigor. But the sourcebook will be of no help to the Canadian lexicographer when he comes to the purely Canadian items of vocabulary, which are far more numerous than most people imagine. Here he will need his own collection of citation slips. Without them, he may have no real idea of which Canadianisms to enter, and he will have too little guide as to the admissible spellings of many Indian-derived words. Here, again, arbitrary decisions may not be useful. The purpose of the Canadian dictionary must be to describe Canadian English, not to prescribe it and still less to invent it.[6]

Dr. Walter Avis, a distinguished student of dialectology and lexicography, had commented a few years before on the general permissiveness in pronunciation and in dialect which was gaining ground in the English-speaking world. He further clarifies:

...this view does not imply that "anything goes" by any means; it does imply, however, that vain attempts to stamp out variants, either British or American, which are in general used among educated Canadians should cease. Furthermore, it must be recognized that certain pronunciations which are in widespread educated use in Canada, though perhaps not elsewhere, should be received as acceptable usage...[7]

Perhaps the controversy, implied in Dr. Avis' statement, regarding what is "acceptable (oral) usage" is one of the reasons why Canadian universities and even colleges of education have been reluctant to include classes in speech in their curricula. The Canadian student is supposed to know how to speak *before* he enters university or college. However, since the truck driver's son as well as the son of the college professor now enrolls in university the argument is obviously spurious.

During the entire decade of the sixties, Canadian linguists continued their important contributions. *The Intermediate Dictionary* was published in 1963[8] and the *Dictionary of Canadian English: The Senior Dictionary,* in 1967.[9] Based on the Thorndike Barnhart Dictionaries, *The Senior Dictionary* was augmented with material from the file of some 30,000 words gathered by the Dictionary Committee of the Canadian Linguistic Association. Three divisions of "Canadianisms" were added: (1) words whose purpose is to represent things peculiarly Canadian and also words in general use which have acquired a particular significance when used in Canada; (2) pronunciations which are Canadian in that they are used by educated

Canadians in preference to established British or American pronunciations; and (3) alternative spellings where the preference of
educated Canadians is not clear.

Also published in 1967, an impressive and sizable offering to
Canada's centenary, was *A Dictionary of Canadianisms,* which
endeavors to treat in depth the characteristic developments of the
English vocabulary in Canada.[10] Major credit for its production
should go to its distinguished editor-in-chief, Dr. Walter Avis.

Pondering the advance and gradual expansion of Canadian
English, it may come as something of a surprise to learn that speech
per se is not a teaching subject in the secondary schools. Hence
teachers in training, even though deeply interested in the subject, are
not able to include it in their programs as a teaching major.
Nevertheless, some progress is being made. Changes which are
beginning to be apparent in the last half decade will be discussed in
some detail after the brief examination of the total educational
system to which we now turn.

EDUCATIONAL SYSTEM—SCHOOLS AND UNIVERSITIES

The character of the school system in Canada has passed
through two main phases. From the middle of the nineteenth
century to about 1920, there was a continuous striving toward a rigid
uniformity in methods and textbooks. The government exerted
control by means of examinations and grants of money. The system
was designed to surmount the inefficiency of the pioneer period.
Since 1920, the tendency has been toward less exacting standards
and toward a curriculum more vocational in extent.

Quite a degree of uniformity exists in the organization of
provincial education across Canada, but there is much diversity at the
level of university education. In the early years, churches as well as
Old World universities set an imprint on many Canadian universities,
especially in the eastern provinces. Efforts were made to adapt the
system followed at Oxford, at Cambridge, and at Scottish universities
to Canadian needs and conditions. This influence was reinforced by
the importation of British professors. After 1900, the influence of
American universities grew increasingly strong, partly through the
bringing in of American professors and partly through the training of
Canadians in American graduate schools.

A wide range of professional faculties and schools is maintained
by Canadian universities. Pedagogy, or education, is one of these.

Most of the universities operate faculties, colleges, or departments for the training of teachers. Today, differences in the thinking of Canadian and American educators in universities and colleges tend to be largely one of emphasis. Intellectuals in both countries are aware of the need to learn more about the structure on which our thinking in education is supported. Both have chosen not to lend exclusive support to the implementation of any one system, be it realist, materialist, idealist, or pragmatist.

One of the respected leaders in Canadian thought during the two decades, roughly 1945-65, was Vincent Massey. Reflecting on the purpose of the schools and upon ways in which we might relate the claims of liberal education to the training for a profession, he comments:

> We recognize the fact that education and training are two different things. One is concerned with the equipment for a career, the acquisition of the necessary knowledge and techniques; the other with the training of the intellect. The candidate for one of the professions should be enabled to receive both. Whatever his task, he can perform it better with what a liberal education can give him.[11]

The line is hard to draw, says Arthur Bestor.

> The fundamental test of an educational system is not whether it produces successful men, as success is popularly measured, but whether it produces educated men, that is, men who can deal successfully with intellectual problems. If the two concepts of success are confused, the argument of immediate utility can be—and has been—turned as devastatingly against pure science as against literature, philosophy, or history....[12]

It is this drawing of the line, the somewhat different placing of values, that causes diversities in the educational thinking of Americans and Canadians. They are often not readily apparent. Says Denis Wrong:

> The emphasis on vocational education in English-speaking Canada is somewhat less pronounced than in the United States, and the influence of the point of view that defines the school as a "center of democratic living" rather than merely a place where elementary intellectual skills are transmitted, has been rather less marked....Although the same controversy as to whether the goal of the university should be to turn out the specialized expert or the cultured humanist is waged as in the United States, there is rather more vocal support for the latter, and opposition to the trend toward a purely vocational education is stronger.[13]

Moving now to 1968, subtle changes in outlook become evident. Concern about education due to rapid social modification is evident in the report of eight Royal Commissions and numerous other conferences held within the last few years. Since education tends to follow or reflect changes in other sectors of Canadian society, it is reasonable to expect much change in Canadian educational patterns. Canadians are now distributing themselves differently over the 3,500,000 square miles of their country. They are moving from farms to cities or towns. In the thirty years from 1961 to 1991, it is estimated that double the facilities will be required for education and that by A.D. 2000 half of Canada's population will be in nine giant metropolitan areas.[14] Whenever a society experiences a rapid social change, protests arise against basic assumptions in that society. That opinion in Canada has passed from concern to protest is evident in the subject chosen by Dr. Frank MacKinnon, the lecturer in the 1968 Quance Lectures in Canadian Education—"Relevance and Responsibility in Education."[15]

The schools must be "turned on" says Dr. MacKinnon. Healthy criticism and debate must not degenerate into a continuing state of protest. Ample and acceptable scope for criticism and debate within our social institutions must be provided. Emphasis in education must be placed less on aims and structures and more on persons—on the practices associated with the characteristics and relationships of the people involved. The school should be thought of as an academic community, not a public service organization—as an interesting place in which to live; a place where there are things to do besides book learning; a place where there are chances to become involved, to communicate, to express oneself. Throughout his lectures, Dr. MacKinnon enlarges on several other aspects of his philosophy. The best and most lasting interests and abilities of the student are those that he finds and develops by himself. Adults must do less dominating; librarians must be able to deal with people as well as with books; more responsibility should be given to the young. Lounge and coffee shops are educationally valuable places, for here young people can find an outlet for self-expression and the exchange of ideas.

For the last address in the series, Dr. MacKinnon chose the topic, "The Relationship Between Government and Education." Effective change results from leadership of a few, which, when it works, is followed by the many. The elements of imagination, interest, and enthusiasm, so necessary to any successful change, are best secured by action on the part of those directly responsible. Efforts to solve problems by turning them over to government is dealing with troublesome matters by proxy. If contemporary protest is an indication of a wish for more personal responsibility, it should be supported. The giving of responsibility must come by way of the schools, for democracy in the schools becomes democracy in the universities, then in the institutions of society, and finally in the state itself. The reasoned opinions expressed by this Canadian representative are highly significant when viewed within the context of the development of speech education in Canada in the last half decade.

SPEECH EDUCATION

It is probably true to say that the meaning of the word "speech" when used in educational circles in Canada is slowly changing from an earlier elocutionary meaning to one more closely approximating "speech communication." There are several reasons for this change. A strong belief in the value of attention to speech education has resulted in excellence and personal commitment to the teaching of the subject. Examples of this kind of dedication are to be found in all the provinces of Canada from the Atlantic coast to the Pacific. Professor Layman of Memorial University provides an up-to-date illustration. In the fall of 1968, she went to live and work for three months with deprived youngsters along the bleak coast of Newfoundland. In the dead of winter she moved to the Northwest Territories north of the northern reaches of Alberta, to repeat, with energy and enthusiasm, her research experiment designed to demonstrate the value of speech communication and educational drama. Two Ph.D. theses in speech education as well as several related studies have also helped to evolve the speech communication connotation.[16] Three other forward steps are of significance. In 1966, the Department of Speech and Drama within the Faculty of Education at the University of British Columbia formally set up a master's program.[17] In 1967, the Canadian Speech Association was founded, and in the spring of 1968, the first issue of *The Canadian Speech Communication Journal* became available.[18]

Further evidence not only of the interpretation of speech as speech communication, but also of a growing agreement in basic philosophical viewpoint is seen when one compares the statements of Dr. MacKinnon, of Prince Edward Island, with these expressed in the same year (1968) by an educator 4,000 miles away in British Columbia.

> ...The primary question (of choice of university) is whether the offerings of a particular department will give the student an opportunity to carry on

a program which will have meaning for him. What of the psychosocial environment? Is it one which he is likely to find challenging? An initial interview with the head of the department concerned or with a major professor should help him to decide whether responsibility and dedication are considered the concern of both faculty and student. The soundness of any graduate course is guaranteed by the basic integrity of the person who teaches it. The graduate student should have instructors who enjoy sharing insights they have gained. Once it has been established and there is sufficient compatibility of values and of interest and that routine requirements set up by the graduate office can be met, the exploration can then turn more specifically to the field that he has chosen.[19]

In the spring of 1968, a questionnaire having to do with various aspects of speech education was circulated among Canadian speech instructors. A sampling of the questions and of the answers which were received is set forth below.

Question: What do you see as the relationship of speech education to the total educational system?

"Speech is a skill just as mathematics is a skill. It is the practical use of good speech habits (and I don't mean elocutionary competence) that makes other subjects come to life and become purposeful and meaningful to the learner."

—Professor Grace Layman, Memorial University, Newfoundland

"My - - -, we communicate (educate) basically with speech! What is the relationship of water to oceanography?"

—Dr. Phillip Spensley, Guelph University, Ontario

"A vital relationship—one that is the key not only to the personal development of the individual students in the system—but to the very system itself."

—Professor Mary Lynch, Xavier College, Nova Scotia

Question: Is this need different than the need for special education in other countries?

"I think so:

1. Canada's neglect appears more serious and long-standing.
2. The vastness of our country creates a special type of speech education problem (higher incidence of regional dialects, etc.).
3. The need is different because of our bilingual nature and multiracial population.
4. The need is different because of the frustrating seesaw influence of speech exerted by traditional but far-away Britain on the one hand, and progressive near-by 'Uncle Sam' on the other."

Question: Considering the "average" Canadian, how does he look upon speech
education? Does he like the use of the word "speech"? Does he feel
that there is need for this kind of thing?

"Most people look upon speech as something that must be corrected.
As long as this view is held and unless the what and how of one's speech is
accepted as an outpouring of a unique personality, speech education will
remain the poor relative of the general curricula."

Further examination of the answers to the 1968 questionnaire
revealed that although the respondents mentioned the same difficulties which were felt to be of first importance at the time of the
1957 doctoral study,[20] the problems now had a different focus.
Thus faulty voice production, slurred or imperfect articulation, or
lack of inflection were considered problems in the sense that they
tended to hinder the individual's growth in ability to communicate
effectively as a human being. To the initiators of *The Canadian
Speech Journal* this is of first importance. As the fly leaf indicates, it
is "a journal dedicated to deepening the foundations of human
communication and cooperation through insights gained in the field
of speech."

There are no major institutional programs of speech now in
existence in Canada, but there are several healthy beginnings.
Starting at the east coast and proceeding westward, the names of the
institutions which have speech education programs and the speech
persons involved are as follows:

Memorial University, St. John's, Newfoundland
Professor Riach, Professor Grace Layman

Xavier College, Antigonish, Nova Scotia
Professor Mary Lynch

Faculty of Education, University of Toronto
Miss Esme Crampton

Faculty of Education, University of Manitoba
Professor Harold Turner, Mrs. Sheila Maurer

Faculty of Education, University of Brandon
Dr. Virgil Logan

Faculty of Education, University of Calgary
Professor Laura Muir

Mt. Royal Junior College, Calgary, Alberta
Mrs. Leona Paterson

Faculty of Education, University of British Columbia
Dr. Read Campbell, Dr. Irwin Shaw
Professor Janie Stevenson, Professor Dorothy Washington

All the speech instructors mentioned above are members of the Canadian Speech Association. Programs are being expanded as rapidly as possible. The Faculties of Education in the University of Saskatchewan and the University of Alberta have recently appointed a speech instructor, while several other centers of learning are offering at least one course in speech. The situation changes as new colleges and faculties come into existence.

In all the universities or colleges mentioned above where speech education or speech communication is taught, creative or educational drama is given a serious place. The same could be said of remedial speech. For anyone interested in knowing what drama courses are being given across the country the best source of information is probably the Canadian Theatre Centre, 280 Bloor Street, Toronto, Ontario. The National Theatre School of Canada, 407 St. Lawrence Boulevard, Montreal, Quebec, has a deservedly fine reputation. The actor-training methods of this school are the subject of a Ph.D. thesis which will be completed by Professor Spensley of the University of Guelph from Wayne State University in Detroit in the spring of 1969.

It is possible to get an advanced degree in clinical speech or speech pathology at only three universities in Canada—McGill, Montreal, and Toronto. At the University of British Columbia, a proposal to offer a graduate program in audiology and speech sciences was submitted by the Faculty of Medicine Department of Pediatrics to the Faculty of Graduate Studies in December of 1968. It is considered likely that the Senate will approve the proposal early in 1969. The University of McGill, mentioned above, offers a somewhat similar type of program. It is labelled a Ph.D. in experimental audiology and speech communication. The University of Windsor, at Windsor, Ontario, offers a M.Sc. in communication sciences. Since to date the recruitment of personnel into this field in Canada has had to come from other countries, research on a national level in experimental phonetics and audiology is practically non-existent. The need for individuals trained in this field as university teachers, research workers, and service-oriented professionals is now being increasingly recognized.

In another field somewhat related to speech education, a recent forward step was taken. A national association formed for the purpose of serving the professional needs and interests of educational radio and television broadcasters was formed in Toronto in January, 1968. Two aspects of the emerging program of this association, called the Educational Television and Radio Association of Canada, appear particularly worthy of comment. One is the establishment of an information exchange on television research in Canada and the setting up of a study to attempt to phase a television project with an educational system without antagonism between professional educators and professional producers. The other has to do with the setting up of a computerized program information and storage system in a phased development which would include a comprehensive listing of program material available in Canada and elsewhere along with dubbing storage facilities and distribution procedures for educational television productions. Several classes in television and radio work are offered by the Ryerson Polytechnical Institute, 40 Gould Street, Toronto 2, Ontario.

The Royal Conservatory of Music, in Toronto, has had a speech course for many years. Interested secondary school teachers and private speech teachers sometimes sponsor speech festivals and speech contests of various kinds. Sometimes these have been elocutionary and have prejudiced Canadian educators into believing that this is the only thing that the study of speech has to offer. At times, however, and in certain localities, this movement has brought about a richness in the expansion of the English curriculum and has paved the road for a further development of speech interest, and for speech activities in other aspects of education within the school and the community.

Since many universities have only one person teaching speech, not much research is possible as yet. Nevertheless, in 1968, research studies were conducted by Professor Layman of Memorial University, Professor Muir of the University of Calgary, and by Dr. Read Campbell and Dr. Irwin Shaw, both of the University of British Columbia. In addition, at the University of British Columbia in the Department of Speech (within the Faculty of Education) four masters' theses are in progress.[21]

Questions regarding any aspect of the work of speech education in Canada may be directed to Mrs. Leona Paterson, president of the Canadian Speech Association,[22] or to any other member of the Canadian Speech Association.

FOOTNOTES

[1]Chester Martin, *Foundations of Canadian Nationhood* (Toronto: University of Toronto Press, 1955), p. 13.

[2]Attention is drawn again to the fact that this paper deals only with English-speaking Canada. Today French-speaking Canadians are equal partners with English-speaking Canadians in the Canadian federation. A study of the development of speech in Quebec—and in other smaller French-speaking areas—would demand a separate study.

[3]George W. Brown, *Canada in the Making* (Seattle: University of Washington Press, 1953), p. 7.

[4]M. H. Scargill, "Canadian English and Canadian Culture," *Journal of the Canadian Linguistic Assn.* I, No. 1 (March, 1955):27.

[5]F. E. L. Priestly, "Canadian English," as quoted in Eric Partridge and John W. Clark, *British and American English Since 1900* (New York: Philosophical Library, Inc., 1951), p. 73.

[6]P. D. Drysdale, "Dictionaries for the Schools," *Education* (Gage), IV, No. 17:107.

[7]Walter S. Avis, "Speech Differences Along the Ontario-United States Border," *Journal of the Canadian Linguistic Assn.* II, No. 1 (October, 1956):55.

[8]*Dictionary of Canadian English: The Intermediate Dictionary,* ed. Walter S. Avis *et al.* (Toronto: Gage, 1963).

[9]*Dictionary of Canadian English: The Senior Dictionary,* ed. Walter S. Avis *et al.* (Toronto: Gage, 1967).

[10]*A Dictionary of Canadianisms on Historical Principles.* Editorial Board: Walter S. Avis (Editor-in-Chief), Charles Crate, Patrick Drysdale, Douglas Leechman, M. H. Scargill, C. J. Lovell (to 1960). The Lexicographical Centre for Canadian English, University of Victoria, British Columbia (Toronto: Gage, 1967).

[11]Vincent Massey, *On Being Canadian* (Toronto: J. M. Dent and Sons, 1948), p. 65.

[12]Arthur Bestor, "The American University: A Historical Interpretation of Current Issues," *College and University* (Menasha, Wis.: American Assn. of Collegiate Registrars and Admissions Officers), Winter, 1957, pp. 184-185.

[13]Denis H. Wrong, "Leisure and the Arts," *American and Canadian Viewpoints* (Washington: American Council on Education, 1955), pp. 19-20.

[14]B. Y. Card, "Education and Social Change," *Canadian Education and Research Digest* (Toronto: Canadian Education Assn.), VIII, No. 1 (March, 1968):9.

[15]Frank MacKinnon, "Relevance and Responsibility in Education," *Quance Lectures in Canadian Education* (Toronto: Gage, 1968).

[16]P. Read Campbell, "Speech Education in the English Speaking Teacher Training Institutions of Canada" (Ph.D. thesis, University of Wisconsin, 1957); L. L. Wilson, "Speech Education in Canada: Curricula, Facilities and Personnel" (Ph.D. thesis, University of Alberta, 1966).

[17]A brochure may be obtained by writing to Chairman, Speech and Drama Department, Faculty of Education, University of British Columbia, Vancouver 8, Canada.

[18]For a subscription or courtesy copy, write to I. R. Shaw, Editor, Faculty of Education, University of British Columbia, Vancouver 8, Canada.

[19]P. Read Campbell, "Graduate Work in Speech Education in Canada," *The Newfoundland Teachers' Journal,* June, 1968, pp. 38-40.

[20] Campbell, *op. cit.*

[21]The establishment of the (small) Department of Speech and Drama would not have been possible without the initial and continued support and encouragement of the Dean of Education, Neville V. Scarfe.

[22]Leona F. Paterson has probably made a greater contribution to the growth of the discipline of speech and drama in western Canada than any other educator.

SPEECH EDUCATION IN FINLAND

Lahja Salonen
Inkeri Lampi
Irja Innola

INTRODUCTION

It is said in Finland that the Finnish landscape has made Finns frugal with words. The landscape is extremely rough, with rocky hills, ridges, valleys, and hollows which usually contain lakes. The country is snowbound for about five months of the year in the south and up to seven months in Lapland. In older times the houses were widely separated, especially in the western part of the country, and people did not come into contact with each other very easily.

The history of Finland, including 700 years of Swedish and 100 years of Russian occupation, may also have had some influence on the reserved and uncommunicative nature of Finnish people. The country has been independent only 50 years.

A BRIEF HISTORY OF SPEECH AND SPEECH EDUCATION IN FINLAND

Nonacademic Speech

The Finnish country population has always been a vital element of the nation. The farmers were never serfs. Thus the greater part of the cultivated land has always been owned by independent farmers, and this ancient heritage of freedom has left its mark on the folk culture—an important part of Finnish culture as a whole. Therefore, the native oral tradition of epic poetry, legends, stories, proverbs, and riddles began and was preserved. They have been collected, and at present the folklore archives have developed into the largest of their kind in the world (1,550,000 catalogued items).

These old poems, stories, and proverbs were interpreted in living rooms of farm houses on long dark winter evenings either by speaking or by singing. Children learned the poems by listening to these interpretations and, in turn, taught them to their own children. Among these interpreters, there were always some who were more capable than others, and thus the old traditions were enriched with their personal interpretations. Some of the masters were living in the nineteenth century in the eastern part of Finland; their presentations were used to compile folklore into *Kalevala,* the national epic collection.

In addition to the rich epic and lyric tradition, which no doubt was the first means of speech education in Finland, there were several spiritual and intellectual movements which developed the speech proficiency of ordinary Finnish people. Among the oldest were religious movements, led both by priests and laymen, including men and women. Some of them were born speakers whose way of speaking—moderate and yet deep—is still admired by many. The requirements of the religious speakers were rather high; if the speaker could not interpret his inner feelings or if he had nothing worthwhile to say, the audience interrupted him by singing a psalm. This type of audience reaction may even nowadays take place in a religious meeting.

The Finnish Youth League, aimed to meet intellectual needs of rural youth, and the Labor Movement, the purpose of which was to increase the cultural level and political activity of working people, were both established at the end of the nineteenth century. The role of these movements as developers of Finnish speech is most important, since, in their meetings and festivals, they offered opportunities for speakers, discussants, and interpreters to develop their skill in real speaker-audience situations. Little by little, both movements added speech to their activities, and as early as 1905, there came into existence the first Labor Speech Club in Finland. These two movements have also trained speakers for Finnish social and political forums and even for the Finnish Parliament.

Drama is said to be the most characteristic way for a Finn to express himself. It has been said, too, that every Finn has acted at least once in his life. In a country of less than 5,000,000 people, there are thirty-six professional theaters and more than six thousand dramatic clubs. These clubs, located both in towns and in the countryside, offer valuable speech training to people who otherwise would not get any speech training at all.

There are many other forms of adult education in Finland; for instance, one- and two-year peoples' colleges, workers' evening schools, and peoples' institutes. During the school year of 1967-68, every twentieth Finn was registered in these volunteer and nonprofessional schools. All these institutes offer speech in various forms: public speaking, discussion, interpretation, and dramatics.

Academic Speech

In 1155, the Swedish King Erik the Good invaded Finland and secured the position of Christianity with the aid of the English-born Bishop Henry of Upsala. For 300 years the Catholic Church had a dominating position in the country, and the first medieval schools in the thirteenth and fourteenth centuries were based on the Catholic tradition. In these schools, the curriculum was divided into two parts: *trivium,* including Latin grammar, rhetoric, and dialectics, and *quadrivium,* including theology, music, arithmetic, and astronomy. Speech, together with theology, formed the core of the curriculum in the Middle Ages in Finland, and later on speech was considered to be more important than ever in the Finnish school curriculum, a tradition which has continued up to this date.

The first university, the University of Turku (later the University of Helsinki), was established in 1640, but because of the lack of research in the field it is hard to estimate how much it influenced the development of speech education. As late as 1928, the University of Helsinki began to offer courses in interpretation and voice training.

SPEECH EDUCATION IN THE FINNISH EDUCATIONAL SYSTEM

Compulsory School

The Finnish compulsory school is going through important changes from the old school to the so-called basic school, which resembles the Swedish and American school systems. The children come to the primary school at the age of seven and stay in the same school four years according to the old plan. Then they may choose between the upper primary school, which leads to the vocational schools, and the lower secondary school, which leads to upper vocational colleges and to the upper secondary school, which, in turn, leads to university studies. The Parliament has already passed the law establishing the basic school that will do away with the duality of the upper primary and lower secondary school and keep the pupils in the same school up to sixteen years of age. Then the pupils will choose between the trade schools and the upper secondary school.

Speech is taught in all Finnish primary and secondary schools as well as in most of the trade schools as a part of Finnish language courses. As a separate subject it is taught nowhere; in some secondary schools the pupils may, however, study speech as an extracurricular, elective subject. According to the Finnish educational philosophy, all teachers are speech teachers too and are required to pay attention to their students' oral proficiency.

In practice this philosophy has turned out to be most unsatisfactory. There are several factors that prevent effective speech education as a part of Finnish. First, time devoted to Finnish is less than the time devoted to the vernacular in other Scandinavian countries and in the Soviet Union. In the curriculum of the primary school there are from nine to six weekly periods of forty-five minutes each in Finnish; in the secondary school there are from three to four periods. Second, the number of pupils in one class—an average of forty—is far too great. There is no time and no place for individual contact between the teacher and the student, and under these circumstances effective speech education does not take place. Knowing this, it is difficult to say how much speech is taught in Finnish classrooms, since it depends on the personal interest of the teacher, and since teachers in Finland may decide to a great extent what they teach and how they teach.

Aims and Purposes of Speech Education in the Compulsory School

The aims and purposes of primary speech education were defined as follows:

1. To increase the child's social awareness and participation.
2. To develop the child's distinct, sincere, and pleasant speech.
3. To increase the child's knowledge of written and spoken language, both the similarities and differences.
4. To develop the child's ability to choose and organize speech material.
5. To develop the child's skill in using libraries and other sources.
6. To increase the child's audience awareness.
7. To increase and develop the child's vocabulary.
8. To remedy the child's speech and articulation defects as a lasting and careful process.

While planning the course content the teacher should:

1. Allow the child to choose the speech topics;
2. Offer the child opportunities to practice speech in social situations: in conversations and discussions;

3. Offer the child new and worthwhile material to increase his listening skills;

4. Lead the child slowly from dialects to standard Finnish.[1]

Improvised dialogues and plays are mentioned as proper student activities in the primary grades. In the intermediate grades, short reports and discourses on various subjects are recommended.

In teaching reading, the teacher should help the child to maintain natural speech intonation. This is extremely important while reading Finnish, in which intonation carries meaning to a large extent.

The above recommendations do not meet the needs of modern methods such as creative dramatics, puppetry, choric interpretation, and pantomime. Audio-visual equipment is also needed.

Recommendations for teaching speech in the secondary school are much more inadequate. The pupils in the lower grades should practice reading and tell freely of their hobbies in front of the class. In the intermediate grades, demonstration speeches and short discourses are mentioned as proper student activities. In the upper secondary school, book reports and longer discourses as well as unprepared activities, like discussion and debate, are suggested. In all grades a free, natural, pleasant, and interesting way of speaking is emphasized.[2]

In the 1960s, some secondary schools have added extracurricular speech to the curriculum. Lahden Yhteiskoulu, a private secondary school located in the city of Lahti, is the first, and thus far the only, school in Finland to own a closed-circuit television system. In this school and several other schools, extracurricular speech is found to profit the whole curriculum since methods used in the speech class are often accepted by other teachers. The titles of speech courses, such as speech, public speaking, interpretation, voice improvement, and dramatics show how much the course content may vary from school to school.

As was mentioned earlier, the Finnish compulsory school system is undergoing changes from the old school to the basic school. Several curriculum experiments are now going on in various schools. A temporary plan for teaching speech to grades 1 to 9 was developed by a specialist group of Finnish language teachers and speech teachers chosen by the Ministry of Education. Because the experiment is not yet finished, the results and the suitability of the plan are difficult to estimate. It is, however, obvious that not even this plan will provide effective speech education since speech is still considered to be taught as a part of Finnish.

The aims and purposes of speech education in the basic school are defined below:

1. To increase the student's skill in using standard spoken Finnish.
2. To increase the student's skill in expressing his thoughts orally in various speaking situations in a relaxed and natural way.
3. To enrich and increase the student's vocabulary, genuine Finnish expressions, and Finnish intonation.
4. To improve the student's voice and develop proper and careful articulation and pronunciation.
5. To develop the student's listening skills from appreciative to critical listening.

The stated aims and purposes of teaching reading are:

1. To increase the student's ability in finding the main points on the written page.
2. To increase the student's ability to understand what he reads.
3. To increase the student's skill in reading aloud and interpreting both fiction and nonfiction.
4. To increase the student's skill in using libraries and other sources.[3]

As far as the course content is concerned, discussion, voice improvement, improvisation, and reading are mentioned as student activities in every grade. In the lower grades (1-3) topics for share-and-tell periods and those for conversation and discussion are chosen from the child's own experiences and surroundings. Discrimination of sounds and the repetition of short stories told by the teacher or classmates are emphasized as listening activities. In the intermediate grades (4-6) conversing about current events, demonstration speeches, oral reports, and conversation form the core of students' activities. Listening, note-taking, and improvisation exercises gradually become more difficult. In the upper grades (7-8) demonstration speeches on various subjects such as maps, diagrams, and tables should be used. The students move from conversation to problem-solving discussion and learn the duties of the leader and the participants in a discussion. Critical listening and note-taking are emphasized. Dramatics, choric speaking, and interpretation also form a part of the speech programs. In the ninth grade, the speech program consists mainly of basic public address.

A plan for speech education in the three-year gymnasium, or upper secondary school, has not yet been defined. However, speech teachers have recommended a concentrated one-year course meeting twice a week as most suitable. The course should be planned to meet the needs of speaking situations in adult life.

Speech Education at the Universities and Other Institutes of Higher Learning

There are six universities and ten institutes of higher education in Finland, but none of them has a special speech department. Yet universities offer some speech courses in connection with Finnish or phonetics. As a matter of fact, academic speech education is intended to increase the speech proficiency of future teachers, especially those majoring in Finnish and primary-school teaching. In addition to these two groups, some other groups such as future teachers at technical institutes, institutes for home economics, textiles and clothing, and nursing colleges as well as future officers, priests, and lawyers are required to take speech courses.

Since academic speech education is intended for those preparing to become teachers, their own speech articulation and voice training are most emphasized. This philosophy results in the neglect of communicative speech and methods courses. The following discussion will give a more detailed description of the aims and content of various academic speech programs.

Teachers Training Colleges and Pedagogic Institutes

Up to 1968, primary-school teachers were trained in two-year teachers training colleges. The students were required to take speech in every fourth semester, from seventy to a hundred hours altogether. In addition, some speech training was given during the student-teaching period. According to the new plan, the three-year pedagogic institutes will offer a basic speech course with 15 hours of lectures and 30 hours of recitals. This means that the new plan offers even less speech to the students than the old one. However, a student wanting to specialize in teaching speech in the basic school may choose an extended course with 250 hours of speech.

The aims and purposes of speech education in the pedagogic institutes are as follows:

1. To test and to increase the student's own speech.
2. To improve the student's own communicative speech and interpretative reading.
3. To increase the student's skill to teach speech to others.

It is suggested that the course follow the lecture-recital method. The teacher should give lectures on the following problems:

1. voice improvement
2. organs of speech
3. relaxation and correct breathing
4. voice resonance
5. standard language and its proper articulation and pronunciation
6. the most common speech defects
7. children's speech
8. various aspects in speaking and speechmaking
9. methods of teaching speech, listening, improvisation, pantomime, choric speaking, creative dramatics, and puppetry

For recital sessions that take place in groups of sixteen students, the following exercises are recommended:

1. relaxation, correct breathing, and making vocal organs flexible
2. social speeches like telephoning, applying for a position, testimony of an eyewitness, reports, interviews, discussion, conference speeches
3. impromptu speeches (2-3 minutes) and extemporaneous speeches (3-4 minutes)[4]

Evaluation after student performances is intended to encourage and is given orally by the teacher and the classmates.

In addition to the required course the students may choose extracurricular speech, mainly dramatics, interpretation, and parliamentary procedure.

The above-mentioned extended course is planned to give the student a deeper and wider understanding of speech and the teaching of speech. More attention is paid to methods courses. In lecture-discussion sessions, problems such as language and structure of poetry, interpretation of folklore, and children as interpreters are discussed. To a great extent, recital sessions are planned and carried out by the students. Written research is required. The students are also required to participate in supplementary courses taught by specialists outside the faculty. The length of a supplementary course is thirty hours, and every student must choose six out of the following: Public Speaking, Discussion and Debate, Parliamentary Procedure, Interpretation, Dramatics, Pantomime, Improvisation, Puppetry, Radio-Television Teaching of Speech Didactic, and Speech-Correction for Classroom Teachers.

University Speech Programs

Since 1928, some speech courses, mainly emphasizing articulation and voice improvement, have been offered at the University of Helsinki. In 1956, the university began to extend the speech program. But phonetics and physiology are even today an important part of the speech program.

At this moment, the universities offer a three-semester speech program, including two series of lectures on physiology, communication psychology, theory of speech-making, and interpretation. The length of the compulsory course, including lectures and recitals, is about sixty hours. More advanced students may choose elective, extended courses in interpretation, conference techniques, and the teaching of speech. These courses are open for those students who have successfully completed the basic courses in voice improvement, interpretation, and public speaking.

Even if the university speech courses are mainly aimed at students majoring in teaching, the teachers are not wholly satisfied with the university speech programs since they tend to be too theoretical and to neglect teaching methods. The teachers find themselves imcompetent as speech teachers and prefer teaching Finnish and literature, which are taught much more extensively at the universities than speech.

The Institute of Technology and the School of Economics do not offer any speech courses. The students themselves have tried to better this situation by arranging speech clubs and hiring speech teachers at their own expense. An experiment of educational television is in progress at the University of Oulu.

Suomen Puheopisto (The Finnish Speech Institute)

Suomen Puheopisto, the only institute that trains speech teachers, was founded in 1947 as a private enterprise, though it is now supported by the city of Helsinki and by the state. One of the founders and the president of the institute is Professor Antti Sovijarvi, professor of phonetics at the University of Helsinki. There are three levels of instruction in accordance with the background of the student. The purpose of the institute is to develop and improve Finnish speech, conduct, research, and produce literature and publications in the field of speech. The institute also prepares its students to treat functional speech defects.

Most of the students of the academic department of Suomen Puheopisto study at the same time at some university or other institute of higher learning. Most often they choose three of the following subjects for their master of arts degree: Finnish, literature, phonetics, psychology, education, political science, sociology, or social politics. Before registering, the applicants take an examination that tests both their academic competence and their speech proficiency. In the fall of 1968, 44 out of 128 applicants were chosen. Altogether 144 students have graduated from this department.

Before graduating from the academic department, the students have studied five semesters at Suomen Puheopisto. The classes meet mostly in the evenings, and the students may choose one of the following majors: public speaking, interpretation, or speech correction. Some choose two majors. Subjects compulsory to all majors are phonetics; spoken Finnish; language, communication, and speech psychology; radio and television performance; relaxation and improvisation; the teaching of speech. Every student is required to submit a written research project.

The institute also offers shorter speech courses, for instance, a forty-hour course including public speaking, voice improvement, and parliamentary procedure. According to need, even shorter courses, planned for businessmen and other people interested in the practical aspects of speech, are offered.

Sibelius-Academy

Sibelius-Academy, the leading music institute in Finland (founded in 1885), has offered speech courses from the beginning. Speech is an obligatory minor required of students majoring in singing, music pedagogy, and church music. Course content consists mainly of the interpretation of poetry, and the remedy of speech and articulation defects. Instruction is individual; the teacher and the student meet half an hour a week during two semesters. Some lectures are also given. In 1968, there were about one hundred speech students at Sibelius–Academy. All other music institutes, both private and state-owned, offer similar speech courses.

Suomen Teatterikoulu ("The Finnish Theater School")

The most thorough speech education is given by three institutes that train professional actors and actresses. The following speech program is offered by the Finnish Theater School, the leading and the oldest (founded in 1943) institute in the field.

During the first year of the three-year program, the students are taught basic theater speech twenty hours a week. Group activities are most common during the entire first year, and the aim of education is the unity of speech and improvisation as well as the unity of speech and physical activity. During the second year, group activities give room for more individual programs, and every student has speech from five to six hours a week. Main attention is now paid to problems in expression. During the third and last year, individual speech training is given according to the needs of the students.

The number of students at the Finnish Theater School is very small; in 1968, there were only forty-five students. This means that from twelve to eighteen new students may register every year. Also the speech groups are small, and the teachers, applying team-teaching methods, know the needs of their students. However, vocal expression of Finnish actors and actresses is often criticized, and the suggested cause is inadequate speech education in the compulsory school.

Speech Correction

In Finland there are six phoniatrists, and five hospitals with phoniatric clinics. These clinics treat all kinds of speech and voice defects. The phoniatrists are assisted by a special faculty team, including speech correctionists, psychologists, kindergarten teachers, pediatrists, psychiatrists, and audiologists. At the phoniatric clinic of the University of Helsinki Hospital, there were, in 1967, more than one hundred new patients, and over twelve thousand were treated. Children with cleft palate are operated on at the age of two. In addition to operations, the treatment consists of speech therapy and dental care. Hospitals and establishments for giving treatment for mentally defective persons have hired thirty-four speech therapists.

More attention than before has been paid to the speech correction of hard-of-hearing children. The first school for deaf children was founded in Finland as early as 1846. Today there are six schools for deaf children in Finland, and at only one of them are children taught by sign language. Since 1966, about four thousand children have been tested every year in order to find hard-of-hearing children as early as possible. The youngest child who was given a hearing aid was two months old. The father of the screening test is Dr. Aatto Sonninen, the pioneer of phoniatry in Finland.

Functional speech and voice defects are treated at the phonetic department of the University of Helsinki. The president of the department, Professor Antti Sovijarvi, has developed a procedure to examine defects of the thyroid cartilage and the hyoid bone. In treating the patient, both voice exercises and various apparatus designed and developed by Professor Sovijarvi are used. One of these apparatus is a so-called tube resonator: a glass tube submerged into water picks up vibrations from the patient's vocal cords.

Speech correction for kindergarten children is arranged in only two Finnish towns. Speech correction for primary school children was begun in 1943 in Helsinki, but today children with speech defects are treated in twenty-seven localities. In 1967, there were 760,000 primary school children in Finland, and 12,750 of them were treated by speech therapists. However, there is a shortage of specialists in the field, since it is estimated that about 15 to 20 per cent of the primary-school children suffer from speech defects. S and R defects are most common. Classroom teachers are supposed to be able to remedy the lightest defects, but their help can be used only to a small extent.

Training of Speech Therapists

Training of speech therapists in Finland is not consistent at this moment. Some study phonetics at the universities or graduate from the Finnish Speech Institute. One short but difficult course was arranged especially for those working at mental hospitals. Since 1966, the University of Jyvaskyla has offered courses leading to a certificate for school speech correctionists. Only competent primary school teachers with two years of teaching practice are allowed to study toward this certificate. Up to this date eighteen speech correctionists have graduated from this university.

Training of speech correctionists is arranged according to the following guidelines: the applicant must have a B.A. degree with a minor in phonetics and education or psychology. In addition, he must have had six months of practical experience under the guidance of a phoniatrist. The course consists of 250 hours of lectures and 600 hours of practice. It is estimated that from 90 to 130 speech correctionists are needed in Finland.

There are some associations for speech correctionists in Finland: Puheterapeuttiliitto, Koululogopedit, and Logopedisfoniatrinen yhdistys (founded in 1963). The latter is a member of the International Association of Logopedics and Phonetics.

University Speech Teachers

University of Helsinki

Antti Sovijarvi, professor of phonetics
Ritva Ahonen, M.A., Speech Institute certificate
Urho Vapaavuori, licentiate of philosophy, Speech Institute certificate

University of Turku

Kaija Tuominen, M.A., Speech Institute certificate

University of Tampere

Timo Leino, M.A., Speech Institute certificate

University of Oulu

Esko Vierikko, M.A., Speech Institute certificate

Teachers Training Colleges

Teachers Training College in Helsinki

Lahja Salonen, M.A., Speech Institute certificate

Teachers Training College in Jyvaskyla

Ossian Leisimo, M.A., Speech Institute certificate

Teachers Training College in Oulu

Kaakinen Iikaa, M.A.

Teachers Training College in Turuku

Otro Kontturi, Speech Institute certificate

SUMMARY

In spite of an honorable tradition of speech education in medieval Finnish schools, including rhetoric and dialectics, and a rich folklore, interpreted orally for hundreds of years, modern speech education is rather young in Finland. Nonacademic speech was mainly developed by several intellectual and spiritual movements such as religious movements, the Finnish Youth League, and the Labor Movement, beginning during the second half of the nineteenth century and continuing to the present. In addition, dramatic clubs and various institutes of adult education have influenced the development. The first academic speech course was offered in 1928 at the University of Helsinki.

The Finnish compulsory school is going through important changes from the old school to the basic school. In the old school, speech is taught as part of Finnish, and teachers of the whole curriculum are considered to be responsible for the students' speech proficiency. This philosophy has not guaranteed effective speech education. In the teaching plans for the basic school, the importance of effective speech education is admitted, but it is still suggested that speech be taught in connection with Finnish by Finnish language teachers. There are some experiments going on to show the suitability of the teaching plan, but it may be stated that speech teachers doubt the effectiveness of the marriage of speech and Finnish.

At the universities and other institutes of higher learning, speech is required mainly for those majoring in teaching. However, the student's own speaking skills rather than communicative speech and methods courses are emphasized as the core of speech programs. Teachers Training Colleges and the Finnish Speech Institute have a broader philosophy of speech education that includes both the enrichment of the student's own speech and the development of skill in teaching speech. Finnish university courses are being revised, and it seems obvious that the scope of speech programs will be widened soon.

Among professional schools, Sibelius-Academy and the Finnish Theater School have developed speech programs to meet the needs of future singers, music teachers, actors, and actresses.

The importance of screening and treating children with speech and hearing defects is admitted. Speech correction for primary school children was begun in 1943, and at this moment twenty-seven localities have been able to arrange for this care. However, the lack of speech therapists prevents all children in need of treatment from receiving it.

The training of speech therapists in Finland is under revision too. According to the new plan, the applicants must have a B.A. degree. The course is planned to consist of 250 hours of lectures and 600 hours of practice.

However, it seems obvious that in twenty years speech will be considered a more important subject than today, since public opinion—especially technical people and people in business—recognizes the value of speech in modern life. Tomorrow's speech education will no doubt be structured along the following lines:

1. Speech should be taught from the child's first school day using methods that are tested and found most suitable for each grade. At vocational schools speech education should be planned to meet the needs of the student's adult private and vocational life.
2. The final aim of all speech education should be the relaxed and pleasant speech of every individual.
3. Speech should be seen as a part of the whole curriculum and the whole educational plan.

4. All teachers should be responsible for the enrichment of the student's speech.

To meet the above aims the following suggestions should be considered as soon as possible:

1. All schools, universities, and other institutions of higher learning should arrange speech courses taught only by speech teachers. Speech therapists should be available to treat students in the speech defects.
2. The universities should arrange academic speech training of speech teachers by founding special speech departments.
3. Research on various aspects of speech and on teaching methods should be initiated.
4. Speech teachers should be provided with opportunities to get acquainted with speech education in foreign countries.
5. Speech textbooks and books suitable for collateral readings should be published in Finnish.

FOOTNOTES

[1]Kansakoulun opetussuunnitelmakomitean mietintö ("Statement of the Primary School Teaching Plan Committee") II (Helsinki: 1952).

[2]Asetus oppikoulujen lukusuunnitelmista sekä valtion oppikoulujen oppiennätykset ja methodiset ohjeet ("Statute of Teaching Plans for the Secondary School, Required Achievements of State-Owned Secondary Schools, and Methodical Recommendations"), (Helsinki: 1944).

[3]Väliaikainen peruskoulun opetussuunnitelmakomitean mietintö ("Temporary Basis School Teaching Plan Committee's Statement"), (Helsinki: 1968).

[4]Opettajanvalmistuslaitosten opetussuunnitelmakomitean mietintö ("Statement of the Teaching Plan Committee for Teacher Training Institutes"), (Helsinki: 1968).

SPEECH EDUCATION IN GERMANY

John Fred Deethardt, Jr.

INTRODUCTION

Tacitus lamented the decadence and dethronement of eloquence at Rome in *Dialogus de Oratoribus,* and celebrated in *Germania* the practice of German tribes in which one was qualified only by eloquence to speak. Eighteen hundred years later, in 1812, Adam Muller eulogized German eloquence in his *Twelve Speeches on Eloquence and Its Decline in Germany.*[1] Tacitus and Muller were generally ignored in their own day, only to be rediscovered much later at a time when people seemed to be more receptive to the lessons history can teach.[2]

Irmgard Weithase's book, *Toward a History of the Spoken German Language,* provides basic information that may account for the decline of speech from Tacitus to Muller and on to quite recent times.[3] The author[4] has elsewhere traced the historical foundation from the Middle Ages up to the present of speech education in Germany. The present chapter focuses on the major activities since 1948.

THE RENAISSANCE OF SPEECH EDUCATION

In 1948, Marie-Hed Kaulhausen revived the German Society for Speech Science and Speech Education. Out of its first post war convention in Frankfurt am Main, October 12-15, 1950, came a resolution, a petition to the Standing Committee of the Ministers of Education of the States of the Federal Republic of West Germany (1) to make training in speech mandatory for all teachers, especially those presently pursuing studies at universities and colleges, and (2) to include speech science *(Sprechkunde)* in the state examinations for the positions of German teachers in the higher schools. The professional association felt that the two-step program was necessary for the following reasons:

65

(1) Between the theoretical recognition of speech education and its realization in instruction there is a constant discrepancy from which grows detrimental consequences for the pupils, the teacher and the population as a whole. (2) Voice and Speech errors are frequently not correctly recognized as a result of a lack of knowledge and experience. Thus their treatment, which the teachers in the easy cases must undertake themselves, [and] in the more difficult cases refer to the speech therapist or doctor, is left undone. (3) The speaking and reading of the pupil often lacks the readiness requisite for later professional life. (4) Artistic education in the speaking of poetry and in amateur theater falls behind the attainable. (5) The ability to speak and discuss is not cultivated as much as would be necessary for citizenship education. (6) The pupils are therefore not led to that standard of speech training that is desirable for personality training. (7) Those teachers whose individual ability in this area is not sufficient are restrained in the development of their pedagogical possibilities. (8) Frequently teachers suffer from vocal hardships physically and spiritually . . . (9) Through short courses of lessons alone . . . . as valuable as they may be as a stimulus and a refresher . . . these evils cannot be removed, but only through a systematic speech education stretching over a longer time.[5]

With this resolution, the professional association began to pressure the educational authorities and the public in general for reforms in German instruction.

Speech education and democratic behavior, in the long view, are inimical to the European ideal that it is erudition that builds character. Seidelmann effectively and succinctly contrasted American pragmatism with German scholarship: "The goal of American training is not man as a creature of intellectual order with critical and synthetic powers of thought as in the German, but on the contrary, the state citizen, developed individually according to his talents and fitting into the whole, with activated capabilities for his own point of view and for the assertion of his own existence. . . . To the historical-humanistic conception of education he opposes a practical-realistic philosophy of education which stresses the present but is not free of the missionary ideal."[6] The practical philosophies have been politics and rhetoric from the time of Aristotle. Weller believes that the present German government shows a better picture of convergence with pragmatism than the Weimar government. "However," he says, "parliamentary oratory still suffers from the lack of foundation, namely, an accustomed way of viewing public address and discussion from youth up."[7] Members of Parliament can neither speak extemporaneously nor debate, in spite of standing orders in the parliament to do so since the orders took effect January 1, 1952. The frequent error on the part of campaigners for political office is to give a lecture *(Sachvortrag)* instead of a public address *(Rede)*. "Without a doubt," Weller concludes, "the lack of interest in politics will not be avoided without civic education in speaking and discussion.... Since the reestablishment of democracy, no systematic schooling in speech has been pursued on the whole and therefore the most important means of civic education and political activation has been omitted."[8] He calls for experiences in speech and debate for teachers-in-training at the colleges, especially for future teachers of German in the higher schools *(Gymnasien* and *Mittelschulen)*.

KULTURPOLITIK AND THE GERMAN EDUCATIONAL SYSTEM

A brief word about *Kulturpolitik* might be appropriate while we are standing on the bridge between politics and education.[9] In all cultural matters the states *(Länder)* have sovereign powers, i.e., legislation and the execution of legislation regarding schools and extrascholastic education. Above the states, on the highest level of government, exists cultural federalism.[10] The Federation only deals with tasks relating to the promotion of knowledge in general or to foreign policy in education. Consequently, any consideration of the German educational system first would have to consider the individual characteristics of the system of the eleven sovereign states: Bavaria, Baden-Württemberg, Saarland, Hesse, Rhineland-Palatinate, North Rhine-Westphalia, Lower Saxony, Bremen, Hamburg, Schleswig-Holstein, and Berlin. (Berlin, Bremen, and Hamburg are city-states.) An attempt is made to achieve some uniformity within diversity through the work of the Standing Conference of Ministers of Education at the federal level, and by and large the essential and common features can be fixed in a brief description.

The trunk of the system is the first four years of primary schooling (beginning at the age of six, there being no obligatory preschool education). All children attend this junior division in common. The tree has three limbs; the branching begins at the end of the fourth year. As for the first limb, the main body of the population continues in the senior division of the primary or people's schools *(Volksschulen)* to complete eight, nine, or ten years. In the junior division (basic school, *Grundschule* or *Unterstufe)*, play is superseded by the learning of elementary skills. The senior division (main school, *Hauptschule* or *Oberstufe)* aims at developing all practical talents. Many states are adopting the option of adding a year or two to accomplish the change-over from schooling to employment.

The second limb of the system, the intermediate school, or secondary school shorter course *(Real-* or *Mittelschule),* takes about 7½ per cent (according to 1955 figures) [11] of the pupils from the primary schools after the fourth year. Some intermediate schools have a four-year course, taking pupils from the sixth class of primary school, and some have a three-year course for pupils after the seventh primary year, but the standard intermediate school has the six-year course. Pupils leave with the intermediate certificate of maturity *(Mittlere Reife)* and go into careers as officials of the executive grade in public administration and the social services, or attend vocational schools, technical schools, or advanced technical schools, or change over to secondary schools in order to obtain a certificate of maturity *(Reifezeugnis)* for entrance into a university.

The third branch, the secondary school *(Gymnasium),* is important as preparation for the university. According to the 1955 figures, about 17½ per cent of the pupils entered from the junior division of the primary school. There are several types of secondary schools: the classical-language school *(altsprachliches Gymnasium),* the modern-language school *(neusprachliches Gymnasium),* and the mathematics-physical sciences school *(mathematischnaturwissenschaftliches Gymnasium).* About 40 per cent of those entering succeed in obtaining the certificate of maturity *(Reifezeugnis)* after passing the culminating examinations *(Abitur).* The standard secondary school follows the fourth class of the primary school and continues for nine years. Class designations are either (1) equivalent to the year in school, numbered consecutively from the first year in the primary school and continued into the secondary (e.g., the fifth class is the first year in the *Gymnasium, etc.);* (2) numbered separately in the primary and in the secondary schools (e.g., the first year in the *Gymnasium* is the first class, etc.); or (3) given Latin names (e.g., *Sexta* being the first year in the secondary school, followed in order by *Quinta, Quarta, Untertertia, Obertertia, Untersekunda, Obersekunda, Unterprima,* and *Oberprima,* being the ninth and final year). Continuous numbering may become the uniform system in the future. The most important drive for reform in the secondary school, however, is in increasing the number of entrants and in lowering the high rate of attrition.

Quite simply, in summary, branching in the United States occurs within one school, the high school. In Germany, by contrast, branching occurs between schools, and the type of program the pupil desires determines the school he will attend. If such a school is not available, he must change his program. In the United States one can climb the mountain as high as he wishes or is able, but in Germany the attempt is made to put on the mountain only those who can and will climb to the top.

Guidelines *(Richtlinien),* lesson plans *(Lehrpläne),* or school orders *(Schulordnungen)* appear in each state under the direction of the chief education official *(Kultusminister).* The syllabuses for courses in the curriculum are constructed by the ministry, usually with the specific authors chosen from the foremost university scholar-specialists who remain anonymous (although often they can be identified by their style of writing or by their colleagues).

Speech education appears under the heading of German instruction in the guidelines. In the states of Hesse and Bavaria, speech education is given a position of lesser importance, behind reading, writing, spelling, in the lower level of the primary schools.[12] In Bremen, speech education is treated in first position.[13] In the guidelines for the intermediate schools, Hesse ranks speech education first in its consideration of German instruction, and Bavaria makes no special mention of speech education at all. In the secondary schools of both Hesse and of Bavaria, speech education is of the highest order of importance since that aspect of German instruction is described before all other activities. In the opinion of the writer, the order of the treatment has been the force of official preference. Furthermore, speech education is deemed more important for the small number attending secondary schools; unfortunately, this is comparable to the status of speech studies as an elective in American high schools. Under which system speech education obtains the broadest exposure has not been studied.

The guidelines all specify the hours of instruction per week to be given to each subject in the curriculum. The case of Hesse illustrates the great difficulties of consummating in practice the desires of the policy-makers. There, history, German, and political instruction are lumped together in seven hours per week. Moreover, German instruction is clearly subdivided into the four areas of speech education, composition, grammar, and literature. The picture becomes blurred with a multitude of teacher and pupil activities in a bit more than an hour a day for six days a week. Wilhelm Poethen, in an article, "The Guidelines for German Instruction in the States: A Critical Overview," testifies to the overloading of the curriculum:

> In a few states speech education in the narrow sense is missing completely or is only considered in very general terms. Others provide for exercises in breathing, voice and speech training in a systematic structure, but one must reckon with the fact that here something exists on paper that can scarcely be realized. Quite correctly the Hessian guidelines emphasize that speech education in the German school still is in a bad way and is not prosecuted by the teachers for the most part with the requisite devotion and methodical care.[14]

The pragmatism of oral skill and the need for pragmatism in German education, as an alternative to the antidemocratic grip that the European emphasis on scholarship has in education, are quite clear to Poethen. "There should, in the last analysis, no longer be a German teacher who has not procured in university exercises or in speech courses the assumption that actual instruction in speech education can be a basis for artistic education as well as for the training of volition, for the development of the communal spirit and the formation of character, that it leads to an engaging style of speech which forms in the language of speech the natural counter-weight against the style of writing."[15] Speech education is seen as one alternative force not yet realized in Germany. The trouble lies in the classroom teacher. Walter Wittsack, speaking for the Departmental Association of the Academic Representatives of Speech at the Universities of the Federal Republic of Germany, an arm of the professional association, outlined the studies that should be necessary for all matriculating German teachers.

1. Fundamentals of Speech Work (work with the questions of Language as Speech Performance, that is, insight into its structure and exercises toward its mastery in the area of the mother tongue, inclusive of exercises in standard German speech).
2. Interpretative Speaking (that is, working of the oral manifestations [*Schallformen*] of German verse and prose in interpretation [*Nachgestaltung*]).
3. Extemporaneous Speaking [*Freigestaltendes*] (that is, experience in the area of German discourse, therefore in conversation, discourse and discussion, as well as exercises in the style of speaking and writing).[16]

There is no doubt that when the policy-makers go to work, the program in speech education they devise has the requisite qualities of

identity in academic respectability, continuity over the years, scope
in forms and fundamentals and guaranteed enrollment of each pupil.
But that is only the official promise. So much for *Kulturpolitik.*

The three basic areas outlined by Wittsack constitute the field
of speech in Germany. Speech correction is affiliated with the
faculties of medicine in the universities. Theater in most of its
practical phases is too highly associated with professionalism to be
accepted into the academic community of the universities; special
schools exist for those interested in theater. Radio and television are
adjuncts, as audiovisual aids, to all instruction. The chief production
center of all aids is in Munich.

THE FUNDAMENTAL: *HOCHSPRACHE*

A fundamental of speech is a property of speech universally
present in situations of oral communication, i.e., voice, articulation,
listening, language, emotional adjustment, and bodily action (other
than articulatory movements). In the United States when one speaks
of the fundamentals of speech, one includes all the properties named;
in Germany only voice and articulation have become a major focus in
speech education. Among a number of articles on speech education
appearing between 1945 and 1965 in the leading journals, *German
Instruction, Mother Tongue,* and *Effective Word,*[17] only one was
concerned with bodily action.[18]

Regarding bodily activity, one takes a hint from Reclam,
writing on German choric interpretation, that "the Germans, who
have not the gift of moving as the peoples of other nations, remained
more static in their performances."[19] No section of the most
comprehensive and definitive work on German speech, *German
Speech Science and Speech Education* by Christian Winkler and Erica
Essen[20], gives discrete identity to the subject of bodily action. Nor
does listening merit identity in this book. "Language," or style,
could come under Winkler's headings of "The Thinking Performance" *(Denkleistung),* "The Sentence as a Basic Form," "Word
Meaning," "Vocabulary," "Word Usage," etc. The lesser term,
diction, rather than the larger term, style, is the extent of interest in
oral language. Put another way, Winkler seems to be more interested
in correctness and clarity than in embellishment in language. It is
understandable since the speaker in the German classroom is more
likely to be an oral interpreter than an extemporaneous speaker and
thus is not likely to be himself the creator or inventor of the style he
speaks; he does not invent the language of his performance.

The director of the German Library *(Deutsche Bibliothek)* in Frankfurt am Main, Frau Dr. Schall, granted the writer an interview in June, 1966, in which it became clear that speech education *(Sprecherziehung)* is a nonpolitical, academic course, giving training in the oral expression of fine writing, correct breathing, and articulation. Political themes are not a part of speech or speech education. In Germany there is really no good or exact word for political speaking. Political matters are the theme of training in the political parties and political assemblies, and even though Dr. Schall is interested in political affairs, she does not belong to a political party. The journalists, especially, must study politics so that they may report political affairs. One can truly speak of a "journalistic democracy" in Germany, which is something less than a mediated or representative democracy.

Wittsack, as previously quoted, described what may be termed as one fundamental and two activities of speech. The fundamental was cited as "work with the questions of *language as speech performance,* that is, insight into its structure and exercises toward its mastery in the area of the mother tongue, inclusive of exercises in standard German speech." Wittsack clearly separates the investigation from the inculcation of speech. Weller's *Lexicon of Speech* defines the differentiation that is so important in German speech: "Language *(die Sprache)* as physical-mental event, language *(die Sprache)* as speaking or, better still, as speaking activity. Language *(die Sprache)* is here action, practice, volition, effect. It is comprehended as biologically functional, concerning the act of its production, coming aurally into being, (and) concerning the act of its reception. With the investigation of this world of speech, speech science *(Sprechkunde)* occupies itself; with the full educational use of the results of investigation, speech education *(Sprecherziehung)* stands alongside in a close relationship."[21] Unfortunately, the dichotomy among interested Germans becomes a class distinction between speech "scientists" and speech "educators," separating queen bees from workers.

The research and teaching of *Hochsprache,* or standard speech, constitute an age-long goal of German instruction: a dialect-free pronunciation *(Rechtlautung)* by the German people. Related goals are the vocal training *(Stimmbildung)* of pupils in the normal events of speech technique and the hygienic maintenance of the organs of speech *(Sprechhygiene).*

Such a fundamental concern for voice and articulation produces a lively strain of interest in speech in elementary education and in initial instruction in reading. Gustav Wenz, in *Speech Education as the Basis for Language Instruction in the Basic School,* enumerates four specific causes of the lack of speech skills in the pupil: (1) the nature of beginning instruction in reading; (2) lack of the practice of speech education in the schools; (3) lack of speech education in teacher training institutions; and (4) neglect by the periodicals of speech education in the primary schools.[22] The chief fault is in the instructional method which aims at activities of passive reception and appeals to intellectual understanding. This sample of Wenz's approach shows one chief feature of all writing—its polemic of justification.

Wenz sees the task of the teacher in initial reading instruction to be to lead the child from his particular oral usage to the language of more general usage and, in the process, to prevent writing, reading, and arithmetic from becoming inhibiting factors in the child's general spiritual and mental growth. The emphasis is on correct speaking, but the desire for colorful expression is indicated in this passage:

> Such a habit of correct speaking forms the foundations of all speech education and remains a constituent of German instruction in all classes. The goal is correct sounding speech, physically healthy speech organs and mental cultivation of language, and building on that, speaking that is filled with sense and richly expressive, the impromptu conversation, extemporized speech, the extemporized lecture, ability in discussion, and finally, sensible expressive reading.[23]

One antithetical form of expression to be attacked is *das Leiern,* the grinding, monotonous, singsong of schoolroom recitation. A second problem is the shallow breathing of silent sitting in the classroom, which requires instruction in breathing. A third issue is the level of diction, whether it should be the low, middle, or high dialect *(Mundart),* some acme form of speech such as Sieb's stage diction *(Bühnenausprache),* or the printed language of books and periodicals *(Schriftsprache).* A fourth issue regards pedagogical method. Should there be fundamental drill in correct speech proceeding systematically and structurally from individual phonemes to words, to phrases, to sentences, and so on? Or should one take seriously the desire to preserve a child's joy in self-expression through the silent and repressive years of initial reading, writing, and mathematical instruction? Is correctness in speech so much better that it should get the chief emphasis over rich expressiveness in the primary school? Speech education is primarily concerned with correctness and clarity, which are bound up in problems of delivery, to the neglect of appropriateness, and impressiveness tied to invention and arrangement. Is this a general hallmark of elementary speech education that is unquestionably appropriate for the elementary-school pupil?

Christian Winkler, the grand old man of German speech science, professor at the University of Marburg an der Lahn, and prolific writer in the field, expresses a synthesis in his article, "Leading Thoughts in Present Day Speech Education." An all-embracing task is posed for speech education. "Whoever intends it to be a matter only of voice and articulation drill, of that which was called in a mechanistic age 'speaking technique,' fails to recognize its character completely."[24] Winkler sees its task as making speech "transparent" for the mind. He then expresses a satisfactory, though subtle, resolution in the conflict between older and newer methods.

> To the conveyance of sense also certainly belong the individual parts of the production of expression: a hygienically faultless breath and voice control, a formation of sound in a dialect suitable at times or in standard speech and an emphasis and diction that conforms to the intended sense. But all these individual parts in the production of speaking may be separated at most in theoretical contemplation, but never in the practice of speaking. Indeed, one cannot separate them from the creation of sense and fashioning of thought without destroying their fine construction. When the old speech technique drilled certain sounds of standard speech, it taught first how the so-called organs of speech work and then, in connection with other sounds, exercise further in syllables and words. But as soon as the pupil spoke spontaneously, it all fell apart again . . . . Indeed, those peripheral functions in expression have been for so long so far automated in the school child that in ordinary self-expression the incentive to go from the language of thought over to expression is sufficient to let them run off as by themselves. Whoever would want to attend to a certain beat of the tongue would no longer be able to speak, let alone think: we are, when we speak, near *what* we want to say, scarcely even near the *how* of it. If one therefore, wants to work at the accent, then he must be cautious not to destroy that fine interplay of the production which scarcely ever becomes known—stuttering could be the result. The exercise material should be so chosen that just the parts of the performance of expression, which one desires to train, will play a special role in the speech, that this sentence here, for example, demands a specially careful arrangement of breathing or the expression of especially sharp consonants and fricatives. Then diction serves the sense, and the speech pupil moulds his speaking for the sake of understanding.[25]

Speech education, he says, is not a course or branch of German instruction (even if there it has its special place, if only for the convenience of administration), but *a basis of all instruction.*

Gunther Buehl in an article, "Speech Education, A Principal Item of Instruction in the Mother Tongue," corroborating Winkler's view, outlines several ways speech education has expanded its conception:

1. Opening up the way for verbal understanding
   Habits of correct use of the native tongue (Standards, listening exercises, speaking exercises).
   Purging speech of errors and impurities (Consideration of the idiom of the age level and of the region, improvements, technical exercises).

2. Development of the capacity for verbal expression
   Enrichment of the verbal repertoire (Experiencing things, images, words, etc.).
   Exercises in expression (Communication, telling original and other stories, plays, reports).

3. Preservation of the joy in speaking
   Ties to the idiom of the language of the home and the dialect (Songs, rhymes, poems, instructional conversations, choric interpretation, etc.).
   Richly varied exercises stressing enthusiasm (Improvised plays, tape recordings, occasional expression, etc.).

4. Becoming aware of the speech process through phonetic exercises
   Significant use of the speech organs (Breathing exercises, cultivation of voice, instruction in singing).
   Precautions against defects of speech (Special exercises for children with inhibited, disturbed speech).[26]

It may be deduced from all the articles put together that there is something more fundamental in German speech education than voice and articulation. Nearly all writers express a concern for the relationship the learner exhibits for his speech. The usual list of fundamentals contains the elements almost universally present in contexts of oral communication; most of these are visible and audible dimensions. Perhaps the list should be extended beyond behavioral objectivity, as is the case with listening, to include such descriptions of a fundamental relationship.

Weithase, in a discussion of six "Problems of Speech Education," further defines such a fundamental. In educating one "for speaking through speaking," the first major problem resides in the fact "that the pupil believes himself already to be able to do that for which he is to be trained. To him it is not a question of imparting unknown material or of inculcating new skills."[27] *The relationship of the learner to his speech must be basically changed. His naiveté must be disturbed, along with the whole phenomenon of his speech.*

Weithase then poses other problems of speech education: standard speech, mechanistic drill, the future use of speech skills in all areas of instruction, educating all teachers as speech models (all teachers teach speech), and advanced college level courses beyond the fundamentals, which she defines thus: "The fundamentals of speech education consist of education in hygienic and esthetically faultless speech as well as the command of standard German speech."

ORAL INTERPRETATION (RE-CREATIVE SPEAKING)

Speech educators in Germany have long made oral interpretation bear the burden of education in the speech fundamentals, rather than have oral interpretation serve literature. It is a matter of priorities. A typically German analysis is given by Weller in his *Lexicon of Speech.* He states that among actor, interpreter, and speaker there are degrees of (1) audience orientation, (2) performance identity, and (3) dependence on words only.[28] (1) The actor is more distant from the audience than the interpreter, and the latter is more distant than the speaker. (2) The three arts progressively include more of the performer's ego and also of his moral responsibility for what is said. (3) In the three arts, as separated, the performer stands to a greater or lesser degree alone with his words, unsupported by other arts such as scene design, costuming, and literature. Weller says the basic differences are that the actor is dependent on transformation, the interpreter on revelations, and the public speaker on intended action or a recital of facts. If the actor is successful, for the moment one is not aware of the personality of the performer. If the speaker is successful, one is completely aware of the character of the speaker. The interpreter treads some middle ground between the two.

The phrase *nachgestaltendes Sprechen* may be translated as "interpretative speaking." There is an affinity for the native word rather than the foreign noun, *interpretation,* or the verb, *interpre-*

tieren. Nachgestaltendes Sprechen is distinguished from *selbst-* or *freigestaltendes Sprechen.* One "fashions" or "forms" *(gestaltend)* according to *(nach)* some given text or model in oral interpretation. On the other hand, one "fashions" or "forms" freely *(frei* or *selbst)* in impromptu and extemporaneous speaking. Winkler points at the historical rise of interpretative speaking in distinguishing the two forms: "While the old rhetoric only considered the *selbstgestaltete* word, speech, since Lessing, aimed at the *nachgestaltete* word, especially for the actor."[29] Another form of the possible variations of the word is given by Krech as *nachschaffend Gestaltendensprechen:* "The *reader* does not give the form of presentation to the text, but discovers the form of presentation placed in the text by the *author.* "[30]

In most cases, the text for interpretation is verse. German speech has enshrined the German lyric as the focus of worship. The cultural-political guidelines for the schools manifest this observation, as do most of the articles in the journals. Verse makes obvious demands on fundamental skills of rhythm, sound, and articulation. As Kaulhausen has said: "The most difficult chapter of all of speech education is the speaking of verses. It is an art with its own body of laws precisely like music. But while the future music teacher must establish his knowledge and skill in his area before he can hope for a position, the speaking of poetry remains purely an act of dilettantism left to the arbitrary judgment of the individuals."[31] Further on she asserts that "no other branch of speech education really offers such possibilities of using and ennobling all the powers of the heart and intellect as objective *(Objektgebundene)* speaking of verses, that is, subordination (of the interpreter) to the lively form of poetry." She desires the student to submit himself reverentially to the author and his text.

Kaulhausen and most others seek the objective performance, "objectivity" being nearly equated with "infallibility" of interpretation. Psychologizing theory is pressed into the service of attaining objectivity. Magda Ferenbach discussed these psychological bases of theory:

> A good forty years ago, 1908, Ottmar Rutz published his sensationally stirring *New Discoveries of the Human Voice,* which rested on the experiences of his father Josef Rutz. Josef Rutz, a teacher of singing, had found that (1) movements of the muscles of the trunk, which lead to a continuous "adjustment" of the muscles, are an expression of human emotional behavior, that (2) the sound of the voice depends on the

adjustment of the musculature of the trunk, that (3) each person possesses a typical talent for emotion along with the appertaining specific adjustment of the trunk muscles, and that (4) the correct, that is objective, rendering of works of sound and speech requires the voluntary and conscious adjustment of the trunk muscles, which is adapted to the author's type.[32]

This theory suggested that the way to the objective, to the ideal, to the inhering form of sound, meaning, the form of sound which inheres within the poet and composer, dwelling latent within the images of notes and language, now appeared accessible. The individual peculiarity of the re-creative musician or speaker, his subjective view, could, it was claimed, be eliminated. A typology of sound *(Klangtypus)* became possible, and many subsequent authors picked up and perpetuated this notion that seemed to have the authority of the developing science of psychology behind it. After a fair discussion of the rather complex ramifications of the theory, Kaulhausen attempts to lay it to rest for all time in suggesting an alternative to the objective oral performance. Speaking that is "faithful to the work" *(das werkgetreue Sprechen)* she hopes will become a popular prescription. *"Getreu* (faithful) means more and less than objective: more, because faithfulness as a moral behavior requires the responsible disposition . . . of the speaker; less, because the personality of the speaker is not eliminated, is only subordinated to the work."[33]

Whether the oral interpreter views himself as a virtuoso (self-aggrandizement), a midwife (cooperation, subjectivity, faithfulness), or a radio (self-effacement, complete objectivity), at least the achievement in oral performance is the analysis itself. The traditional endeavors of the usual teacher of literature, bound as he is by training to the historical-critical method, could be consummated in the revelations of the oral recital of literature, if only he had the requisite training. Again, the polemical vein in the articles is rich in attack and justification. Perhaps Ferenbach exhausted the vein of typology in German speech education for the purposes of oral interpretation, but it may still be too early to tell.

An apparent contrast between German and American views of oral interpretation becomes clear in a simple inspection of the published writings. Innovation in forms comparable to the development, for example, of chamber theater in the United States, seems to be lacking in Germany. Several reasons for the lack may be suggested. First, there is a lack of advanced courses in all areas at the university level and consequently a lack of anything more than a fundamental interest in any area. Second, the conception that the lyric constitutes the ultimate test of proficiency, fostered by Kaulhausen and many others, inhibits innovation. In the United States, chamber theater came about through a deeper analysis of prose literature for the purpose of oral performance. The more essential properties of prose fiction, such as the often overlooked drama inherent in narration and its angle of vision, were usually being deprived of meaningful interpretation. The luxury of advanced students in advanced classes not devoted exclusively to one genre in the pursuit of a goal peripheral to it, as in oral interpretation in the United States, serves the exaltation of literature and the deeper excavation of its experience. In such a condition, a mastery of fundamentals may be presumed.

Choric interpretation in Germany is viewed with suspicion in general. The guidelines of Hesse give this warning: "Choric speaking is only to be employed with caution. The speech chorus can give especial effectiveness to individual works, but should only be made the object of work in exceptional cases."[34]

After World War I, Wilhelm Leyhausen gave choric interpretation its ultimate form in Germany. In his hands it took on international and professional characteristics that may have discouraged educators, who also avoided the diction of the stage as too professional a model to be held up to pupils for imitation. A repugnance to anything with a taint of professionalism may be a healthy view in the interests of education. Professionalism has been cited as the cause for the breaking up of the field of speech in the United States.[35]

Kaulhausen sees something inherent in choric interpretation that is to be rejected.

> After the first world war there came into Germany a form of speaking association unknown up to then: the speech chorus . . . Fortunately, the schools drew back from this form of poetry speaking. Speaking in a chorus, in a manner necessarily mechanical, is not consistent with the character of our language. It spoils the natural feeling for what is correct or idiomatic in language in the young and educationally only has the value that discipline and unconditional subordination to the chorus leader is required. It is not formative of personality. Also, there are only a few German poems that justify a choric treatment.[36]

Choric interpretation of a crude kind was used by Hitler's Youth to chant propaganda slogans and drum up hate and nationalistic feeling.

Perhaps that is why Kaulhausen felt the subordination of the youth to the uncertain arbitrariness of the chorus leader was more unhealthy than his submitting himself to the poet.

EXTEMPORANEOUS SPEAKING (CREATIVE SPEAKING)

Two recent publications bring something new to Germany. They are inexpensive paperbacks put on the popular market and are viewed by this writer as major, remarkable straws in the wind to be studied as cultural innovations. One is Walter Magass's *The Public Silence: Are There Rules for the Art of Public Address in Germany?*[37] and the other is Ekkehart Rudolph's *Extemporaneous Speaking and Persuasion: An Art That Is Capable of Being Learned.*[38] A third book should take its place alongside the other two. It is *Adam Muller's Twelve Speeches on Eloquence and Its Decline in Germany,* with an essay and a postscript by Walter Jens.[39] Muller's speeches were delivered in 1812, but have increased relevance now. The chief aim of all three is to reactivate the art of extemporaneous speaking and its tie to persuasive discourse. They attempt to revivify ancient rhetoric, the roots of a tradition long lost in Germany. The books cited constitute implicit criticism of German society. In order to rejuvenate speech education in Germany, the current emphasis on oral interpretation, on the aesthetic basis of speech, must be changed, and the small voice of criticism is heard in a few such as Friedrich Fikenscher, who shall be quoted at length.

> We have previously spoken almost exclusively about free speaking in which the pupil produces oral expression from within himself as he dresses a subject in his own words; only now do we concern ourselves with the speaking of given words, verse. The usual methods of German instruction proceed in reverse fashion. What they have to say about speech education is dealt with completely in its segments in expressive reading and in the recital of poetry; free speaking is scarcely touched upon by them. Isn't that remarkable? The pupil in his whole life will not, with 99.5 per cent probability, have to deliver a poem publicly. But the person will need his free speaking daily, and the more we have trained him in it, the better, the clearer he knows how to use it; many even depend on it in their profession, on being able to speak freely and convincingly; it is not at all necessary to think perhaps of the political speaker or of the one lecturing in science; each one in business life must be able to conduct a free conversation in community councils; in association meetings each should

be able to participate in the discussion. How many people are there who are greatly embarrassed when they are to speak freely a couple of words at a jubilee, at a wedding dinner, or at the grave of a respected one! Even in the circles of the so-called educated the fear of speaking is a frequent phenomenon. The school has educated so little in speaking abilities which each person really carries within him as a natural talent. The school has cultivated the performance of poetry . . . from time immemorial, although only a small selection of people attain the role of a *Rezitator.* Therefore, we always maintain the school should educate for life.

I already know what one can reply to this: it is for the sake of artistic education when the school practices the expressive performance of poetry; it is the strongest means by which we lead the pupil to the experience of poetry. I would let the object pass if it were only so since the endeavors of education in the arts; but it was always so even in the times when thoughts of the art experience had not yet been taken up in the pedagogical goals. The cause lies deeper. It lies in the fact that the school more and more in the course of its development reached the point of over-estimating the written language and consequently of a one-sided education in writing. The written and imprinted word is considered everything to it, the spoken was only a necessary means of instruction and educational apparatus, no goal of instruction. The poetic word was a printed word; one may therefore practice oral expression on it. It even went so far that they believed that through reading and recital of poetic works, style and purity of written expression would above all be developed, which is a fallacy; for poetic language lies on a plane not yet attainable by the child. One can be convinced again and again by simple observation how little the style of the reader goes over into the style of the children in essay writing; that (transfer of training) is only the case on a level of the intellectual development of style and mostly does not fall within the scope of the people's school, and is only accomplished in those fifteen or sixteen years old. But on each age level the path leads straight from speaking to writing. The logic and purity of language are more easily developed in the speaking child than in the roundabout, laborious way through written expression and its correction. Therefore, the cultivation of free speaking is to be denominated as the true, the most effective basis of German instruction.[40]

With this lack of an art of public address, the men and women of German speech have become specialists in what may be classified more comfortably under the heading of "free speaking," which, for reasons of brevity, was not translated accurately in the heading for this section as "extemporaneous speaking": they are specialists in "conversation" *(Gespräch),* a peculiarly German adaptation to a condition in which public address has not been possible. Conversation annihilates the distance between communicators, where the unmoved objectivity of discussion and societal relations is "nothing other than the elimination of the most dangerous possiblity of losing distance."[41]

Conversation in the United States is classified among the activities of informal speech because Americans have specialized in the subtleties of form in discussion, debate, and public speaking, all of which from the beginning axiomatically preserve a three-way distance among the speaker and the listener, the speaker and his subject, and the listener and the subject. Americans take the distance perhaps too much for granted in their practice and must constantly be reminding one another of the nature of discussion in a society *(Gesellschaft)* with its division of labor. However, the Germans are firmly rooted in community *(Gemeinschaft),* and forms are distinguished by the way they increase or lessen the distance between members. Germany has a history of throwing off foreign or other internationalizing influences that would effect an increase in the distance among members and consequently work against community: Judaism, Communism, Catholicism, democracy, etc. As a result, German speech resists discussion and debate as activities and as terms. An interesting study could be made of this question under the broad explanatory statement of the Sapir-Whorf hypotheses, the principle of linguistic relativity which infers the existence of correlations between linguistic structure and nonlinguistic behavior.[42]

That the overriding concept of *Gespräch* is hurtful is attested to by Schmidt-Hidding. He takes up a discussion of those forms of discussion in which the German finds something strange to his way of life.

> The youth of Anglo-Saxon lands learns to debate already in the *debating clubs* of the schools and colleges. The competitive character of *debate* particularly appeals to the youth of the debating clubs. The role of *proposer* or *opposer* is frequently allotted without the youth concerned being asked about his personal opinion on the problem raised. It is considered as a special achievement when I win an opinion that I do not myself share. The educator may justly object it is dangerous to teach young people to represent an opinion behind which they do not stand. This favors opportunism.[43]

The fact that Schmidt-Hidding sees danger in debating against personal convictions stands as one bit of evidence that Germans have

a "cultural decision" favoring *"überzeugen"* and not *"überreden."*
Winkler says: "Persuading remains forceful and according to our
definition, like an order: it intentionally looks beyond the person
being addressed and aims only at his external behavior."[44] Holding
to a conviction-persuasion dichotomy is also hurtful, especially since
psychology teaches that persuasion acts on immediate, small behavior, and this in turn contributes to the ultimate deepening of
conviction. As Professor Clarence Simon of Northwestern University
has said, Hitler's command of the "big muscle" behavior of all
Germans, i.e., the strictly external behavior of the Nazi salute for
citizens and soldiers alike, was instrumental in regimenting the
convictions of most Germans for Hitler's own purposes. Compliance
is prerequisite to internalization. The extremely idealistic view of the
"Gespräch" (exemplifying "German inwardness") put blinders on
the speech educator where alternative conceptions are possible.

Schmidt-Hidding himself asks if there are superior forms and if
Germany could adopt them.

> The (English) talk, conversation, discussion have one attitude in
> common, the threefold distance: one keeps one's distance as well from
> oneself, as from one's partner and generally also from the topic of
> conversation. It belongs to good form (etiquette) in English conversation
> that one considers himself with self-irony and always stresses that one
> could also be mistaken. Obstinacy is out of the question, forbidden, taboo.
> Already in the syntax of the modern English language there is provided a
> continual consideration of the person addressed. In addition, one is not
> supposed to want to win one's partner over personally. It must be left to
> his judgment whether he becomes converted to our point of view or not.
> To sum up, self-irony, humor, readiness to compromise and tolerance have
> humanized the English conversation. At least one must pretend to think
> unassumingly of oneself and to respect one's partner. To the distance from
> oneself and from one's partner often is joined the distance from the topic
> of conversation which then is not taken so seriously as it is with the
> German way of conversation. Such humanized forms of conversing, to
> which is added a minimal volume of voice, determined greatly the English
> intellectual atmosphere. This atmosphere is unfavorable to all radical
> solution, perhaps, however, also for keen *(hart)* intellectual decisions . . .
>
> Let us now assume from long experience, we have arrived at the
> conclusion that English forms of and attitudes toward conversation are
> superior in all practical situations of life. What can we do then? Can highly
> developed forms of conversation simply be taken over from another
> culture, as perhaps the English debate? Will it fit organically into the

German conversational behavior? As we saw, the black-white design of the Anglo-Saxon lands, the bi-polar thinking of debate will be profitably supplemented by the *multi-valued orientation* of discussion which brings to light the complexity of the subject. Besides, the general English conversational attitude of the threefold distance of Anglo-Saxon debate often takes the sharpness away. From our general conversational attitude we mistake all too easily an objective difference of opinion for a personal fight and suspect that the objective opponent wants to find fault with us personally. It would be for us a national gain if we could learn from the Anglo-Saxons the threefold distance in the discussion of practical matters of this life; for English forms of conversation combined with the basic German conception of conversation could easily have a destructive effect. Idiomatic tropes flatly requires us "to be plain spoken" *(kein Blatt vor den Mund zu nehmen)* and "to speak one's mind frankly" *(frei von der Leber weg zu reden).* In public life, however, one may not give free rein to his feelings . . . .

Though we frankly acknowledge the superiority of the English attitude to conversation in the practical and political areas, yet we may really hope that the "conversation" *(Gespräch),* as it developed in the continental and German tradition, and as the Anglo-Saxons fully lack it, is especially suited for spiritual contact and for the discussion of questions which concern human existence. When man is at stake, the threefold distance is not the suitable attitude. *"Gespräch"* with the Anglo-Saxons remains sometimes unsatisfying . . .[45]

Schmidt-Hidding implicitly advocates the view that universals in speech education exist, that is, that superior forms could be instituted in Germany. There is no doubt that there is diversity among the nations in their views of fundamentals and forms of speech, but the search for uniformity within the diversity of practice should be the goal of anyone who professes an international interest in speech. Similarity in practice among nations is not meant by the word uniformity; what is meant is that a practice has international value. To piece together the best practices of all countries would be to recognize the special contribution of each country to a universal speech education. If each country has a special interest in one aspect of speech education, as Germany has specialized in conversation, and as the United States has developed public speaking activities, then a universal speech education is possible, growing out of a comparative speech education. It becomes a question of educational strategy not to run roughshod over resistance. In other words, it becomes a job for persuasion and one of its special settings, education.

Toynbee, in *Change and Habit: The Challenge of Our Time,* stresses the historical necessity of education (change) outracing disaster (habits); he implies that persuasion must put whole peoples on a new high road of survival. A supranational speech education, with a central concern for training in the free speaking and political forms of oral communication, will not come about through a courteous withdrawal from debate about the best forms and national contributions, adopting the slogan that it would be national arrogance to debate. It will only be realized in the supranational spirit of a vigorous search for universal axioms, for the *Weltanschauung* of speech education, naturally at the cost of provincial, national habits.

It does not seem to be too remote to suggest in this context that the Association in the United States could provide the leadership in establishing an international newsletter on the order of *Spectra* with reports from colleagues around the world. Thus a practical first step would be taken to facilitate the search.

It is evident that Schmidt-Hidding's emancipation from a national interest in German speech education arises from a posture critical of German practice, and, to a certain extent, Fikenscher also may be included. Criticism from within, in the articles and books, is a rare thing when one looks for it.

THEATER

By a series of free decisions by municipalities and separate states, in other words, by no federal, central or unified policy, is the German theater subsidized. Some universities (Berlin, Göttingen, Hannover, Cologne, Mainz, and Vienna) offer training in drama *(Theaterwissenschaft)* as a separate course of study leading to the academic and scholarly degree of doctor of philosophy with the primary emphasis upon dramatic literature and history rather than upon practical theater activities. Special schools for theater and music are in Frankfurt am Main *(Frankfurter Schauspielschule)* and Wiesbaden (acting school).[46]

Taken historically, the beginning of a movement in amateur theater *(Laienspiel)* in 1914 was coincident with the youth movement in Germany.[47] The Richert guidelines of 1924 in Prussia gave official impetus to the classification of theater activities in the core curriculum. In the course of time, the special, pedagogical form of school theater *(Schulspiel)* developed.[48]

Presently the German writers jealously guard the amateur status of school theater through subtle definition. Rudolf Mirbt, a pioneer in the theater for laymen, distinguished among the professional actor, the dilettante player, and the true amateur player.[49] He puts in the dilettante category the Oberammergau passion-player who uses the professional actor's means without the professional actor's abilities. In other words, there is no amateur theater as a profession. The true amateur player lets the human being, not the artist in himself come to words. Amateur theater is communal play *(Gemeinschaftsspiel)* in which fidelity *(Treue),* not effect *(Leistung),* is the aim.

This kind of theater puts the pupil in a situation for the unfolding of his character and personality. It is seen as an enrichment and completion of German instruction in permitting the direct experience of dramatic literature. The chief value, according to Ferenbach, resides in its quality of play. From childhood, through adolescence, to adulthood, play never ceases facilitating self-discovery and social adaptation.[50] The articles all put a premium on the invention and discovery of dialogue of powers of imagination, movement, and rhythm. This amounts to creative playmaking, providing systematic development of spontaneous powers, not artistic productions. In Germany, school theater is creative dramatics as an educational method, according to the articles, our sources of theory. One cannot vouch for abusive practices in the schools as representative of knowledgeable intent. The scope and continuity of creative theater in Germany are truly amazing, and what the speech educators are striving for must be regarded as worthy of emulation everywhere.

SPEECH EDUCATION IN COLLEGES AND UNIVERSITIES

A broadening of the field of activity is generally the felt need among members of the German Society for Speech Science and Speech Education, which is equivalent to the Speech Association of America. Frau Ingeborg Geissner-Nida, technical assistant to Dr. Walter Wittsack in the Institute for German Speech at the Johann Wolfgang Goethe University, said in a personal interview with the writer in the summer of 1966 essentially what Marie Hed-Kaulhauser reported in the official publication of the professional association in 1959: "In sum, one can say that the powers of speech investigators for getting their work done in Germany are still extraordinarily limited and also probably can never so develop and perhaps should not so develop as in America, but that a reasonable expansion is urgently necessary and would be justified through the scientific work and corps of teachers presently concerned."[51]

At the time of the interview with Frau Geissner-Nida and Dr. Wittsack, about seventy-five students, almost all of them future teachers of German in the *Gymnasium,* were taking courses in the Institute, among which was the required course, Language as Oral Performance *(Sprache als Sprechleistung).* Two other courses are Poetry in its Oral Form *(Dichtung in ihrer Klangform)* and *Rhetorik.* The speeches, lectures, readings, and discussion in all three center around literary-philological themes paralleling the interests of the students in *Germanistik.*

Dr. Christian Winkler told the writer that the course required at the University of Marburg an der Lahn is called "Basic Training in Speaking." Witsack said that students have suffered in expressing themselves since World War II and that *nachgestaltendes Sprechen* (oral interpretation) gives them a speech experience they must have to overcome the pain of expressing themselves.

The areas of speech that readily lend themselves to instrumentation and exact measurement, phonetics and logopedics, have academic respectability within the faculty of medicine and in linguistics. The others, the speech scientists and speech educators, in nearly all they have produced for publication, have in no way dimensionalized or quantified aspects of the normal speech performance. The literature is speculative, anecdotal, and stylized. The vast literature of German scholarship in rhetorical theory often cited by American writers is not deemed to fall within the purview of this chapter.

Biennially, the professional association meets and discusses a theme. The formal contributions have three times resulted in a publication, about the only official organ identifiable as a scholarly journal. The fourth volume had no theme and did not grow out of a convention.

Semiannually, the *Communications* of the German Society for Speech Science and Speech Education is sent to the membership by the president.[52] It is the equivalent of the American Association's *Spectra,* giving personal items, notes of those who have passed the examinations for the title of certified speech educator, new members, reports, a bibliography, and other information. A recent expansion of the contents included one of the examination lectures for *geprüfte Sprecherzieher.* Such a step may indicate the future growth of this organ and the association, as it struggles for identity for itself and the field it represents.

A FINAL WORD

Speech education in Germany has not yet achieved a major position in the elementary, secondary, and higher schools, but the retardation is more pronounced in Germany where the elemental bases are speculative philosophy and aesthetics. The characteristic emphasis on the ideal and the resultant ideologies, the emphases on the natural, beautiful, genuine, true, healthy, and correct, reminds the writer of the motto on the opera house still standing monumentally in ruins in Frankfurt am Main. It reads, *Dem Wahren, Schönen, Guten,* (to the true, the beautiful, the good). The inscription has survived a devastating war as Plato's writings have survived and lived beyond their time. But the actualization, the thing that gives such inscriptions substance, is the extent to which man can crystallize his dreams through pragmatic communication, and such workaday function of the oral word seldom survives its own utterance or captures the imagination of the group for which it works. One sees in the Frankfurt opera house a symbol of two coexisting worlds, the classical and revered idealism of writing (the irony of Plato's *Phaedrus* notwithstanding) and the contemporary and dishonored pragmatism of speaking, a monument to man's aspirations and his shortsightedness. It signifies the shortcomings of ideology and the failure of pragmatism. If Hannah Arendt can see the banality of evil in the Adolph Eichmanns of Germany,[53] then a viewpoint of the banality of Germany's salvation, speech education, is the point seeking consummation in this chapter.[54]

FOOTNOTES

[1] Adam Müller, *Zwölf Reden über die Beredsamkeit und deren Verfall in Deutschland* (Frankfurt am Main: Insel-Verlag, 1967).

[2] See, for instance, Leonard Steven's *The Ill-Spoken Word: The Decline of Speech in America.*

[3] Irmgard Weithase, *Zur Geschichte der gesprochenen deutschen Sprache* (Tübingen: Max Niemeyer Verlag, 1961).

[4] John Fred Deethardt, Jr., "A History of Speech Education in the Volksschulen, Mittelschulen and Gymnasien of the West German State of Hessen, 1945-1965." (Ph.D. dissertation, Northwestern University, 1967.)

[5] *Sprechkunde und Sprecherziehung: Vorträge gehalten auf der ersten Nachkriegstagung des Deutschen Ausschusses für Sprechkunde und Sprecherziehung in Frankfurt am Main* (Emsdetten, Westf.: Verlag Lechte, 1951), pp. 146-147.

[6] Karl Seidelman elaborates further on this in "Bildungsprobleme in U.S.A. and in Deutschland," *Pädagogische Wegweiser* (Jg. 4. H. 5. May, 1951), p. 29.

[7] Maxmilian Weller, *Das Buch der Redekunst* (Düsseldorf: Econ-Verlag, 1954), p. 168.

[8] *Ibid.,* p. 172.

[9] For a more detailed discussion see either Joachim H. Knoll, *The German Educational System* (Bad Godesberg: INTER NATIONES, 1967), or Erich J. Hylla & Friedrich O. Kegel, *Education in Germany* (Frankfurt am Main: Hochschule für Internationale Pädagogische Forschung, 1958).

[10] Cultural Federalism was abrogated only during the Hitler regime.

[11] Hylla & Kegel, *op. cit.*, p. 77.

[12] See the major decrees of 1957. "Bildungspläne für die Allgemeinbildenden Schulen im Lande Hessen," *Amtsblatt des Hessischen Ministers für Erziehung und Volksbildung* (Jg. 10. Sondernummer 4. Wiesbaden, March, 1957). "Bildungsplan für die Bayerischen Volksschulen," *Amtsblatt Bayerischen Staatsministeriums für Unterricht und Kultus* (Jg. 1955, Nummer 17. Munich, November 15, 1955).

[13] See the decrees of 1961 and 1959. Senator für das Bildungswesen, Lehrplan für Grundschule im Lande Bremen (Bremen, 1961).

[14] In *Wirkendes Wort* (Jg. 3. 1953), p. 356.

[15] *Ibid.*

[16] "Sprechkunde im Studienplan der künftigen Deutschlehrer," *Mitteilungen der deutschen Germanisten Verbandes* (Jg. 2. Nr. 3, 1955), p. 4-5.

[17] *Der Deutschunterricht: Beiträge zu seiner Praxis und Wissenschaftlichen Grundlegung* (1943-); *Muttersprache: Zeitschrift zur Pflege und Erforschung der deutschen Sprache* (1949-); *Wirkendes Wort: Deutsches Sprachschaffen in Lehre und Leben* (1950-).

[18] Werner Beutler, "Die Pantomime im Dienste des Deutschunterrichts," *Der Deutschunterricht* (Jg. 7. H. 4. 1955), p. 86.

[19] Herta Reclam, "Choric-Speaking in Greek Tragedies Performed by Students," *Speech Teacher*, XI (November, 1962): 287-288.

[20] Christian Winkler and Erika Essen. *Deutsche Sprechkunde und Sprecherziehung* (Düsseldorf: Pädagogischer Verlag Schwann, 1954).

[21] Maximilian Weller, *Das Sprechlexicon: Lehrbuch der Sprechkunde und Sprecherziehung* (Düsseldorf: Econ-Verlag, 1957), p. 277.

[22] Gustav Wenz, *Sprecherziehung als Grundlage der Sprachbildung in der Grundschule* (Stuttgart: Gustav Wenz Verlag, 1950), p. 5.

[23] *Ibid.*, p. 30.

[24] Christian Winkler, "Leitgedanken zur heutigen Sprecherziehung," *Blätter für Lehrerfortbildung* (Jg. 9. H. 5., March, 1957), p. 130.

[25] *Ibid.*

[26] Gunther S. Buehl, "Sprecherziehung, ein Kernstück muttersprachlicher Bildung," *Blätter für Lehrerfortbildung* (Jg. 14. H. 6. 1962), p. 219.

[27] Irmgard Weithase, "Probleme der Sprecherziehung," *Internationale Zeitschrift für Erziehungswissenschaft*, VII (1964): 299.

[28] Weller, *Sprechlexikon*, p. 263.

[29] Winkler and Essen, *op. cit.*, p. 15.

[30] Hans Krech, "Fifty-five Years of 'Sprechwissenschaft' at the University of Halle," *The Speech Teacher*, XI (January, 1962): 16.

[31] Marie-Hed Kaulhausen, "Vom Sinn der Sprecherziehung," *Schola* (H. 5. Jg. 4. 1949), p. 346.

[32] Magda Ferenbach, "Alte und neue Wege zum nachgestaltenden Sprechen," *Bildung und Erziehung* (Jg. 4. 1951), p. 517.

[33] *Ibid.*, p. 579. For a more complete discussion of the terms of the theory, see the writer's dissertation, "A History of Speech Education in the Volksschulen, Mittelschulen, and Gymnasien of the West German State of Hessen, 1945-1965," Northwestern University, 1967.

[34] "Bildungspläne für die allgemeinbildenden Schulen im Lande Hessen: Das Bildungsgut des Gymnasiums," *Amtsblatt des Hessischen Ministers für Erziehung und Volksbildung* (Jg. 10. Sondernr. 4. March, 1957), p. 442.

[35] Wayne C. Minnick, "Professionalism within the Liberal Arts Tradition," *Spectra*, III (February, 1967): 1.

[36] Marie Hed-Kaulhausen, "Sprecherziehung im Deutschunterricht," *Der Deutschunterricht* (H. 8. Jg. 1950), p. 63.

[37] Walter Megass, *Das Öffentliche Schweigen: Gibt es Maszstäbe für die Kunst der öffentlichen Rede in Deutschland?* (Heidelberg: Verlag Lambert Schneider, 1967). This book was the winning answer to the prize question posed by the German Academy for Language and Literature in the year 1965.

[38] Ekkehart Rudolph, *Frei Reden und Überzeugen: Eine Kunst, die Erlernbar Ist* (Munich: List Verlag, 1967). List Pocketbook #327. *Überzeugen* actually means conviction, not persuasion, but the writer feels there is a shift in meaning without a concomitant shift to that hated word *Überreden.*

[39] *Adam Müller: Zwölf Reden über die Beredsamkeit und deren Verfall in Deutschland,* mit einem Essay und einem Nachwort von Walter Jens (Frankfurt am Main: Insel Verlag, 1967).

[40] In *Die Sprecherziehung in der Volksschule: Unter-und Oberstufe* (Ansbach: Michael Prögel Verlag, 1950, and third ed., 1963), pp. 41-42.

[41] Gustav Mahlberg, "Erziehung zum Gesprächsfähigkeit im Deutschunterricht," *Wirkendes Wort* (Jg. 7. 1956-57), p. 291.

[42] John B. Carroll (ed.), *Language, Thought, and Reality: Selected Writings of Benjamin Lee Whorf* (Cambridge, Mass.: The M.I.T. Press, 1956), pp. 26-31.

[43] Wolfgang Schmidt-Hidding, "Das Gespräch im Deutschen und im Englischen," *Die Neueren Sprachen* (NF. Jg. 2. 1953), pp. 390-391.

[44] Christian Winkler, "Über das Gespräch," *Der Deutschunterricht* (H. 4-5. Jg. 1951), p. 34n.

[45] Schmidt-Hidding, *op. cit.,* pp. 396-397.

[46] Alfred Glenn Brooks, "The Subsidized Theatre in Western Germany, 1945-1960," (Doctoral dissertation, University of Illinois, 1962).

[47] Kurt Gerlach, "Dramen und Laienspiele der Gegenwart als Schulaufführungen," *Der Deutschunterricht* (Jg. 6. H. 3. 1954), p. 81.

[48] Ignatz Gentges, "Das Lainspiel in der Schule," *Wirkendes Wort* (Jg. 5. 1954-55), p. 224.

[49] Rudolf Mirbt, *Laienspiel und Laientheater: Vorträge und Aufsätze aus den Jahren 1923-1959* (Kassel: Bärenreiter-Verlag, 1960), p. 10.

[50] Magda Ferenbach, "Laienspiel in der Schule," *Der Deutschunterricht* (Jg. 1. H. 8. 1947-1949), p. 67.

[51] "Sprechkunde als Studienfach in den USA und in Deutschland," *Sprechkunde und Sprecherziehung,* v. IV (Emsdetten, Westf.: Verlag Lechte, 1959), p. 139.

[52] Currently, Dr. Hellmut Geissner, University of Saarbrücken, 66 Saarbrücken 15.

[53] Hannah Arendt, *Eichmann in Jerusalem: A Report on the Banality of Evil* (New York: The Viking Press, 1963).

[54] This chapter is based in part on the writer's doctoral dissertation.

SPEECH EDUCATION IN GREECE

Eugene Bahn
John Cambus

INTRODUCTION

Modern Greece is a land of nearly eight million people in contrast to a mere fraction of that number in ancient days. Its major products are olives, olive oil, raisins, wine, minerals, and tobacco. The distance between urban and rural life, in terms of education, mode of living, and cultural opportunities, is great, yet many Greek farmers would not think of changing their way of life for that of their Athenian friends. Only a relatively small portion of the land is cultivated, little beef is grown, and meat and butter are not generally a part of the average daily diet.

The land itself leaves one with an impression of brilliant golden sunshine, rugged mountains, hills and wide valleys where shepherds, in their long black cloaks, tend their sheep. Yet this brilliant land of sunshine can have a demonic force when heavy rains fall and the sharp Vardar winds blow in from the west; the difference is so great that the transparent land of sunshine seems, for the time, to be gone forever. Yet the gloom never lasts very long, for Greece *is* a land of sunshine and brilliance.

Such is the nature of the land and of the people. Intelligent, cheerful, outgoing, talkative, with few repressions, yet with tremendous courage and bravery and a profound sense of personal honor and national patriotism, the Greeks are a people to be admired.

EDUCATIONAL BACKGROUND

After the victorious, but long, war of independence (1821-1829) which freed Greece from the Ottoman Empire, Greece was faced with manifold problems of governmental, social, and educational reform. In 1822, the First National Assembly proclaimed the abolition of slavery and the nobility and the universal right to free education. Some sought advice and technical help from Thomas Jefferson in the organization of a democratic state. This, unfortunately, was not realized, and a monarchy was set up under Otto of Bavaria. Thus, the Bavarian plan of education was organized, with ancient Greek as the language even in the elementary school.

Many changes took place in the educational system. For example, between 1909 and 1921, the period of great national expansion when the state area and the population were doubled, there were numerous progressive changes in education. Some of the most important were the constitutional enforcement of free elementary education, health, and welfare policies (1911); curriculum reform, with emphasis on national ideals, skills, art, physical education, and exact sciences (1912); and introduction of the demotic language in the elementary school (1917). By 1933, 98 per cent of the children were enrolled in elementary schools. Between 1933 and 1940, teacher training colleges were established for the preparation of elementary teachers, and there was a better distribution of educational opportunity, especially in the North.

In World War II the schools and the pupils, along with the entire nation, suffered. War pressures and the destruction of about 70 per cent of the school buildings were major problems. An estimated 350,000 children were orphans, and it was estimated that about 600,000 were not enrolled during the Occupation. After this problem was nearly solved, the internal war caused additional difficulties. Even so, the concern for education did not lessen; the country continued its effort to produce an informed electorate. The Greeks are proud of the Greek constitution, which states that "primary education shall be free and compulsory for all," and since 1963-64, education has been free at all levels, including college, regardless of the financial status of the students.

Among the schools of higher education in Greece are the University of Athens, the University of Thessaloniki, the National Technical University, the College of Economics and Commerce, the Athens College of Agriculture, the Panteios School of Political Science, the Academy of Fine Arts, the Colleges of Industrial Studies at Piraeus and Thessaloniki, and and the Academy of Science and Letters, which is traditionally the highest cultural institution in the country.

There are other lesser institutions, both public and private, serving the needs of higher education in Greece; they have a total of 53,150 students and 1,703 teachers.[1] Undergraduates are enrolled after an entrance examination which must be taken regardless of the student's high-school record. The courses are highly specialized without several years of general education in a liberal arts faculty, and there are no elective courses. There are few extracurricular activities in a Greek university. There is little organized sports activity, and there are few, if any, clubs such as exist in an American university.

The University of Athens has five faculties and a dentistry department. The faculties of this university include a Faculty of Theology, Faculty of Philosophy, Faculty of Law, Faculty of Medicine, and Faculty of Physics and Mathematics. In the Faculty of Theology, there is a provision for the study of sacred oratory and the liturgy. The University of Thessaloniki has seven faculties, including the five mentioned above, plus a Faculty of Agriculture and Forestry, and a Faculty of Veterinary Medicine. The National Technical University has five faculties: Civil Engineering, Electrical Engineering, Architecture, Chemical Engineering and Metallurgy, and Surveying.

Yearly examinations, as well as graduation examinations, are held at all the above universities. The period of study varies from four to six years according to the university and to the size of its faculty. The academic year begins in October and ends on June 30.

Certain relatively recent developments in education merit mention. In 1964-65, 538 classrooms were completed and an additional 1,012 were started. Compulsory education was extended so that pupils must now attend school for nine years instead of six; this means that pupils attend school from the ages of six to fifteen. The courses at the teachers' colleges have been increased from two to three years.

Ancient Greek and Latin have been removed from the gymnasium, the lower three-year level of secondary education. Instead, Greek literature is now taught in Modern Greek translations. In the upper level *(lycée)*, the curriculum consists of Christian literature, ancient Greek literature, elements of philosophy, introduction to sociology, elements of economic science, and economic geography. New textbooks have also been published for ancient Greek literature. Other textbooks, either already published or in the process of publication, include religious textbooks, a history book, and translations from ancient Greek authors to be used in teaching Greek literature in the gymnasium.

There are certain general aspects of Greek life which will help in an understanding of its relation to the speech arts. First of all, in

Greece there are really three languages in use: one of these is the purist, or Katharevousa; another is the demotic, or language of the people; and the third is the ecclesiastical language of the church. Many of those who favored a return to the classical past supported the Katharevousa language along with the revival of ancient plays, dances, and customs, and an interest in classical archeological remains. This language was established to serve in legal, official, and polite usage. This group originally violently opposed the demotic language of the people. In fact, when a theatrical troupe attempted to stage the *Oresteia* in modern translation some fifty or more years ago, Athenians rioted in the streets, and a short time before this a few students rioted in an attempt to keep the gospels from being put into the modern language. The demotic language has persisted, however, and is used by a large portion of the population; it is used by many writers and in the schools.

ANCIENT CLASSICAL SPEECH EDUCATION

Before reviewing the extent and nature of speech activities in Greece today, it is of interest to see what preceded it in ancient Greece and whether or not there are any influences from the past which are now at work in various aspects of speech education.

The oral tradition in ancient Greece, as in other civilizations, was of prime importance. It was the acknowledged tradition to such an extent that the Ancient Greek said, "I heard it, therefore I know it is true."

In the education of youth in early Greek days, there was relatively little emphasis on the ability to write. In fact, reading and writing were not esteemed as much as they are today. In Sparta the boys were required to know old heroic legends. In Athens the poetry of Homer and Hesiod was memorized and recited. By the time of Plato (427-347 B.C.), a boy read great poetry at school and learned many tales, words of praise and encomia of great men by heart so that he might become as noble as they were.[2]

From the age of three to six, the child was taught fairy tales of the highest quality, and he learned to recite or chant poetry. Aristotle (384-322 B.C.) warned those in charge of a child's education to be careful what tales or stories were told to the children. He specifically advised that youths not be allowed to hear satirical iambic verses or see comedies until they can drink "strong wine," for by that time, they will be past the impressionable age.[3]

As the young man in ancient Greece grew, he attended one of the schools of rhetoric. Athens, famous as the source of ancient culture, was so renowned for its training in oratory that young men came from distant lands to be trained by the great teachers of rhetoric. One of the most famous of these teachers, Isocrates (436-338 B.C.), a pupil of Gorgias, established a school of rhetoric. He believed that oratory provided a means of carrying on the great democratic ideals of Greece. He observed that ". . .Athens is looked upon as having become a school of all able orators and teachers of oratory."[4] This was due, he said, to the opportunities there were in Athens for prizes, the practical experience available, the cosmopolitan speech of the Athenians, and the mental agility and interest in letters which, at that time, existed in Athens.[5] He believed that if a person is able to find and learn the truth, willing to work, has a good memory, a good voice, clear diction, and self-assurance he may become a great orator.[6] Of all of these he considered natural ability and self-assurance to be of major importance.[7] Understanding was paramount to Isocrates just as it was later to Roman Quintilian, and, still later, to modern man. Isocrates sees its relation to speaking when he says ". . .the power to speak well is taken as the surest index of a sound understanding."[8]

He also saw good speaking as related to human values and ethical standards. He maintained that one can become a better person if he has a deep desire to speak well and a strong urge to persuade his hearers.

Socrates, too, related good speaking both to understanding and to moral values. He observed that if a youth understands the inner meaning of the great literature he memorizes and recites, it will help him grow to be a "good man."[9] Plato, too, obviously regarded the art of discussion as contributing to man's moral and intellectual stature, for he used it as a teaching method. This understanding the student sometimes obtained by listening to the teacher, memorizing as he listened and, as Plato saw it, engraving it on his heart and then reciting it. He memorized the laws of the land and learned quantities of poetry. He memorized the lines of Homer in the *Iliad* and *Odyssey*. Homer's verses could further be implanted in his mind almost constantly, for it is said that the rhapsodes recited from Homer nearly every day. Great ideals also came to the young man through Greek drama. This ancient tradition, dating back to Thespis in the fifth century B.C., was a potent force in the development of religion, philosophy, and the theater arts.

SPEECH EDUCATION IN MODERN GREECE

With this remarkably strong orientation in speech in classical Greece one may well ask, "What is the nature of speech education in Greece today?" This term, as used in the United States, would mean very little to Greek educators. There is a logical reason for such a reaction, for there are normally no courses in the speech arts in any Greek school. Such courses are not required by law, nor are they provided as electives in the Greek school system. Even the American colleges in Greece—Anatolia, Athens, and Pierce Colleges—and the American Farm School, under the Greek Ministry of Education, do not have courses in speech. One may well wonder why speech courses are excluded in Greece, the ancient home of the speech arts, where they, especially rhetorical training, were given such a prominent place in education. There are a number of reasons for such an omission.

First of all, the required curriculum in the Greek high school is very heavy and includes mathematics, foreign languages, modern Greek literature, six years of ancient Greek (up to 1964), sciences, and other subjects. By the time all of these courses are taken, there is scarcely any time left for additional studies. This is further complicated by the fact that there are usually no study periods during the school day. This means that the students must do their studying at home. In addition to the courses they are studying in the gymnasium, the students in the upper class are generally being tutored in the later afternoon, after they arrive home from school, in preparation for the difficult university entrance examinations. Another major fact is the tendency of the Greek educational system to be conservative, which results in a hesitancy to relinquish an educational system that was influenced by German education in the nineteenth century.

Inasmuch as the Greek is a very articulate and dramatic person, one naturally expects to find some means for teaching the speech arts in the educational world even though they are not specifically provided for in the curriculum. Is there such a means? If so, where is it, and how is it activated?

Actually, in the school system speech is generally interwoven into the subject matter of a variety of classes the pupils take. This means that the pupils may actually never hear the word "speech" as it is used in American education. It also may mean that they will not be aware that they are having any opportunity or experience in the practice of the speech arts. Yet, the fact will remain that very probably a number of the speech arts will be used in every school year that a Greek child attends school.

Public Address

Training in public address, for example, is provided by the use of oral reports which pupils give in their classes. Very often, in fact, some say this is usually the case, the class hour proceeds as follows: The instructor will give a short lecture of some fifteen minutes based largely on the material in the textbook. On the following day, or whenever the assignment is to be prepared, the pupils are called upon to give a résumé of the instructor's lecture. This will be memorized, and its excellence will be considered in proportion to the exact reproduction by the pupil of what the instructor said, both in context and wording. With the Greek ability to memorize, which never ceases to amaze a foreigner, this is not at all an insurmountable task. Such a résumé may be given by the pupils in front of the class. In one hour a number of pupils will go to the front of the room and repeat as closely as possible the material they have heard the instructor give a day or two before. This repetition, which takes place particularly in mathematics, science, history, and literature, gives the students extensive practice in oral delivery before the class. When this procedure is continued throughout the entire school year, and for each year of schooling the child receives, one can see that there is considerable emphasis upon a certain part of public speaking, namely, the vocal and bodily aspects. The matter of organizing material, however, is not achieved through this practice. Suggestions as to how the student is to speak are not usually given unless there is some obvious difficulty. Oral reports are given in all classes at Pierce College and at the American Farm School, and they are given in all English classes at Athens College and in some classes at Anatolia. At the *Deutsche Schule* oral reports are given in the tenth and twelfth school years.

Debate

Formal debating is usually not practiced in most schools, either in the classroom or as an extracurricular activity. There are, however, significant exceptions. For example, debate is found in some schools such as Anatolia College and other colleges where American and English influences have left a mark. In the three colleges sponsored by the Near East College Association, there has been debate activity. At Anatolia College, there has been a tradition in debate for some years, and the debate club has generally been a popular activity. One recent project involved certain dramatic exercises in which debate was used. At Pierce College and at Athens College, the pupils participate in debate in the classes in English, although there is no debating club. At the American Farm School, students occasionally take part in debates. There is activity in debate at some of the teacher training colleges. At Florina, for example, debating is practiced within the classroom. At the teacher training college in Rhodes, the students participate in debating in the classroom, but there is no debating club. At the same type of institution in Myteline, the students also take part in debates within the classroom.

It has been said that whenever two Greeks meet there is an argument. This often appears to be the case, for Greek people enjoy an argument and like to discuss abstract ideas. Often, however, the emotions expressed are not as violent as they appear to foreigners because of the emphatic gestures and tone that are used. For the Greek this freedom to express his ideas is a part of the democratic heritage, and open and frank discussion is the means of exercising this right. Discussion is a vital factor in the life of every Greek; he can no more avoid discussion and lively argument than he can stop breathing. This is as true of the grammar school boy as of his grandfather in the *Kafeneion*. In school he tests his argumentative wits against those of his classmates, not with a cool rationalism, but with the heat of intense emotion. In the classroom he has less opportunity to put this to use. Yet he will present his argument to his teacher to defend himself. He will start out with his most logical arguments and, if and when these fail, he will move down the scale in the range of logical proof. If he is finally cornered, he will give up and accept his fate as a sensible human being, but the important thing is that he tried to defend himself. This art of discussion is not taught as a subject in the schools, but its roots are instilled in a child in the closeness of the family circle where wit is matched against wit to win a point. As to radio and television courses, these are not taught in a class, but, in rare instances, pupils participate in such programs.

Discussion

Discussion is also fostered by clubs which have been prominent in schools such as Anatolia College. These clubs have been set up to meet the various student interests and show a remarkably well planned range of opportunities. The Correspondence and Stamp Club, Music Study Group, Psychology Club, Modern Greek Literature Club, Glee Club, Press Club, Mavrorachi Welfare Club, International Relations Club, Debate Club, and Drama Club are among the organizations which thrive. However, discussion perhaps needs less emphasis in Greek education than do the other speech arts, not only because of its age-old tradition, but also because it is such an integral part of daily life.

Other Speech Activities

Extracurricular activities also provide opportunities for training in public address. At Anatolia, the pupils have frequently given talks in the school assembly. At Athens College, all of the boys are required to speak before the assembled school, and there is some instruction in this field in connection with the English course. At the American Farm School, training in public speaking is included in the fourth class seminar (third year of the gymnasium) in a course entitled Application of Farm Principles. The students are required to give four speeches a year in seminar, and later in the general assembly, on their specific plans to relate what they have learned at school to their own particular agricultural situation. There is further training in public speaking at the American Farm School: At the regular Sunday evening assembly, the students give prayers, make announcements, and also read from the Bible. The student council also provides training in both public speaking and discussion.

At most of these colleges, speeches or orations are given at the graduation ceremonies by outstanding pupils of the graduating class. These events are attended by the pupils, parents, and many friends and relatives, so the challenge to a young speaker is very real. Problems such as inadequate projection, poor diction, or poor posture will be brought to the speaker's attention by the teacher in charge.

Teacher Training

In the teacher training colleges of Greece, there are generally no specific courses offered in speech. However, as far as it has been possible to ascertain, there is one exception to this. One specific course in speech, entitled Introduction to Speech Education, was given at the Lamia Teacher Training College. This course was given only in the year 1967-68 and was then dropped. In it there was specific training in public speaking and in the oral reading of literature.

The students at Lamia are encouraged to give oral reports at every possible opportunity so that they will become accustomed to speaking in public. Occasionally they give reports to the pupils in the high school. As in numerous schools, the outstanding students give speeches or orations as a part of the graduating ceremonies.

At the teacher training college in Myteline, oral reports are given in all classes, and the outstanding students give addresses at graduation, directed by the instructor in literature. At the teacher training college in Rhodes, there is training in public speaking in the course in Greek literature, and the students give oral reports in Greek literature, education, and psychology. Outstanding students give speeches at graduation, directed by the teacher of Greek. The teacher training college at Florina reports that oral reports are given in the sixth class of the primary school and that the students participate in debating although there is no debate club.

Speech Correction

The field of speech correction is not overlooked in Greece. It is not, however, as closely allied to schools, colleges, and universities as it is in the United States. Rather, it is apt to be channelled through clinics concerned with such problems. The first speech education center in Greece to be organized for speech correction is located in Theotokos Institute in Athens. The director of this center is Dr. Constantine Kalantis, who studied pedagogy and psychology at the University of Vienna and specialized in speech education. He is the author of *Speech Disorders in Childhood: Voice — Speech — Reading and Writing,* a treatise of 250 pages, published in 1957. At the Theotokos Institute, Dr. Kalantis and his staff treat children with speech disorders such as stammering, stuttering, dyslexia, dysorthogaphy, and "agrammatism." In 1968, seventy-four cases were treated. The treatment is collective as well as individual.

Oral Interpretation

Reading aloud is an important part of the Greek educational system. This activity starts in the first grade and is continued through the high school. As a result of this extensive training, the Greek students read aloud very well. This subject is not taught as a separate course, but it is used as a tool for the study of other subjects, particularly literature. Most, and often all, of the material that is studied in the class in literature is read aloud by the pupils, either at their desks or in front of the class. Suggestions on how to read may be given more emphasis than instruction on how to speak. The pupil may be given advice on tone, diction, tempo, volume, and vocal changes in characterization. The literature he reads is drawn from his textbook in modern Greek, which is prescribed by the Greek Ministry of Education and is used in all Greek high schools throughout Greece.

In the choice of textbooks and in the list of readings for the fourth, fifth, and sixth forms required throughout Greece in both public and private schools, the Ministry of Education shows a certain concern for speech education.

In the fourth form (the approximate age of the pupils at this time is sixteen years), the students are required to read from ancient history, oratory, and poetry. In history, they read from Xenophon's *Historia Graeca*. In the field of oratory, they read several speeches of Lysias, one speech of Isocrates, and one part of Homer's *Odyssey*. The speech aspects of Lysias and Isocrates are obvious, as is the reading of Homer's *Odyssey*, since in ancient Greece Homer's poetry was always recited. In the fifth form, Plato's *Crito* and two speeches from Thucydides' history are required study. In addition, the tragedies of Euripides are read, one in the original ancient Greek text and the other in a modern Greek translation. From Homer two parts of the *Iliad* are read as well as selections from Greek lyric poetry.

In the sixth form, two tragedies of Sophocles are studied, one in the original ancient Greek and the other translated into modern Greek. Thucydides is represented by the funeral speech of Pericles, and selections from Plato's "Phaedo" or "Protagoras" are included. The poetry of Homer is again chosen with two parts from the *Iliad* and, finally, the *Idylls* of Theocritus complete the list. The emphasis on speech composition and on the oral recitation of literature are obvious. The degree to which these will be read aloud or recited from memory will vary from school to school and with each instructor. But it clearly indicates that the ancient oral tradition is fostered in the modern Greek school and that the pupil is learning the overall oral approach, certain principles of oral composition, and a depth of feeling and intellectual richness that was known to his ancestors 2,500 years ago. This exposure has permeated the thinking of generations of Greeks and has undoubtedly had its effect upon the educated as well as the uneducated. Departments of speech in American high schools, colleges, and universities might do well to infuse more of this same ancient tradition in their curricula.

In addition to the above required reading list, the textbook in modern Greek, also prescribed by the Greek Ministry of Education for use in all Greek high schools, generally contains speeches, stories, memoirs, biographies, chronicles, essays, criticisms, science and philosophy, descriptions, character studies, travels, prose, and humor. In addition, folk songs, modern poetry, poetic drama, dialect poems, and some foreign literature are included. Some of this material, such as the speeches, stories, poems, and plays, readily lends itself to the speech arts and is frequently read aloud.

As we look at this classification, we can readily see a relationship to at least three of the speech arts. The first section of the book used fairly recently is devoted to the study of famous speeches. These are of national interest and include a speech of the late King Paul and a speech by a hero of the Greek Revolution of 1821 as well as others. These speeches are sometimes read aloud and analyzed just as they might conceivably be handled in a speech composition class. Thus, there may be a study of speech composition within the class in literature and, inasmuch as these speeches are usually not memorized, there is practice in oral reading as well. The stories and poems are also read aloud, again giving emphasis to oral reading. Poetic dramas are also read; this requires some study of dramatic structure and characterization. In some instances, each pupil may read the lines of a specific character, which brings us nearer to the art of the theater. Besides this book, the students, in their ancient Greek classes, read the epics, histories, and dramas of classical Greece in the original. This, however, is apt to be more a study of the language and of the ideas presented than of the speech arts.

In the classes in modern Greek, the students are frequently required to write weekly themes and essays to provide training in literary composition. In this practice, the development of an idea, organization, grammar, and language are emphasized. Often the best themes in class are read aloud by their authors, thus providing an additional opportunity for experience in speech. It would appear that one of the prime purposes here is to develop in the students an appreciation for the expressive possibilities of demotic Greek. In the *Deutsche Schule* pupils also read aloud in literature classes and memorize and recite about five literary selections in a school year.

In the colleges under the sponsorship of the Near East College Association, reading aloud has been relatively important in connection with the study of literature. At Anatolia College, students read aloud in their study of literature. One year (1950-60) the students gave group readings from *The Most Dangerous Game* by Richard Connell, *The Devil and Daniel Webster* by Stephen Vincent Benét, *The Snow Goose* by Paul Gallico, *Macbeth,* and the poetry of Robert Frost and Vachel Lindsay. Especially fascinated with the strong rhythms of Lindsay's poetry, the students remarked with wide-eyed wonder: "We have never heard poetry like this before." Some of this material was presented in the college assembly and some at noon-hour reading programs.

At Pierce College, the students read aloud and recite poems that they have memorized, and this occasionally includes the recital of ancient Greek literature such as Homer. The oral reading of literature is done in connection with Greek and English courses, and, occasionally, ancient Greek. Athens College students read aloud in literature classes, and each student recites several memorized poems each year, especially in junior high school. They also memorize selections from ancient Greek literature such as Homer. At the American Farm School students read aloud in classes in modern Greek literature and in English, especially from poetry and essays. The students recite in ancient Greek every day, and memorize classical literature such as Homer. At the Sunday evening assembly, they read from the Bible in Greek and English. In teaching English, the instructor uses the oral-aural approach, reports Mr. Phil Foote, chairman of the English department.

The teacher training colleges also foster reading aloud and the recital of poetry. At Lamia the students memorize and recite two or three poems a year and read aloud in literature classes. Florina Teacher Training College has its students memorize and recite some six or seven poems a year, including material from ancient Greek literature; they also read aloud. The students at Rhodes Teachers Training College read aloud in the course in Greek Literature, where they study folk songs, Cretan poetry (from the fifteenth century to the present), Byzantine literature, Cyprian and Medieval literature, and extracts from the ancient classics. They also memorize and recite at least two or three literary selections in a year. At Mytilene, Greek literature is read aloud in the course of that title, which includes outstanding poems of ancient or modern literature and other significant material. Students also memorize and recite some literary selections, including Homer.

The recital of literature is by no means limited to the classroom. The recital of poetry, rather than the reading of it, is a feature of many Greek celebrations, and family gatherings and birthdays are often the occasion for the reciting of poems either composed for the event or drawn from literature. Since a number of the assembled group may join in the recitation, such a program may last a considerable length of time.

The oral tradition in reciting today is closely linked to the patriotic tradition in Greece just as it was in ancient days when the Greek gods and heroes were exalted. On national holidays and on days concerned with patriotic events, pupils recite with considerable fervor patriotic poems in praise of the great heroes of Greece.

The national holidays in Greece, particularly, October 28th and March 25th, are days of major celebration and thanksgiving. In the schools, at all levels, including the teacher training colleges, these days are commemorated. In some classes each child recites a poem to his classmates and to the assembled parents in honor of the holiday. At one school, each of the fifty pupils recites a poem to the guests. Obviously, such a program may last for quite a long time. Poems are frequently recited in connection with a play. Some of these patriotic poems are "The Rock and the Wave," (in which the wave, symbolizing the Greek nation, undermines the rock, representing the Ottoman Empire), "The Song of the Sacred Battalion," and "The Greek Soul." Class programs are supervised or directed by teachers of literature or of other subjects.

A unique aspect of recitation is to be found in the fascinating island of Crete. The Cretans have the remarkable gift of being able to compose verses almost instantaneously. An amusing incident in a schoolroom can bring forth a rhyme. At a wedding celebration a guest may start a rhyme to which another will add a verse; this is continued by one after another of the guests until a story in verse is complete. It is said that marriages are even arranged as a group of assembled friends develop a poem around the eligible pair. A Cretan will compose rhymes to define a word. Or he may spontaneously compose and recite a verse to a girl he admires, and if she likes him, she may reply in verse.

Much of the instruction in reciting in Greece is so indirect that the teacher is unaware that he is teaching, and the pupil is unaware that he is being taught. Without stressing the niceties of grammar or the purity of tone, the Cypriot peasant teaches his son to project his voice across the valley to communicate with an unseen friend in the next olive grove. In just such a manner the peasant learned to do this from his ancestors. The end result, however, is a well-projected voice, clear diction, and good diaphragmatic support. Such is the natural, unsophisticated way of learning one of the speech arts in rural areas.

He learns, too, those ancient proverbs which have come down through the centuries. Some of them date back to Hesiod's *Works and Days* or come from the same source composed in about the 7th century B.C. that Hesiod relied upon:

1. Cultivate a field never before cultivated to break your bad luck.
2. If you are successful in surface cultivation do not tell your son about it. Let him find his own strength.
3. Do two things side by side. If you have a farm, try to have a dairy along with it.
4. Do not plant an olive tree near a wall.
5. A garden can feed one hundred people who *work* there.
6. Only the earth can make you stand. If you cultivate the earth you help create social and economic stability.
7. A field that buys, buy; a field that sells, sell.
8. When you choose a cow or donkey, look it over. Do not buy it if it has a hump. It is the same with a wife.

The Cypriot farmers also use speech for pure entertainment as they work in their olive groves. They chant stories in verse across the fields to each other, often about the unhappy lover who is filled with grief over his lost love; they tell jokes, and they enjoy the sentimental. But as their children work by their side in the olive groves, they learn these verses, and they learn how to recite them as have their older brothers, their parents, and their ancestors for untold generations. Here again speech is being taught, far away from academic halls though it be.

In the same way the Cretan youth learns to recite hundreds of lines from *Erotokritos,* a very long narrative poem by Kornaros, just by hearing his own parents recite it or his relatives and elders recite as they sit around a winter's fire or out-of-doors, which they especially enjoy. He does not realize that he is being given instruction. He may be only half-listening, but he is absorbing into his memory, subconsciously perhaps, over and over again these same endless lines, and with his natural bent for memorization, he learns them without knowing he is doing so. This poem has been heard so many times by every child in every generation for hundreds of years that the poem itself and the methods of chanting reciting it are learned early in life.

Erotokritos, based on a fifteenth century romance, and written in the seventeenth century, tells of the love of Arethusa, daughter of the Athenian King, and the son of the King's councilor. In this poem both the characters speak, and the poet speaks as narrator. It is sometimes sung, sometimes chanted, and sometimes recited, by memory, of course. Both its content and its methods of delivery have been handed down through the centuries, and each new generation learns from the preceding generation both the words and how to deliver the words.

A very important educator in modern Greece, although his teaching is indirect, is Mr. John Tavoularis, a rhapsode attached to the Royal National Foundation. Mr. Tavoularis recites from the *Iliad* and the *Odyssey* to countless numbers of people, both adults and school children, throughout Greece, just as did the ancient rhapsodes. His presentation is memorized, and he gives his material with a certain regal dignity befitting the gods, goddesses, and heroes about whom he tells. The Greek government is to be congratulated for keeping this ancient tradition alive.

The tradition of folk legends, too, has been handed down from parent to child for many centuries; many of these stories can be traced to Aesop, or at least to the same source from which he drew. They have been told to children who have learned to tell them, just as they heard their mothers and fathers and their grandmothers and grandfathers tell them while they sat beside them. This, too, was a teaching situation in which inflections, pauses, and vocal qualities were consciously or subconsciously imitated by listeners through the centuries. The numbers of these ancient storytellers have dwindled in the last decades, but some Greek scholars have realized, as radio and other means of communication have developed, that there is danger of losing a vast wealth of oral literature. So, Professor Politi, of the University of Thessoloniki, and Paraskevas J. Miliopoulos, of the Institute for Macedonian Studies, made recordings and collected stories in many Greek villages. Mr. Miliopoulos realized that many of the stories he heard were the same as he went from village to village. Many of these stories are about animals, and the storytellers are mainly shepherds and farmers who have observed the domestic and wild animals firsthand and have seen in them traits not unlike those of human beings. From these stories children learn about human behavior as well as the art of storytelling. Mr. Miliopoulos has synthesized the elements in the various versions of the same story in order to catch its essence and has read these stories on radio to Greek children for a number of years.

Reading aloud is also taught in the monasteries on Holy Mount Athos where the Bible and the Lives of the Saints are read daily when the monks gather in the refectory for their simple meals. The young monks hear this religious material repeatedly and learn, in turn, the traditional way of reading as it has been practiced for centuries in the Greek Orthodox Church. In like manner, the liturgy of the church is handed down from one generation of priests to another, in addition to the actual training young priests receive while they study in the seminary.

Perhaps the most significant bearer of the ancient tradition of the rhapsode of the fifth century B.C. and later can be found in the Greek Orthodox Church, where the priest chants the services. The three major liturgies in the Greek Orthodox Church are those of St. James, St. Basil, and St. John Chrysostom. There is also the liturgy of the Presanctified, which is performed on the weekdays of Lent. When the priest, reader, and choir recite and sing the gospel and utter the various responses at the end of each prayer, they are probably following a tradition carried down from the rhapsodes.

Theater

The theater, as one might expect from a nation whose people are as expressive as the Greeks, is prominent in Greek life. There is some evidence of this, though limited, in the schools. This interest is, no doubt, partly restrained by the rigors of the classes, which demand considerable preparation. In addition, the production of plays in the high school does not have the same kind of tradition that it has in the United States. In Greece most of the plays that are presented have a major focal point, which is to commemorate the great national holidays. Others have a religious theme.

The major occasions when the regular Greek high school gives dramatic productions are the national holidays of Independence: October 28th, "Oxi" or "No" Day, when the Greeks refused to capitulate to the Italians in World War II, and Greek Independence Day, March 25.

In the colleges under the aegis of the Near East College Association there is considerable interest in dramatics on the part of the dramatically inclined Greeks. At Anatolia College, a number of superior productions have been given in recent years, including *Life With Father, Our Town, The Rainmaker,* and *A Midsummer Night's Dream. A Midsummer Night's Dream,* given for the seventy-fifth anniversary of the founding of Anatolia College, was presented three times on the campus and also in Kavalla, the Neapolis of St. Paul's day. Other more recent productions by the Drama Club, under the direction of Dwight Holbrook, include (for 1956-66) *The Confrontation* written by Mr. Holbrook (a stylized interpretation of the Epiphany); *Oedipus Rex* (a reading in English); and *The River*

Merchant's Wife: A Letter, choreographed by Mr. Holbrook. In 1966-67, *The Boor* by Anton Chekhov and *Our Magnificent Mice,* by Euripides Tsakarides, a student, were presented. In 1967-68, *My Heart's in the Highlands,* by William Saroyan, *The Long Stay Cut Short or The Unsatisfactory Supper,* by Tennessee Williams, and another play by Euripides Tsakarides were given. In addition to this, Mr. Holbrook worked with some of the students on the first chorus in *Agamemnon* in ancient Greek. *The Long Stay Cut Short or The Unsatisfactory Supper,* was the most successful in terms of audience appreciation, according to Mr. Holbrook. Most of the plays are given in English, which presents a particular problem for the director in terms of such facets of expression as intonation.

Pierce College, in Athens, usually presents two or three plays a year plus many single scenes or acts from modern and classical Greek plays. Recent productions included Thornton Wilder's *Our Town* (in English) and James Barrie's *Quality Street* (in Greek). Some of the plays in Greek are centered around patriotic holidays or have religious significance. In Athens College, several plays are produced annually. For example, *Journey's End,* by Sherriff, was given in Greek. In 1967-68, *Philoctetes* by Sophocles, was presented in Greek and *Billy Budd,* by Coxe and Chapman, and *My Heart's in the Highlands,* by Saroyan, were given in English.

The American Farm School's major dramatic events include two plays to celebrate national holidays. At Thanksgiving and Christmas the students give plays in English. An informal show consisting of skits is given on alternate Saturday nights. In April there is one night on which plays are given in English by each class. At the end of the school year an impressive pageant which has many dramatic elements is held out of doors.

The teacher training colleges sometimes provide impressive dramatic fare. The college at Lamia has presented *The Persians* by Aeschylus, another "patriotic" play by Theotokas entitled *Katsantones,* and a religious play on the theme of the prodigal son. The teacher training colleges at Florina, Rhodes, and Myteline have presented patriotic plays. Myteline has also given religious plays as well as some which did not come under either of these classifications.

The professional theater is prominent in Greek life. There are numerous theaters in the two major cities, Athens and Thessaloniki, as well as in the smaller cities, and there are also many theater schools where acting and other aspects of the theater are taught.

The Greek National Theater Company and its drama school are major factors in providing education in the theater arts in Greece. A

Royal Theater was opened in 1901, which lasted until 1908. It was in 1930 that a National Theater was established, significantly enough, through the efforts of the Ministry of Education, supported by the Greek Government. It opened in 1932, presenting for its first plays *Agamemnon,* by Aeschylus, and the *Divine Dream,* by Xenopoulos.

This theater made great strides and proved a real contribution to the art of the theater in Greece as well as internationally. It has given a great range of plays representative of international drama such as those of Shaw, Molière, Pirandello, and, of course, Shakespeare. It has toured through western Europe, Cyprus, Egypt, and the United States. One of the major objectives of the National Theater was to bring about a rebirth of ancient Greek classical drama, as its very first production, *Agamemnon,* indicated. Since 1954, the National Theater has presented seasons of ancient Greek drama in the Odeon of Herodus Atticus at the base of the Acropolis in Athens, and at Epidaurus. The National Theater has been a major factor in educating the Greek public in the arts of the theater and in bringing to it a knowledge of its own great dramatic heritage as well as the heritage of world drama. To bring about the revival of classical drama was one of its major objectives. This process is not merely confined to educating the citizens of Greece, for thousands came from western Europe, America, and the Middle East to see these interpretations of classical dramas as the Greeks understand them. The National Theater wanted to bring to its productions a vital human experience so presented that they would have depth of meaning and beauty today and would not appear only as museum pieces. In this they have been successful in staging, costuming, acting, choral work, and choreography. Perhaps to the Western world the intricate and sensitive movement and vocal work of the chorus is of greatest significance, for it is entirely new and shows how the chorus contributed to, and reinforced, the total dramatic impact.

One of the outstanding contributions of the National Theater is its festival at Epidaurus, which is held in the ancient theater at Epidaurus in the Peleponessus. This theater, seating 14,000 people, was built in the fourth century B.C. by Polycleitus, the younger, a great sculptor and architect. Plays by the ancient playwrights—Aeschylus, Sophocles, Euripides, and Aristophanes—have been presented to thousands of people who have attended these outstanding performances. The festival presented its first experiment at Epidaurus in 1954 with *Hippolytus,* and in 1955, it was definitely established. This project was made possible by the combined efforts of the leaders in the Greek world of art. The simple staging, authentic costuming, good acting, and superb choral work give it a stellar place in the theater world. The Greeks, as well as foreign visitors, are moved by these productions, and fathers can be seen explaining the meaning and significance of a play to their little children just as fathers must have explained it 2,500 years ago in the same theater. This, too, is a part of speech education.

The National Theater has also established its own drama school. Here it has trained its own actors and also has supplied actors for private theaters throughout Greece and in other countries. This school gives training in all phases of the theater arts, and it is certainly one of the most potent forces in speech and drama education in all of Greece, in its formal education for the professional theater, as in the production of Greek plays for the national and international audiences. The National Theater of Greece and its school of the theater have been major forces in the theatrical life of Greece for many years, both as examples of good theater and as teaching media for future theater personnel and for general cultural development. A National Theater of northern Greece, founded in 1961, with headquarters in Thessaloniki, has also given both indoor and outdoor productions.[12] One of the other outstanding theaters in the Near East is the Art Theater in Athens. Its director, Karolos Koun, is himself a historical figure in the history of the modern Greek theater. He attended school in Constantinople and later studied for a year in Paris. In 1929, at twenty-one years of age, he began to teach English at Athens College. Simultaneously, he played the role of Osborne in *Journey's End,* by R. C. Sherriff, which was being presented on the stage in Athens. It was from this point on that he became a significant part of the Greek theater. For his students, he himself wrote little plays, and by 1932 his students gave *The Birds* and *The Frogs* of Aristophanes, Euripides' *Cyclops,* and Shakespeare's *A Midsummer Night's Dream;* in 1932 a Cretan drama, *Stathis,* was presented.

In his Popular Stage, a semi-amateur group, Koun developed a style of acting in "the manner of the people." That is, he wanted the actors to catch the mode of expression of the modern Greek in contrast to the formalistic style of earlier acting, and along with several others, namely Kontoglou and Tsarouhis, he wanted the actors to convey the sorrow and joy that have grown out of their ancient tradition. On April 20, 1934, with D. S. Debaris as general manager, J. Tsarouhis as scene designer, and Koun as director, this theater presented *Erophile*, and in December, 1934, produced *Alcestis.*

An important aspect of Koun's philosophy of the theater appeared in the program of *Erophile*—important in that it shows his belief in psychological involvement in the theater: "We believe that every nation (or peoples) is capable of producing and putting forward only as much as they know in themselves."[13] Unfortunately, this theater was dissolved in 1936 due to lack of funds.

In 1941, Koun established his Art Theater. Some of his early followers included B. Metaxa, E. Hadjiargyris, K. Lambropoulos, M. Janakopoulos, P. Zerbos, L. Kallergy, B. Diamamtopoulos, M. Plorites, A. Nomikos, G. Sevastikoglou, and K. Hadjiargyris. During the war years his dedicated students existed on raisins, yogurt, unsalted bean soup, and dreams. There was a break in his theater in the years 1949-1952, during which time he directed plays at the National Theater of Greece.

In 1952, Koun founded his own drama school. His insight and experience made it clear to him that there was an innate histrionic quality in the Greek people and that the very climate of Greece helped "give form to things." Although he used the Stanislavski approach to a considerable extent, he realized that it had to be adapted to the needs and temperament of Greece and its people. He puts more stress on the biological side of acting than on the psychological approach of Stanislavski. For example, Koun sees Ibsen as psychological and Tennessee Williams as "organic" in approach—as stressing the whole man rather than only the cerebral. The theater, says Koun, has to do with the senses.[14]

As a teacher and director, Koun's genius is notable. Although he is concerned with producing able actors, he does not rush his students into plays. Instead, he has them study for six months before giving them roles in a public production. He rehearses a play from five weeks to two months, depending upon the play. His rehearsal methods also depend upon the play; his system is flexible. Usually he does not block out the action until ten days after rehearsals are started. Koun likes the play to develop without too much preconceived inflexible planning and does not use a "regie" book. Rather, he likes to "feel" how the play goes and to bring this feeling out through the actors. He does not favor actors learning their lines too early because this tends to stabilize the wrong inflections and to solidify a concept which prevents further growth in interpretation.

Koun believes that technique can help the artist arrive at a deeper understanding. Yet he emphatically believes that external appearance, without inner substance, is by no means art.

As a teacher, as a director, and as a person, Koun speaks quietly and is patient. He has deep faith; he is courageous; he is enthusiastic; and of course, he is persistent. As a director, he is described as sitting with his eyes focused intently on the actor, with his mouth half open, and with a shortness of breath. He lives into the role of the actor with the intensive depth of feeling that he hopes the student actor will sense. Suddenly he may jump up, stand over the actor in seeming fury to say some of the lines with abrupt, rapid movements, yet with depth of feeling and truth.[15]

Koun's Art Theater presents a comprehensive range of plays representative of world drama, including those by Brecht, Garcia, Lorca, Chekhov, Ibsen, Pirandello, Anouilh, Rattigan, Inge, Priestley, Gorky, O'Casey, Wilder, Shaw and many others, including, of course, the plays by the ancient Greek dramatists. In recent years the National Tourist Organization of Greece has arranged that productions of Greek drama be given in numerous Greek communities so that those citizens, as well as those in Athens, may become a part of this tremendous educational project. It is significant that Karolos Koun and his Art Theater are among the leaders in this project. His theater offered *The Birds,* by Aristophanes, and *The Persians,* by Aeschylus, and again proved Koun's ability to see the past in relation to the present. The educational work of Koun has made for itself a secure place in theater and cultural education.

There are numerous other theaters and theater schools that deserve mention. One of these, unfortunately no longer in existence, is the Theatrical School of Salonica. This school had a rather brilliant existence in its short life. Founded in 1960 by the Greek section of World University Service in Thessaloniki and directed by Kanellos Apostoloy, there were seven instructors, with approximately ten students in each of the three classes. The entire course of study required three years to complete. The curriculum consisted of a course in acting, which all students took. Improvisation (for first year students only) developed from a description of a simple situation to the organization of a one-act comedy. The plot was outlined by the class, but was developed and changed by the students "according to the mood and inspiration of the moment." Finally the entire play was written down and acted. A course in Speech: Voice and Diction, including exercises for strengthening the muscles for breathing, was required of all students. Drills, poetry, and scenes were used to train the voice and diction. A course in dancing, movement technique, and modern dance was taken by all classes. Design was taught to all classes, and scenery and costuming were taught to the second and third classes. Make-up was taught to the third class. World history of art, Greek literature, and ancient Greek theater were taught to all classes. The philosophy of acting could best be described as eclectic inasmuch as it even included influences from the Far East. The actual approach depended upon the specific play being presented and its interpretation. In his class work, each student prepared at least three scenes in a year. The University Players, composed of students at the University of Thessaloniki, were related to this drama school and gave one play each year during University Week. Some of the plays presented by the University Players and the drama school included Molière's *The Doctor in Spite of Himself* and *Tartuffe,* Aristophanes' *Plutus,* Chekhov's *Uncle Vanya,* Anouilh's *Antigone,* Williams's *Suddenly Last Summer,* Synge's *Shadow of the Glen,* Shakespeare's *A Midsummer Night's Dream and Twelfth Night,* Euripides' *Iphigenia in Taurus,* a group of Belgian one-act plays, and plays by Strindberg and Goldoni. Considerable emphasis was placed on the study of ancient Greek drama.

This school stressed versatility in acting, and the students learned to play a variety of characters in order to avoid the pitfall of type-casting, for it was maintained that even type-casting improved with such training. Approximately one-half of the students became actors, although some did not continue in that profession. No textbook on acting was used. This school showed real promise in its group, its sense of purpose, its artistic perception, and its good leadership. It is to be hoped that it can be revived.

SUMMARY

It is apparent that speech education in modern Greece is extensive, yet the pupils, the populace, and perhaps a considerable percentage of the teachers are not aware that it exists beyond the training that actors receive. The method of imparting a knowledge of speech training is far different from that employed in the United States. It is so subtle that the Greeks themselves may not realize they are receiving it and are quite honest in their belief when they say that there is no speech training in their land—the land that first gave speech training to the Western World.

FOOTNOTES

[1]*International Yearbook of Education,* XXVII (1965). Publication #286. International Bureau of Education, Geneva. UNESCO, Paris, p. 158.

114   Greece

[2] Plato "Protagoras" *The Dialogues of Plato.* trans. Benjamin Jowett. (New York: Random House, 1937). I. 96.

[3] Aristotle *Politics.* trans. Benjamin Jowett (Oxford: Clarendon Press, 1908), VII. 17. 11. p. 298.

[4] Isocrates "Antidosis" in *Isocrates* trans. George Norlin (London: Wm. Heinemann, 1956), II. 349.

[5] *Ibid.,* p. 349.

[6] *Ibid.,* pp. 293-5.

[7] *Ibid.,* p. 295.

[8] *Ibid.,* p. 327.

[9] Xenophon "Symposium" in *Xenophon* trans. O. J. Todd (London: Wm. Heinemann, 1922), III, 405.

[10] *Ibid.,* p. 405.

[11] *Epidaurus* (Greek Theatre Organization, 1960.)

[12] *The Oxford Companion to the Theatre,* ed. Phyllis Hartnoll (3rd ed., London: Oxford University Press, Reprinted 1967), p. 410.

[13] Karolos Koun *25 Years of the Theatre* (Athens, 1959), p. 21.

[14] Personal interview with Mr. Koun, June, 1960.

[15] Koun, *op. cit.,* p. 34.

SPEECH EDUCATION IN JAPAN

Takehide Kawashima
Wayne H. Oxford

INTRODUCTION

The history of speech education in Japan began in 1873, when Fukuzawa Yukichi, the founder of Keio University in Tokyo, instituted on his campus the practice of Japanese language oratory and debate based on Western rhetorical principles and the rules of parliamentary procedure. Two years later, in order to establish a "home" for his newly-formed Oratorical Society, he built on the Keio campus his famous, and still-standing, *Enzetsukan* ("Speech Hall"), the first auditorium in Japan to be designed expressly for the presentation of public speeches.[1] Since those early days, speech education has become a firmly-entrenched force in Japanese society.

It should be noted, however, that Japanese speech education has four important dimensions: first, with but a few exceptions, it is not to be found in the classrooms of accredited academic institutions; second, it is concerned almost exclusively with the classical Western concept of "the training of the orator";[2] third, it is closely associated with the use of two languages, both Japanese and English; and fourth, it seems to have a great popular appeal.

Partly as an attempt to clarify the statements above, we will discuss in this chapter the major avenues by which a person living in Japan today can learn to improve his ability to communicate orally with his fellow man.

SPEECH TEXTS

In 1873, the same year in which he introduced to Japan the practice of oratory and debate, Fukuzawa Yukichi published the first speech text ever written in Japanese.[3] In this fifty-four page booklet, entitled *Kaigiben* ("How to Hold a Conference"), Fukuzawa explained how the Western rules of parliamentary procedure could be used to facilitate group discussion in Japan.

Although countless speech books have been published in Japan since that date, it seems as though they have now reached an all-time high in popularity. During the summer of 1968, while on a shopping tour of five bookstores in Tokyo, the authors of this chapter purchased a total of ninety-six different texts—an amazingly high number when compared to the number of speech texts that one would expect to find in five typical bookstores in an American city.

A further check of the availability of speech books was made in four small towns along the remote shore of the Japan Sea near, and including, the ancient castle town of Matsue. Each bookstore that we visited in three of these towns had an average of five speech books on its shelves. However, not one speech book was to be found in the tiny, dilapidated bookstore in the fourth town. When we asked the wizened old proprietress if she had any speech books for sale, she replied, "Oh my! A young fisherman's wife came in this morning and bought my last speech book. I won't have any more for about a week."

These spot checks in Tokyo and along the coast of the Japan Sea would tend to indicate that speech books are readily available throughout Japan and that thousands of Japanese families have at least one of these texts in their homes. It is also probable that, in spite of the widespread popularity of speech contests, the only opportunity that many Japanese have to learn about speech is offered by the reading of these texts.

Therefore, let us now focus our attention on the several different types of speech books that have been written for the mass market. (Following this discussion, a few significant works written for the specialist will also be mentioned.)[4]

Texts Written for the Mass Market

Books on Rhetorical Theory. Probably the books on Western rhetorical theory represent the majority of speech texts available in Japan. (Forty-six of the ninety-six texts mentioned above are of this type.) Some of these are "theory-only" texts; others include brief "model" speeches, which, in most cases, are brief, uninspiring stereotypes that the Japanese reader may memorize, or perhaps read aloud, on the appropriate occasion.

One of the most prolific writers of these texts is Professor Takehiko Egi, founder of the Institute of Speech Science, which will be discussed later in this chapter. Professor Egi has written approximately twenty books of this type, his most popular work being

Hanashikata Kyōshitsu ("The Speech Classroom"), 100,000 copies of which were sold during 1959, its first year of publication. His 250-page paperbacks are well-adapted to the mass market. They contain clever cartoons and are written in a direct and vivid style strongly reminiscent of the Dale Carnegie approach to effective speaking.

Slightly more scholarly in its treatment of rhetorical theory is the 195-page paperback, *Enzetsu no Kagakuteki Jōtatsu Hō* ("Scientific Methods for Improving One's Speeches"), published in 1965 by the Kobunsha Press, Tokyo. This is one of the few mass-market speech texts in Japan that is a translated version of an American text. The original, entitled *The Successful Speaker's Handbook,* was published in 1962 by Prentice-Hall, Inc. Its author, H. V. Prochnow, is vice-president of the First National Bank of Chicago.

Speech Anthologies. Possibly the second most popular type of speech text in Japan is the speech anthology. (Thirteen of our ninety-six texts are of this type.) As speech theory is omitted, the authors of these texts need minimal credentials in the field of speech. A case in point is the author of the paperback text, *Speech Kojiten* ("A Small Anthology of Speeches"), a compilation of 300 banal speeches of dubious origin. According to the blurb on the jacket of this book, the author's many other publications include: *How to Write Letters, What to Name Your Child, Twelve Months of Fishing,* and *Painless Childbirth.*

A far more impressive work is the 690-page *Shikiji Aisatsu Enzetsu Shū* ("Anthology of Ceremonial Speeches, Informal Addresses and Orations"), compiled by the Kodansha Press. It includes more than 400 above-average speeches presented on an astonishingly wide variety of occasions by prominent members of Japanese society.

Wedding Books. A most unusual genre of speech text found in Japan is the "wedding" book. (Eleven of our texts are of this type.) Immediately following the wedding ceremony, the relatives and friends of the bride and groom assemble at a banquet, during the course of which each of the guests is expected to rise and present a brief speech in honor of the newlyweds. Consequently, the typical Japanese wedding book has developed into a curious amalgam of advice to the guest speakers and advice to the bride and groom. An example is the 459-page *Kekkon Shiki Speech Gohyaku Shū* ("A Collection of Five Hundred Wedding Speeches"), the last sixty pages of which deal in extreme detail with sexual matters (including impotence, frigidity, and the use of various contraceptives) and with the laws pertaining to marriage and divorce.

Books on Group Leadership. A fourth major type of speech text deals with the topic, how to be an effective group leader.[5] (Eleven of our texts are of this type.) Though most of the writings in this area are of little note, *Shikai Speech Zensho* ("The Complete Speech Book for Group Leaders") is a unique and highly creative work. Discussed within its 628 pages are: the techniques of preparing and presenting the extemporaneous speech (including the basic principles of outlining one's ideas in logical sequence, which alone marks this as an exceptional Japanese text); the communication problems that arise when speakers use nonstandard dialects; the purposes and moods of almost every conceivable type of speaking situation, from lighthearted telephone conversations to formal meetings at which weighty problems are discussed; and the techniques whereby these purposes and moods can be achieved by those in charge of these situations.

Books on Persuasion. From the descriptions of the various types of speech texts mentioned thus far, it may be readily surmised that most of the Japanese who buy these texts do so because they wish to learn how to perform adequately during the many occasions on which they are expected to stand up and "say a few words" in front of others. Thus, they are apt to regard speech as the art of saying the appropriate thing at the appropriate time, rather than as the art of persuasion.

Consequently, if a Japanese wishes to learn how to speak persuasively, he will find that most of the texts described above are inadequate and that he will need to purchase a book which deals specifically with the techniques of persuasion. There are several competently written books of this type on the market. (Seven of our books are of this type.) Of special merit are Ryū Moroboshi's *Settoku* ("Persuasion") and Professor Egi's *Settoku Seiko Ho* ("Successful Methods of Persuasion").

Miscellaneous Speech Texts Written for the Mass Market. Books which do not fit into any of the above categories, yet which are worthy of mention, are *Kaiwa Seikō Hō* ("Successful Methods of Conversation") by Professor Egi and *Kaigi to Tōgi* ("Conference and Discussion"), which is a Japanese translation of Harold P. Zelko's *Successful Conference and Discussion Techniques.*

Speech Texts Written for the Specialist

Particularly impressive are a few texts which lack the popular appeal and widespread distribution accorded to the speech texts mentioned above. They deal with radio and television and with speech pathology and therapy.

Radio and Television. Written for the professional radio and television announcer, *Terebi Rajio Shin Anounsu Tokuhon* ("New Reader for Radio and Television Announcing") is a well-written, 635-page work which is used as a basic handbook by the announcing staff of the Japan Broadcasting Corporation, Japan's equivalent of the B.B.C. It includes lengthy drills on the speech sounds of the standard (Tokyo) dialect, instructions and exercises for effective oral reading, and the methods of presenting different types of programs such as news broadcasts, sports broadcasts, and interviews.

Speech Pathology and Therapy. The Japan Broadcasting Corporation, better known as N.H.K., publishes a book entitled *Kotoba no Chiryō Kyōshitsu* ("Speech Therapy Classroom") to be used in conjunction with a weekly television program by the same name, which is for mothers of speech-handicapped children. Included in this profusely illustrated text are descriptions of the different types of speech disorders commonly found among children, the types of speech "games" and simple drills that the mother can use with her child, and a useful list of eighty-five primary-school speech clinics in various parts of the country.[6]

Of a much more technical nature are several authoritative English-language texts which have been translated into Japanese. These include Nancy E. Wood's *Delayed Speech and Language Development* and Frank B. Robinson's *Introduction to Stuttering,* both translated by Dr. Gorō Kamiyama, the American-educated director of the National Center of Speech and Hearing Disorders, and Wendell Johnson's *Stuttering and What You Can Do About It,* translated by Professor Hiroshi Uchisugawa.

Texts authored by Japanese authorities include *Domori no Hanashi* ("The Speech of Stutterers"), written by Dr. Kamiyama and Professor Uchisugawa, and Dr. Kamiyama's *Kitsuon Kenkyū Handobukku* ("Research Handbook on Stuttering"), a comprehensive treatise on the major theories of stuttering and the remedial techniques currently employed in the West. This significant work, published in 1967, also includes abstracts of the stuttering research conducted in Japan prior to that year.

SPEECH CONTESTS

By far the most widespread speech training available, in both Japanese and English, is that furnished by the many hundreds (perhaps thousands) of oratorical, oral interpretation, and debate contests held each year throughout the country. Though there are many speech contests for adults, most of the local, regional, and national contests are for high school and university students.[7]

Unfortunately, the limited space available here precludes any discussion of the kaleidoscopic variety of local and regional contests. Therefore, in this section, we will describe briefly only the thirty contests which are held annually on a national scale.[8]

National English-Language Oratorical Contests

The Annual National Intercollegiate English Oratorical Contest (since 1948). Probably the major speech event in Japan. The best speaker from each of approximately one hundred colleges and universities represents his school in one of five district preliminaries held in five cities. Seventeen finalists compete for the coveted Mainichi Trophy and the N.H.K. Trophy. The final round is held alternately in Osaka and in Tokyo during late June or early July. Contestants present seven-minute extemporaneous speeches. Sponsored by *The Mainichi Daily News* and supported by N.H.K. (The Japan Broadcasting Corporation).

The All-Japan Junior High School Oratorical Contest (since 1948). In October, an elimination contest is held in each of Japan's forty-three prefectures. Three winners from each prefecture participate in the semi-final round held in Yomiuri Hall, Tokyo. Eight finalists participate in the final round held in Tokyo in November. Three-minute memorized speeches are presented. Sponsored by *The Yomiuri Newspaper.*

The Churchill Trophy Oratorical Contest (since 1951 or 1952). Open to representatives from all senior high schools in Japan. It is held alternately at Kwansei University, near Kobe, and at Aoyama Gakuin University, in Tokyo, during the fall. Cosponsored by Kwansei University and Aoyama Gakuin University and supported by *The Mainichi Daily News.*

The English Oratorical Contest for Business Organizations (since 1955). The applicant for this contest should be under forty years of age, the only representative from his organization, and he should be a Japanese citizen who was born in Japan and lived in Japan more than twenty-five years or four-fifths of his life. This event is usually held in Tokyo, though sometimes in Osaka, in October. Approximately thirty young businessmen participate each year. Eight-minute extemporaneous speeches are presented. Sponsored by the International

Education Center. Supporters include the Ministry of International Trade and Industry and *The Mainichi Daily News.*

The All-Japan English Speech Contest for Teachers (since 1963). Though open to all teachers in Japan, most of the contestants are high-school and junior high-school teachers of English. Approximately thirty teachers participate each year in this extemporaneous contest held in Tokyo. Most of the 150 audience members are the teachers' students. Sponsored by the International Education Center, Tokyo.

The All-Japan Intercollegiate English Oratorical Contest (since 1965). Sponsored by the English Speaking Association of Waseda University, Tokyo, and supported by *The Japan Times.*

The All-Japan Impromptu Speech Contest for Senior High School Students (since 1967). Contestants select one of two topics presented thirty minutes before speaking. The two topics for 1968 were "School Uniforms" and "Japan and I." Most of the contestants selected "Japan and I." As each contest has only about eighteen applicants, elimination rounds are unnecessary. *The Asahi Newspaper* sponsors this contest held in Asahi Hall, Tokyo.

National English-Language Debate Contests

The Intercollegiate English Debating Contest (since 1950). Each two-man debate team is selected by the English Speaking Society at a large number of colleges. At Asahi Hall, Tokyo, these teams compete in an elimination contest held in September. Finals are held in October. The audience of 1,000 students behaves as though it were at a football game—cheering the contestants and throwing paper tape. The winning team receives three highly-valued trophies and a twenty-four volume set of the Encyclopedia Britannica. This contest is cosponsored by the International Education Center and *The Asahi Newspaper.* Among its many supporters are the Foreign Ministry, the Education Ministry, *The Japan Times,* and *The Asahi Evening News.*

The All-Japan English Debating Contest (since 1957). Five-man debate teams representing various college chapters of the International Student Association of Japan participate in this Tokyo contest held in conjunction with their annual International Student Conference. This event is sponsored by the International Student Association and is supported by the International Education Center.

The Sophia University Invitational Debating Contest (since 1966). For several years, this contest involving representatives from twenty Japanese universities has been staged by the English Speaking Society of Sophia University, Tokyo, and sponsored by the Sophia International Alumni Association.

(The Meiji University team, winner of this contest in 1967, was sent to Honolulu to debate the University of Hawaii team in March, 1968. And in 1967 and 1968, the University of Hawaii debate team went to Japan to compete against seven of the twenty Japanese universities affiliated with this contest.)

National English-Language Oral Interpretation/Recitation Contests

The National Intercollegiate Contest in the Oral Interpretation of English Literature (since 1964). Each contestant records his selection on tape and sends the tape to Aoyama Gakuin University in Tokyo. (Last year, fifty-eight tapes were submitted.) The tapes are then judged, and the top fifteen contestants are invited to attend the finals of this contest held at Aoyama Gakuin University in December. The finalists must present their selections from memory. The sponsor of this contest is the Speech Clinic at Aoyama Gakuin University. The chairman of this event has been Professor Kawashima, coauthor of this chapter.

The All-Japan Recital Contest (since 1965). There are two divisions of this entirely tape-recorded contest: The Senior High School Students Division and the College Students and General Public Division. Contestants in the Senior High School Students Division record a brief and relatively simple selection written in English. (The selection for 1967 was entitled "Mother.") And the contestants in the College Students and General Public Division record a more challenging selection. (The selection for 1967 was an essay written by Foreign Minister Miki, entitled "Forum of Understanding.") The contestants then mail their tapes to *The Japan Times,* where they are evaluated by a Board of Judges composed of four leading Japanese educators and the director of *The Japan Times.* (Three hundred tapes were submitted during the 1967 contest.) Names of the six winners in each division are announced in December. The top prizes include movie cameras and projectors as well as various certificates and gold medals. This unusual contest is sponsored by *The Japan Times* and is supported by the Ministry of Education.

National Japanese-Language Oratorical Contests

The National Oratorical Contest for University Students (since 1946). This contest, held in Tokyo in December, is sponsored by Chuo University and is supported by *The Yomiuri Newspaper.*

The National Oratorical Contest for University Students (since 1949). This event, open to all university students in Japan, is held at Nihon University, Tokyo. It is sponsored by Nihon University's Correspondence Course Division and is supported by *The Yomiuri Newspaper.*

The National Oratorical Contest for University Students (since 1950). This event is sponsored by Tōyō University and is supported by *The Yomiuri Newspaper.*

The National Buddhist Universities Oratorical Contest (since 1950). Participation is restricted to students enrolled in one of the nine Buddhist colleges in Japan. Risshō University in Tokyo is one of the several sponsors of this event. *The Yomiuri Newspaper* furnishes support.

The National Oratorical Contest for High School Students (since 1951). Though the postwar history of this contest does not begin until 1951, this all-Japan event was also held for twenty consecutive years prior to the Pacific War. It is sponsored by Nihon University and is held on its Tokyo campus in the fall. *The Yomiuri Newspaper* furnishes support.

The National Oratorical Contest for University Students (since 1955). This contest is held in June at the Tokyo Keizai (Economics) College. It is sponsored by this university and is supported by *The Yomiuri Newspaper.*

The National Oratorical Contest for High School Night Division Students (since 1956). Each year, Nihon University selects various high schools throughout the nation to participate in this event. (Different high schools are selected each year.) Contestants must be enrolled in the evening classes of these schools. This contest is sponsored by the *Benron Bu* (Speech Club) at Nihon University, Tokyo, and is supported by *The Yomiuri Newspaper.*

The International Speech Contest in Japanese (since 1959). This contest is open to all foreign residents over eighteen years of age who were born outside of Japan, who are of non-Japanese parentage, who speak Japanese as a second language, and who have lived in Japan for a total of less than five years. Contestants present eight-minute speeches on any noncommercial, secular topic. This televised event, staged in Asahi Hall, Tokyo, in May, is sponsored by the International Education Center. Its supporting organizations are the Ministry of Foreign Affairs, the Ministry of Education, the Japan Broadcasting Corporation, *The Japan Times, The Asahi Evening News,* and *The Asahi Newspaper.*

The National Oratorical Contest for University Students (since 1960?). Sponsored by Nihon University's School of Humanities and Sciences. Supported by *The Yomiuri Newspaper.*

The All-Japan Students' Oratorical Contest (since 1960?). This event, held in Tokyo, is open to all Japanese students. During the preliminary round, contestants present affirmative speeches on a proposition. Finalists present negative speeches on the same proposition. Winners are selected on the basis of the total score made on both speeches. The names of sponsors and supporters are not known.

The Asian Students' Oratorical Contest (since 1963). The students from abroad speak in Japanese. Japanese participants speak in English or some other foreign language. Sponsored by the Asian Students' Cultural Association, Tokyo.

The National Sokagakkai Oratorical Contest (since 1965). The sponsor of this event is the Nichiren Shōshū Sokagakkai, probably the fastest-growing religion in the world today. The elimination contest is held in ten districts throughout Japan, and the final contest is held in August in this organization's huge temple near Mt. Fuji. Participants present seven- to eight-minute speeches on any topic.

The National Oratorical Contest for College Students (since 1965). Though this contest, held in Tokyo in May, is sponsored by the Womens' Division of the All-Kanto District Students' Speech Club Association, both male and female students are invited to participate. Active in this contest is the *Benron Bu* (Speech Club) of the Japan Women's Economics Junior College in Tokyo. This is the only women's college in Japan which has a Japanese-language speech club.

A most interesting national "contest," which cannot be classified according to any of the above-mentioned categories, is The Five Official United Nations Languages Contest, sponsored by *The Asahi Newspaper.* This extremely popular, highly complex contest, the final rounds of which are held in Asahi Hall, Tokyo, is actually composed of five separate contests, each involving the use of a foreign language. Below are a few of the basic facts concerning these contests:

Spanish Contest (since 1955). Five-minute memorized speeches. Judged by the Spanish Ambassador. Finals held in May.

French Contest (since 1959). Five-minute extemporaneous speeches. Finals held in October.

Russian Contest (since 1962). Five-minute memorized speeches. Finals held in June.

English Contest (since 1962). Five-minute memorized speeches. Finals held in November. (This is the only contest limited to high-school students. The other contests are open to anyone under thirty who has spent less than six months in the foreign country.)

Chinese Contest (since 1967). Five-minute memorized speeches. Finals held in December.

ADULT SPEECH EDUCATION

In recent years, steadily increasing numbers of Japanese (and foreigners) have been joining, or enrolling in, various adult speech--education programs available in a few of the major cities. To be discussed below are the programs offered by the three best-known organizations which specialize in this field: the Toastmasters International, the Institute of Speech Science, and the Dale Carnegie Course.

The Toastmasters International[9]

From 6:30 to 8:00 P.M. on the first and third Thursday of each month, the Tokyo Toastmasters Club meets in the banquet hall in the basement of the American Club. A visit to the meeting held on Thursday, August 15, 1968, revealed that this organization's program is identical in format to that of its brother clubs in the United States. After dinner, while the members and guests were still sipping their coffee, the chairman called the meeting to order and proceeded to announce the various items on the agenda, the most important ones, of course, being the extemporaneous speeches and speech critiques presented by the members.

Included in this club's roster of thirty-two members are four bankers, including a vice-president of the Bank of America; a well-known atomic physicist presently with the National Science Foundation; several newspaper, aviation, and business executives; staff members of five embassies; and the pastor of the Tokyo Baptist Church.

The main feature which distinguishes this club from its counterparts in America is that only 60 per cent of its members are native speakers of English. The remaining 40 per cent, though comprised largely of Japanese, includes members from a variety of countries, including Turkey, China, Ghana, and Germany.

There are eight other Toastmasters clubs in Japan, most of which are affiliated with the major American military bases. The speech text which all of them use is Dr. Ralph C. Smedley's *Basic Training Manual.*

The Institute of Speech Science[10]

In 1953, the Institute of Speech Science *(Hanashikata Kyō-shitsu)*[11] was established in Tokyo by Professor Takehiko Egi, a prewar professor of law who, during the early postwar years, was head of the cultural division of the Japan Socialist Party. During the past five years, this Institute has become the largest speech school in Japan, with one branch in Kyoto, two in Nagoya, six in Osaka, and nearly fifty branches in Tokyo. To handle its average enrollment of 1,000 students, Mr. Egi employs 213 instructors, most of whom teach speech on a part-time basis.

The standard eight-month course, conducted entirely in Japanese, consists of two 3-hour sessions each week.[12] The first hour of each session is devoted to lectures on various aspects of oral communication, and the remaining two hours are devoted to three-minute student speeches and critiques.

The fee for this course, which includes the cost of eight small textbooks, is astonishingly low—only 3,500 *yen,* or slightly less than $10.00. This helps to explain why the Institute of Speech Science draws most of its students from the middle and lower-middle classes—its student body being composed primarily of housewives, nurses, young men and women in the lower echelons of the business world, and labor-union members. In short, it would be reasonably accurate to describe this as "the poor man's Dale Carnegie Course."

The Dale Carnegie Course[13]

In 1956, Mr. Frank Mochizuki graduated from Michigan State University with a degree in hotel administration and public service. Three years later, while a trainee with the Palmer House in Chicago, he enrolled in a Dale Carnegie Course presented at the Midwest Institute. As an enthusiastic convert to the Dale Carnegie philosophy, he returned to Japan in 1962 to establish the Japan Institute of Human Relations, Inc., the parent organization of the Dale Carnegie Course in Japan.

The first Dale Carnegie class, formed in Tokyo in January 1963, had forty students, of whom 80 per cent were Japanese and 20 per cent were foreigners. During the first two years, all of the Dale Carnegie classes were conducted in English. However, in 1965, Japanese-language classes were added.

In 1965, a branch office of the Dale Carnegie Course was opened in Osaka; and early in 1968, classes were begun in Yokohama. As of September 1968, a total of 2,800 students had graduated—50 per cent from the English-language course and 50 per cent from the Japanese-language course.

Each class, which is now limited to thirty-five students, meets for one three-hour session each week for fourteen weeks. By Japanese standards, the tuition fee of 48,000 *yen* ($133) is quite high. Consequently, only about 20 per cent of the students are "on their own," as it were. The rest are mostly college-educated executives whose fees are paid by the business firms with which they are associated.

Though personality development and leadership are also stressed, the "Schedule of Class Sessions" lists a wide variety of topics related directly to public speaking. These include "How to

Seize and Hold Attention," "How to Make Your Talk Sparkle," "Thinking of Your Feet," "How to Stir Your Listeners," "How to 'Say a Few Words,' " and "A Quick and Easy Way to Learn to Speak in Public."

During each of the fourteen sessions, each student is called upon to present two 1- to 2-minute speeches, after which brief critiques are presented. The first half of the thirteenth session is devoted to a prepared-speech contest. And, during the first half of the fourteenth session (the last session of the course), the students participate in an impromptu speech contest.

The three Dale Carnegie schools in Japan employ a total of nineteen part-time instructors, including two foreigners. The requirements for becoming an instructor are formidable. One must be a president, director, or department manager of a major business firm that has an international reputation. Furthermore, he must be elected by his classmates as being the outstanding student in his class. And, after being thus selected, he must serve as a graduate assistant for several months, without pay, before he is permitted to teach a class of his own.

In addition to a number of pamphlets, the following three textbooks are issued to each student: Dale Carnegie's *How to Win Friends and Influence People, How to Stop Worrying and Start Living,* and Dorothy Carnegie's *A Quick and Easy Way to Effective Speaking.* Students enrolled in the Japanese-language classes receive translated versions of these three books.

UNIVERSITY-LEVEL SPEECH COURSES

As mentioned earlier, formal academic training in speech is extremely rare in Japan. Indeed, below the university level, it seems to be totally nonexistent.[14] Fortunately, we were able to obtain information on the speech courses offered at the following three private universities in Tokyo: International Christian University, Aoyama Gakuin University, and Nihon University.[15]

International Christian University

International Christian University's Division of Languages has played an ever increasing role in the postwar development of speech education in Japan. Listed below are the speech courses and the number of credit hours of each course currently being offered:

Effective Speaking (2)
Introduction to Speech (6)
Language and Thought (6)
General Semantics (3)
Interpretative Reading (2)
Dramatic Interpretation (2)
General Phonetics (3)
Phonetics for Teachers (3)

American Pronunciation (2)
Voice and Articulation (2)
Discussion and Conference (3)
Argumentation and Debate (3)
Parliamentary Procedure (2)
Public Speaking (3)
Advanced Research Seminar (3)

One of the more prominent members of the Division of Languages at ICU is Professor Mitsuko Saito, who obtained her Ph.D. in speech at Northwestern University in 1957. Her dissertation, entitled "Speech Education in Japan During the Latter Half of the Nineteenth Century," is the first dissertation on Japan to be written in the field of speech.

Aoyama Gakuin University.

In April, 1949, a speech program was inaugurated within the Department of English. The courses taught at that time were Speech Improvement, English Intonation, and Public Speaking. In April, 1952, an advanced speech course was started by Dr. Leslie R. Kreps, currently professor of speech at Oklahoma State University. At present, instruction is offered in the following four-credit-hour courses: Speech Improvement (ten sections), Public Speaking (two sections), and Advanced Speech (two sections).

Dr. Takeshi Haruki, who heads the five-man speech staff at Aoyama, is one of the very few Japanese educators who has an impressive background in speech. In 1926, while in junior high school, he won second place in the first National English Oratorical Middle School Contest. During the 1930s, he obtained his Ph.D. from the University of Southern California, where he majored in political science and minored in speech. While Japan was engaged in the Pacific War, Dr. Haruki was a radio announcer and news editor of N.H.K. (the Japan Broadcasting Corporation). And throughout the postwar years, though a member of the political science faculty at Aoyama, he has been active in promoting and teaching speech courses at this university.

Nihon University

Nihon University, the largest university in Japan, has eleven campuses with a total enrollment of over 100,000 students. For several years, at its main campus in Tokyo, speech courses have been taught within the speech division of the Department of English. Current offerings are two sections of English Phonetics (4 credit hours), twelve sections of Oral Expression I (2 credit hours), eight sections of Oral Expression II (2 credit hours), and six sections of Oral Expression III (2 credit hours).

Scheduled for addition to the curriculum in April, 1969 were two sections of Oral Interpretation (2 credit hours), two sections of Public Speaking (2 credit hours), and one section each of Discussion and Debate (2 credit hours), General Semantics (4 credit hours), and Seminar in Speech (2 credit hours).

Also being planned is the establishment of a department of speech-communication within Nihon's School of Humanities and Sciences. The creation of this, the first autonomous speech department at any Japanese university, will mark a major milestone in the development of speech education in Japan.

SPEECH CLINICS[16]

Though a few stuttering clinics have been in operation for about forty years, it has been only during the past ten years that speech therapy has gained considerable influence as a form of speech education in Japan.[17]

The chief figure in this field is Dr. Gorō Kamiyama, who obtained his M.D. in 1958 at the University of Tokyo and his Ph.D. in speech correction at the University of Wichita in 1963. Since his return to Japan in 1964, Dr. Kamiyama has lectured on speech pathology, stuttering, and aphasia at the University of Tokyo Medical School. And, as director of the National Speech and Hearing Clinic (established in 1958), he has conducted an annual one-year training program for 200 school teachers who, upon graduation, are assigned to the ninety public schools in Japan which maintain speech clinics. Assisting him in this program are ten staff members, several of whom obtained their M.A. degrees in the United States.

In addition to the above-mentioned National Speech and Hearing Clinic (sponsored by the Ministry of Welfare) and the ninety public-school speech clinics (sponsored by the Ministry of Education), there are approximately thirty reputable clinics (both governmental and private) in various cities scattered throughout Japan.

Unfortunately, most of these clinics are forced to operate on inadequate funds. And they are woefully understaffed. (At Dr.

Kamiyama's clinic, for example, the usual wait for therapy is two years.) Indeed, to meet the overwhelming demand, Japan is in immediate need of 6,000 additional speech therapists. Yet, though "special training programs" in speech therapy have been offered for several years in a few colleges in Tokyo and Osaka, it was not until April, 1968 that the first B.A. program for speech clinicians was begun at the Tokyo Teachers College. At present, fourteen students are enrolled in this program. Young Japanese who wish to obtain advanced degrees in this field must still go to the United States for their education.

THE JAPAN SPEECH SOCIETY

The Japan Speech Society *(Nihon Eigo Benron Kyokai)* is a newly-formed organization which is expected to function as a Japanese counterpart of the Speech Association of America. Its purpose is "to help develop the knowledge and techniques of English speech in general and further to contribute to the development of knowledge and techniques of Japanese speech which seem to require improvement in a democratic Japan."

Major areas of interest will include public speaking, argumentation and debate, oral interpretation of literature, microphone announcing, radio speech, telephone speech, voice training, and both simultaneous and consecutive conference interpretation.

Its major activities will include periodic conferences, including an annual general conference to be held in December; the publication of speech bulletins; the sponsoring of international speech contests; and the maintenance of close liaison with overseas speech organizations.

Officers of this Society are Professor Juji Kasai, president; Professor Takeshi Haruki, chief director; and Professor Takehide Kawashima, executive secretary. The present address of this organization is The Speech Clinic Office, Building No. 1, Aoyama Gakuin University, 22 Midorigaoka-cho, Shibuya-ku, Tokyo. Its telephone number is 402-811-9, 8123.

CONCLUSION

Speech education in Japan has indeed made remarkable progress since its birth on the Keio University campus almost ninety-seven years ago. Undoubtedly, it will continue to thrive in the form of popularly written texts, speech contests, adult classes, and in the form of more, larger, and better-equipped clinics.

However, there is one great challenge which faces this field as it approaches its second century of development. It must overcome the opinion, widely held in academic circles, that the teaching of speech should be excluded from the classrooms of accredited institutions.

An important foothold has already been gained on the campuses of at least three major Japanese universities. And the formation of the Japan Speech Association, as well as the proposed establishment of a department of speech-communication at Nihon University, are recent examples of further progress that is being made to raise speech education to a higher level of academic respectability.

Hopefully, if a survey of speech education in Japan should be made one hundred years hence, it will be found that speech has been accepted as an integral part of the curriculum of every high school and university across the land.

FOOTNOTES

[1]Masafumi Tomita, *Mita Enzetsukan no Yūrai* [History of the Mita Speech Hall] (Tokyo: Keio University Press, 1947), pp. 1-13.

[2]Modern communication theory, for example, has not yet been introduced even at the university level. And, though fields such as semantics and linguistics are highly developed in Japan, most Japanese scholars in these, and in allied areas, disassociate themselves from the "nonacademic" field of speech.

[3]Kammei Ishikawa, *Fukuzawa Yukichi Den* [Biography of Fukuzawa Yukichi] (4 vols.; Tokyo: Iwanami Shoten, 1932), II, 188.

[4]As the purpose of this section is to present merely a broad overview of the speech literature in Japan, the authors, publishers, and dates of publication of most of the texts mentioned herein have been omitted. Upon request, Professor Oxford will be glad to furnish additional information on any of these texts.

[5]Here, the term "group leader" *(shikai)* refers to anyone who is more or less in charge of any meeting or ceremony. Therefore it is far broader in meaning than the terms "chairman" and "master of ceremonies."

[6]It could be argued that this text belongs in the category, "speech texts written for the mass market." Nevertheless, it is included here because of its close relationship to the following books, which are obviously "written for the mass market."

[7]As a general rule, the students who participate in the English-language contests are members of their school's extracurricular English Speaking Society (E.S.S.), and those who participate in the Japanese-language contests are representatives of their school's Japanese Speech Club *(Benron Bu)*.

[8]The authors are deeply indebted to the following persons who furnished us with copious information in regard to the many speech contests held annually in Japan. (In most cases, we were granted not only interviews, but also unrestricted access to contest files.) Mr. Gashō Nakano, supervisor of speech contests sponsored by *The Japan Times;* Mr. Tatsuo Shibata, editor-in-chief of the *Mainichi Shimbun* ("Newspaper"), English edition; Mr. Namiji Itabashi, Mr. Minoru Saku, Mr. Takahiko Mikami, and Mr. Kenneth Hara, of the International Education Center; Miss Chikako Takashi, contest supervisor for the *Yomiuri Newspaper;* and Mr. Ueda, supervisor of the annual contest sponsored by the *Sokagakkai.*

[9]Interviewed following the Toastmasters' meeting held on August 15, 1968, were Mr. Dennis Wilham, Mr. Larry Oakland, and Mr. Richard Owen—all long-time members of this organization.

[10]Based on an interview with Mr. Shinken Kawamura, one of the administrative officers of the Institute of Speech Science. This interview was held at the Institute's headquarters in Tokyo on September 9, 1968.

[11]A more literal translation of *Hanashikata Kyōshitsu* would be "Speech Methods Classroom." However, the official English-language name of this organization is the more elegant "Institute of Speech Science."

[12]The Institute also offers an intensive graduate course in speech for those who wish to join its teaching staff.

[13]Based upon an interview with Mr. Frank Mochizuki, founder and executive director of the Japan Institute of Human Relations, Inc. This interview was held at Sophia University, Tokyo, during the opening session of Tokyo Class No. 78 Japanese, on September 11, 1968.

[14]A series of phone calls placed to the Ministry of Education, Tokyo, in August, 1968, revealed that speech courses, in either Japanese or English, are simply not offered in Japan's elementary and secondary schools.

[15]Possibly, a few other universities in Japan offer speech courses for credit. If so, the authors would greatly appreciate having these courses brought to their attention.

[16]Based on an interview with Dr. Gorō Kamiyama, Director of the National Speech and Hearing Clinic, Tokyo, on August 11, 1968.

[17]An important factor in the recent growth of this field has been the N.H.K. television program, "Speech Therapy Classroom," mentioned earlier.

SPEECH EDUCATION IN KOREA

Tai Si Chung
Robert T. Oliver

INTRODUCTION

Speech education in Korea has developed only in minor degree, largely on the fringes of the school system; this is despite the fact that quite literally the modernization of the nation commenced through an organization devoted to the study of speech. Korea has a history of some 4,000 years and, although its people and its new republican government are eagerly and alertly interested in the values of modernity, established customs and attitudes are inevitably rooted in its long past. Today there is in Korea an obvious need for broad and serious speech education; there also are strong conservative factors which militate against it. A fair summary judgment is that among the nations of the world Korea is a laggard in the field of speech; nevertheless, significant beginnings have been made from which a substantial growth may be expected.

This survey of speech education in Korea will consider: (1) factors in Korean history which condition the development of speech education; (2) the dramatic role of speech in the emergence of modernism and democracy in Korea; (3) the factors of conservatism which inhibit the acceptance of speech as an academic discipline; (4) the beginnings which already have been made in the promotion of speech contests, the writing of textbooks in speech, the establishment of courses in speech, and the establishment of speech organizations. Finally, (5) the survey will be concluded with consideration of current needs and circumstances in Korean schools and in the Korean nation which favor the eventual growth of speech education.

THE HISTORICAL MATRIX

Education is deeply rooted in Korean traditional culture. Study of the Confucian classics was introduced into Korea by the Han

Chinese who sought refuge at Lolang (modern Pyongyang) during the period 108-313 B.C.[1] The first organized schools in Korea apparently were set up during the Silla dynasty (57 B.C.-A.D. 935). In them young men from aristocratic families were taught a system of ethics and etiquette known as *Hwarang-do,* incorporating principles of loyalty, filial duty, trustworthiness, valor, and justice.[2] In the Koguryo kingdom (37 B.C.-A.D. 668), which was finally defeated and absorbed by Silla, two sets of schools—public and private—were maintained for the teaching of Chinese classics. In A.D. 682 a *kukhak* (state school) with a nine-year curriculum centered around the Confucian classics was established to prepare young men for government service. A hundred years later, in A.D. 788, a state examination system was inaugurated, whereby appointment to public office depended upon the passing of examinations graded into three levels. After the establishment of the Koryo dynasty, which defeated and succeeded Silla, an orthodox Confucian educational system was instituted, chiefly under the leadership of a great scholar, Ch'oe Ch'ung, and a scholarly official, Kim Pu-sik.[3] At this time elementary schools (*sodang*) and secondary schools (*hyanggyo*) were set up in cities all through Korea, with curricula modeled after the Four Institutes maintained in Seoul, all aimed toward the education of the numerous officials who were required for all levels of administration, from village and city through provinces and on up to the capital itself.[4]

Very little is known concerning these early Confucian schools. Of course they did not teach anything like the public speaking and discussion found in modern speech courses. But centered as they were upon the *Analects* of Confucius, and aimed as they were to prepare young men for the duties of officialdom, it is equally certain that they did pay considerable attention to the acquiring of skill in the arts of polite and effective discourse. The youthful students could scarcely fail to have taken note of the affirmation of Confucius that, "Unless gifted with the artful tongue of Ceremony Master T'o and the handsomeness of Prince Ts'ao of Sung, one can hardly get on in these days." And even their teachers must have noted carefully the master's warning: "In rectifying human relationships, a man of virtue must have words to say. In saying words, he must have their practice in mind. The rule is that he should feel no scruple in speaking them." Unskillful speech could greatly harm an official, since "a slip of the tongue is not to be overtaken by the fleetest horses and retrieved." Indeed, the quality of one's speech could be the chief determinant of his career, for "one word from a gentleman reveals his wisdom or ignorance. So speech cannot be too careful."[5] All officials performed their duties in two directions—upward, by giving advice to their superiors, and downward, by conciliating persons having grievances. No Confucian could be in any doubt of the importance of skill in speech. They all would ponder the warning by Confucius which his disciples selected as the final statement with which to close the *Analects:* "One cannot know people without knowing their words."

Under the Yi dynasty (1392-1910), Confucian education became even more firmly established and widespread. In 1543, a provincial official, Se-bung Chu, founded a new kind of school, known as *sowon,* in which students paid tuition, and which, in addition to its regular faculty, also invited distinguished scholars for special lectures. Being less exclusive than the state schools, the *sowon* rapidly grew in number until by 1568 there were more than a hundred of them. The evidence was dramatic and convincing that in Korea even the common people were hungry for education.

These *sowon* schools became centers for academic meetings in which debates were held on matters concerning both scholarship and public affairs.[6] At that particular period of Korean history political factionalism was at fever pitch, and the *sowon* were deeply enmeshed in the contention. As students of Korean history explain: "Philosophic views and interpretations were important determinants of position and prestige. These views depended on school or teacher; ... hence schools of philosophy and certain of their interpretations were connected with and [were] frequently embroiled in politics."[7]

Thus it happened that the rivalries which beset Korean life were centered in and around the schools. Controversy was the atmosphere in which the contending scholars and politicians lived and confronted one another. Debate was their way of life. Like Confucianists in China, they tested both the validity of ideas and the worth of their proponents by subjecting them to the searching and revealing processes of dialectical discussion. If anyone should inquire whether speech was a subject matter of their curriculum, the answer would be, certainly not—they never heard of such a thing. Even so, the attainment of skill in speech, together with an enlargement of their understanding of the ways by which speech unveils the strengths and weaknesses in both policies and character, constituted very nearly the core of their education.

The ancient traditional attitudes of Koreans concerning the uses and the devices of speech were not altogether clear but were generally negative. Such proverbs as the following reveal their suspicion or dislike of undue volubility:

The foolish man always speaks too much.

Seeing something once is worth more than hearing about it a hundred times.

Talkative families turn their sweet soybean sauce to bitters.

One tree blames another for singing too loudly in the wind.

On the other hand, other proverbs stress the prevalence and perhaps even the value of ready speech, as in the following:

A cobweb doesn't stretch itself inside the mouth of a living man.

It is much harder to stop the mouth of people than to stop the water of a river.

More significant are the proverbs which provide guidance for effective speaking and listening. Typical of these are the following:

Don't draw a sword to kill a mosquito.

It is useless to pour instruction into a sow's ear.

Be attentive even to the words of a small child.

Though your mouth is crooked, always speak straight.

And then there are two proverbs that seem contradictory but that actually combine in teaching that effective speech must be highly skilled. The first runs: "Go to the home of sweet soybean sauce, but not to the home of sweet words"; and the second is a cautionary reminder: "Speak gently to others and others will speak gently to you."[8]

For many centuries in Korea, another form of speech activity which was considered very important was dramatic reading. As early as the twelfth and thirteenth centuries, stories from China featuring social satire, humor, and social problems were introduced into Korea. A successful Korean imitation of the social satire genre was Kyun Ho's picaresque *Life of Hong Kiltong,* which combines pungent commentary on political and social conditions with a Robin Hood-like narrative, with overtones akin to Sinbad the Sailor. Still other popular writings consisted of humorous and risque' stories. The Korean novel achieved maturity with Kim Man-jung's *Cloud Dream of the Nine,* in the seventeenth century. A hundred years later appeared the indubitable Korean masterpiece of the novel, *Fragrance of Spring: the Story of Choon Hyang,* detailing the sacrificial struggles of a faithful wife. Since these stories became very popular, and since printed copies were scarce, men of sonorous voice and dramatic ability read them aloud in village parlors, surrounded by eager listeners.[9]

A profession of elocutionists, or readers, developed to render ancient epics as well as modern narratives. These men travelled from town to town, earning their living by recitations presented with theatrical vocal and gestural patterns, often on street corners, surrounded by crowds that paid with donations. This elocutionary entertainment persisted into the mid-twentieth century, for the authors heard such recitations in Seoul after the liberation from Japan. Although superseded by the radio and motion pictures, they gave impetus to a popular sense of the value of skill in speech.

In summing up this brief glance into Korea's educational practices and attitudes of the past, it might be concluded that the development of skills in speaking and listening were far from ignored either in the schools or in social practice, but that whatever was done along this line was done indirectly and largely unconsciously. There is no evidence of a historic interest in rhetoric, in public address, or in the problems of oral communication in the early history of Korea.

THE EMERGENCE OF DEMOCRATIC MODERNISM

A Korean studying abroad in the twenties turned his attention to the problems of education as a means of fitting people to live effectively in a society that enriches their lives and concluded that "neither Confucius nor Dewey has succeeded in finding a basic aim for education which is entirely suited to the needs of Korea." Then he argued for development of new ideas and methods that would arise from "the doctrine of survival-efficiency."[10] Like Dewey, he favored a pragmatic approach to building an education that would help students to meet practically the needs they would confront; and like Confucius he favored an education that strengthened character and stressed social responsibility. But Korea, in the grip of Japanese colonialism, was not able to devise any educational policies for itself.

It may be said that modernism came to Korea too suddenly and too late. In 1882 a series of treaties with the United States, Great Britain, France, and Russia were negotiated to foster "amity and commerce" with the West. In 1894 Japan overwhelmingly defeated China, thereby toppling the confident faith Koreans had had both in the Middle Kingdom and in its culture. Both the nations of the West and a partially-westernized Japan were intent upon seizing on the mainland of Asia whatever seemed of value to them, and this definitely included the peninsula of Korea, with its ice-free ports, its natural resources, and its strategic location. As a Korean scholar notes: "Korea lacked the necessary foundations for making a transformation of her institutions within the time that was available."[11] The changes that were required to fit Koreans to deal adequately with the problems which poured and tumbled around them seem in historic retrospect to have been undertaken all at once; and though in sober fact the period of transition lasted throughout a generation, even this is not much time for fundamental adjustments to be devised and accepted.

In a confused sort of way modernism had made an initial impact on Korea in 1860, in the Tonghak movement, which taught the people, not equality, not fraternity, not democracy, but that in a cataclysmic intervention by heaven the rich and the powerful would be overthrown and the poor would arise to take their place. Not unreasonably, the founder of this heterodox faith, Ch'oe Che-u, was executed by the state for "confusing the people." In the tumultuous uprisings that marked the Tonghak Rebellion, some 36,000 rebels were slain and the disorders gave an excuse to the Japanese to extend their power into the peninsula. Even so, as Professor Lee points out, some genuine good resulted—primarily in the educating of the people to expect that government might be recast so that instead of oppressing it would help them.[12]

Change, at a dizzying pace, was the order of the day. In 1882, for the first time, the King opened the state schools to common citizens. Christian missionaries were admitted to the country, and they began to open schools: Ilwha Haktang, which (in 1910) became Ewha University, one of the largest and most comprehensive women's colleges in the world; Union Christian College in Pyongyang; and Chosun Christian College (now Yonsei University) in Seoul. The King cut his topknot (the peculiar braid of hair worn by all Korean males) and ordered his people to do the same, symbolizing a dramatic break with the past. Not least among the changes was the establishment in Seoul of Pai Jai Haktang, a mission school, by the Methodists. Pai Jai soon became a germinal source of new ideas.

To Pai Jai, as a part-time lecturer, early in 1896 came Philip Jaisohn (So Chae-p'il), who had taken part in the reform movement of 1884, and afterwards earned his M.D. degree in America. Returning to his homeland, he announced his purpose: "to teach the people and to cultivate leadership."

His principal efforts were expended in two ways: through establishment of a tri-weekly newspaper in which he preached doctrines of reform; and through establishment at Pai Jai of a discussion group he called the Independence Club. Both undertakings were exceedingly successful, perhaps for a reason set forth by an Englishwoman visiting in Korea at that time:

Only those who have formed some idea of the besotted ignorance of the Korean concerning current events in his own country, and of the credulity which makes him the victim of every rumor set afloat in the capital, can appreciate the significance of this step and its probable effect in enlightening the people, and in creating a public opinion which shall sit in judgment on regal and official misdeeds.[13]

The Independence Club was organized on July 2, 1896, to meet in a building in Seoul renamed The Hall of Independence. The thirty charter members included three cabinet officers and other high ranking officials and businessmen.[14] At first weekly meetings were held, with random discussions on subjects such as the cutting of topknots and the need for street lights, followed by chess games, social drinking, and conviviality. Jaisohn was disturbed by the total lack of understanding by the members of orderly processes of discussion. His biographer reports:

> Patience, tact, and aggressive guidance constituted his motto. He began by teaching the members parliamentary rules. Being the pioneer in this, it was necessary for him to coin new terms which the members had to learn. When they became familiar with parliamentary rules, he taught them how to think on their feet and translate their thought into words by the holding of debate meetings.[15]

For more than a year, as the *Korean Repository* reported in its issue for November, 1897, "the club remained essentially an educational and social institution and stands aloof from politics."

That winter, however, the Russian government, which had become increasingly aggressive in intervening in Korean affairs, outraged public opinion by leasing an island in Pusan harbor. Hundreds of individuals now sought membership in the Independence Club—so many that its meetings had to be held out-of-doors— searching for means of protesting Russian penetration. Speeches became inflammatory. Among the new members were radicals and agitators who demanded substantial changes in government policies.

By May, 1898, Philip Jaisohn, under constant danger of arrest, returned to the United States. Among new members of the club, Syngman Rhee became prominent as a street-corner orator and agitator. Yun Ch'i-ho assumed the presidency of the club, and Chong Kyo became secretary. Rhee and others organized a massive anti-government demonstration in October of that year, with some 10,000 protestors staging a three-day, sit-down strike in front of the King's palace. These tactics caused the government to establish a new

Privy Council, with half its membership elected by the people. Political intrigue, however, undermined the Council; and on November 21, a new sit-down demonstration was broken up by hoodlums from the Peddlers Guild, acting under governmental instructions. Among Independence Club members arrested was Syngman Rhee, who was subjected to six months of interrogation by torture and then sentenced to life imprisonment—a sentence finally terminated by amnesty in 1904.[16]

While in prison, Rhee wrote *The Spirit of Independence,* a book in which he sought to combine the virtues of Confucianism and democracy. "If your own heart," he wrote, "is without patriotism, your heart is your enemy. You must struggle against your own feelings if they urge you to forgo the struggle for the common cause. Let us examine our hearts now, at this moment. If you find within yourself any single thought of abandoning the welfare of your country, tear it out. Do not wait for others to lead or to do whatever must be done, but arouse yourself. If you do not do it, it will never be done." Then he added to this Confucian admonition an explanation of democracy:

> Generally speaking, a nation is analogous to an assembly in which many gather to discuss various matters. In a nation many people unite together to survive. The officials of a nation are those charged to carry on the business of its organization. The people are the members of the assembly. Without the assistance of the people, the officials have no source of strength. Where the people are not attentive, vice enters in.

The need for a free and open society, with widespread public discussion of the issues and of governmental practices, was reiterated by Rhee, when he said: "Subjects must serve the ruler with reverence and according to right principles, and advise him with wise words."[17]

In 1904, the commencement of the Russo-Japanese War brought a Japanese army onto the peninsula, and Korean independence virtually ended, with formal annexation by Japan taking place in 1910. Until 1945, the Japanese continued their occupation, limiting discussion drastically and seeking stringently to Japanize the Korean people.[18] Not only was the teaching of speech unthinkable during this period, but the very use of speech as a medium for discussing the real problems of the community was sharply restricted. For a dreary generation the people of Korea learned what it means to be deprived of the opportunity to speak their minds.

BARRIERS OF CONSERVATISM

The most friendly interpreters of Korea, and indeed the scholars of Korea as well, have all agreed that basically the people and the society are unduly conservative and have suffered from this characteristic.[19] In at least four very specific ways this conservative cast of mind has inhibited the development of speech education under the Republic of Korea, which was inaugurated on August 15, 1948. The new democracy did not necessarily mean new freedom.

In the first place, when the reestablishment of the Korean nation took place, the people and the government were united in a feeling that above all they wanted a sovereignty and a society that indubitably would be their own, not a neocolonial creation of the paternal state, the United States, which had liberated and restored the country. Both gratitude and a keen awareness of the values of modernism pointed toward progressive liberalism. But the true restoration of their own native Koreanism impelled a simultaneous backward turning toward the cultural characteristics that were deeply rooted in their own past. This feeling was especially strong among the rural people, who constituted fully 75 per cent of the population. It was shared by a great many teachers—who, after all, were sons and daughters of conservative parents, and who (in the early days of the republic) had almost no specialized educational preparation.

Not knowing what education might mean, lacking all modern techniques and equipment, and without even textbooks from which to teach, it was but natural that the beginnings of the new Korean school system turned inevitably inward, toward a dependable and noncontroversial past. This was scarcely a hospitable atmosphere in which to introduce such a new and unknown subject as the study of speech. Meanwhile, the natural conservatism of the people was fully matched by the uncertainty and lack of confidence of the new government officials, not one of whom was qualified by training or experience for the magnitude of the responsibilities. Under the circumstances, the last thing the government wished was the encouragement of public speech, involving as it surely must the criticism of governmental operations.

A second conservative barrier to the introduction of speech into the curricula of the schools was the fact that a large majority of the college and even secondary school teachers had received all their education from either Japanese or Chinese educators, and generally this schooling stressed the anti-Western and traditionally Oriental areas and methods of learning.

Still a third factor of conservatism derived from the small but growing body of Korean teachers who did graduate work in the United States, Great Britain, or another of the nations of the West. As neophytes unacquainted with the Western world, they were far from willing to become innovators or experimenters. What seemed far wiser to them was to enter into the most conservative courses—or, as these areas would be described to them, the "soundest" or the "most reputable" or the "traditional" studies. Few of them ever encountered departments of speech; and if they did notice their existence, it was only to observe that they were not approved by such disciplines as English, philosophy, history, and economics. Hence, the professors of Korean colleges who returned from abroad to share their Western learning with their colleagues did not bring with them any knowledge of or enthusiasm for the study of speech.

Finally, a fourth conservative factor is one that is also responsible in many parts of the world for the retardation of studies in speech. This is the system of nation-wide, standardized examinations, given to all high school seniors who wish to apply for college entrance. As a result, the whole success of the teachers, of the curricula, of the high school administrations, and of the students themselves, is judged realistically by just one standard: how well the students do on the standard examinations. Since these exams are based upon carefully identified and prescribed areas of study, nothing whatsoever that lies apart from these areas to be examined can possibly have much significance for either teachers or students. Genuine educational liberalism must commence with abolition of the standardized examination system.

The Korean educators themselves gradually became more and more dissatisfied with the straightjacket which the examination system imposed upon them. First, in the early 1960s, the standardized examinations for entrance into the high schools were abolished. Then, late in the sixties, the nation-wide college entrance exams were converted into examinations prepared by each college. Even this partial liberalization, however, still left the high-school curricula under the control of the colleges; and the generally conservative cast of the college faculties continued to inhibit hospitality to new subjects, such as speech.

In sum, Korean education, even in the midst of a nation vibrant with new growth in its economics, politics, and social customs, has consistently lagged behind the tenor of the times. If it is true everywhere in the world that the schools tend to educate youth for yesterday's problems by day-before-yesterday's methods, this charge is even truer of Korea than for many other countries. Nevertheless, genuine progress has been made.

SPEECH EDUCATION—SOME PROMISING BEGINNINGS

Despite all the difficulties and handicaps, there are genuinely promising beginnings of speech education in Korea. The number of educators who are interested is small; the programs that have been started are both few and restricted; the available teaching staff is almost wholly untrained; and there is a discouragingly large extent of sheer indifference to speech among teachers and administrators. These factors, however, are all familiar in all nations which have experienced the commencement of curricular programs in speech. Perhaps the development of adequate course work in speech may yet be delayed until a further impetus is somehow provided. But enough has been done to introduce the values of speech education to people who had not hitherto known about it. And where sturdy seeds are planted they tend to grow, especially when favorable conditions exist.

Speech Contests

As has been true in many places, organized academic work in speech has commenced in Korea primarily in the form of sponsored speech contests. These date back at least to the twenties, when Korea's leading newspaper, *Donga-Ilbo*, inaugurated an annual oratorical contest for secondary-school students.

Public speaking as a means of arousing community concern about current issues was virtually unknown in Korea until 1894, when Chang-ho Ahn undertook a series of speeches in Pyongyang to stir up public support for democratic and nationalistic reforms. A political figure appealing to the people through the medium of speeches was a new phenomenon on the Korean scene. The establishment of the Independence Club in Seoul two years later gave impetus to this new form of public appeal. It appears that the arousal of nationalism and the movement for democratic reforms were both particularly congenial to this new mode of intimate and personal communication between leaders and the people.

In 1912, when a nationwide student protest against Japanese rule swept through Korea, and again in 1919-20, during the demonstrations and uprisings that led to the Republic-in-Exile, renewed interest was aroused in the dramatic and inspiring image of a bold leader standing up in full view of the occupation powers to proclaim the spiritual independence of both himself and his listeners. The Korean populace was thus gradually introduced to the concept of public opinion formation through persuasive public speaking. The atmosphere was right for extending the number and scope of speech contests.

Following Korea's liberation from Japan in 1945, and especially after the inauguration of the Republic in 1948, the number of schools at all levels multiplied and student enrollment greatly increased. The war (1950-1953) interfered with this development for a time, but since then the growth in number and quality of schools has continued steadily. Speech contests were broadly sponsored as a means of stimulating student support for a renewed spiritual and political morality to replace the indifference and decadence that resulted from the Japanese occupation policies of stifling nationalism.

In both secondary schools and colleges debating was introduced in the 1940s, and the audiences took the debates so seriously that scuffles and wrangling often broke out, testifying both to the realism of the arguments and to the lack of sophistication of the auditors. Both oratorical and extemporaneous speaking contests were established, with annual or semiannual contests being sponsored by the following universities and colleges:

In Seoul
Seoul National University
Korea University
Dongkook University
Chung-ang University
Sookmyung Women's University
Konkuk University
Kyung Hee University

In Taegu
Yongnam University
Kyungbook National University

In Kwangju
Chonnam National University
Chosun University

In Pusan
Pusan National University
Dongja University

In Taejon
Taejon College

Many junior and senior high schools also began in the fifties to sponsor speech contests, along with extracurricular speech clubs. The

Heungsadang, a political organization established by Chang-ho Ahn, also sponsors annual speech contests, held on the anniversary of his death, which occurred March 10, 1938. Another annual contest is sponsored by the UNESCO Student Club.

Most of these school and university contests occur in April and May, when a new semester is commencing, and in October and November, when another semester is ending. Contests also center around such national holidays as Independence Movement Day (March 1), Arbor Day (April 5), Student Revolution Day (April 19), Military Revolution Day (May 16), Memorial Day (June 6), Korea War Day (June 25), Constitution Day (July 17), Independence Day (August 15), National Foundation Day (October 9), United Nations Day (October 24), Student Day (November 3), and other special commemorative occasions.

Topics for the contests tend to reflect the nature of the holidays they commemorate and also the leading issues and events of the time. In the late forties the contest topics usually reflected the governmental stand on political issues. In the period between liberation from Japan and outbreak of the Korean War, most of the talks dealt with anti-Communism, atrocities perpetrated by the Communists, and the plight of the divided country. After the military coup of May 16, 1961, popular themes for the speeches became modernization of the homeland and dedication to national service.

More recently the range of topics has broadened considerably, with each student selecting whatever subject might appeal to him. Concurrently, the emphasis in the contests has shifted from the subject matter to the speaker's ability to phrase and present his ideas. Skill in style and delivery has become inordinately important. Good speaking per se seems to be more important than sound thinking. The focus, unfortunately, tends to be upon developing an oratory of display.

Still another unfortunate aspect of the emphasis upon speech contests is that they identify speech as an academic subject by identifying and rewarding students who happily possess special abilities in speech, rather than by confronting the need to help every student to make his communicative abilities more effective. It is as though physical education in the schools were conceived of entirely in terms of football, baseball, basketball, and track contests, with a few stars displaying their skill while the bulk of the students remain as spectators.

Professional and Curricular Developments

Such curricular developments in speech as have been achieved are owing directly to the sponsorship by speech associations. There are in Korea two types of speech organizations. In the Korean language there is no generic word for "speech," as there is in English. There is one term meaning "oratorical style of speech," or public speaking in a formal sense; and there is another word meaning "spoken communication." The first has given rise to organizations which sponsor speech contests. The latter is the base of The Korean Speech Association, which was founded in 1965, following the suggestions of Dr. Martin Bryan, professor of speech, University of Cincinnati, who was then a Fulbright scholar assigned to the College of Education, Seoul National University. Under the presidency of Tai Si Chung, secretary general of the Korean Federation of Education Associations, the Korean Speech Association has a membership of about thirty. Among them are Yong-woo Chun, radio announcer, who holds an M.A. in speech from Sungkyoonkwang University, in Seoul; Doohyun Lee, professor of dramatics, College of Education, Seoul National University; Kapsoon Kim, professor of English literature, Ewha Women's University; Keunsam Lee, professor of English literature and dramatics at Sogang Jesuit College, Seoul; and Sung-koo Lee, teacher in the Seoul Boys' Senior High School.

This association has been largely instrumental in the establishment of speech courses at the following colleges: Department of Journalism, College of Liberal Arts, Ewha Women's University; Department of Cinema and Drama, College of Liberal Arts, Chung-ang University; Graduate School of Communication, Seoul National University; Graduate School of Public Administration, Seoul National University; Department of Mass Communications, College of Political Science and Economics, Korea University; Department of Mass Communications, College of Political Science and Economics, Kyung Hee University; Department of Speech, Union Theological Seminary, in Seoul; Republic of Korea Military Academy; Republic of Korea Air Force Academy; and the Seoul Dramatics School.

Textbooks in Speech

The first textbook in speech ever published in Korea[20] was *Effective Speech for Democratic Living,* which was written in Seoul by Robert T. Oliver in the summer of 1957, and published that fall by Minjung-Sugwan Publishing Co., Ltd., under the sponsorship of the Ministry of Education. This book appeared in three separate editions: an English language edition, a Korean translation, and a third edition which incorporated both the others. It has been used in secondary schools throughout southern Korea and is still in use as one of the standard textbooks.

The first textbooks in speech written by a Korean were three books by Tai Si Chung. The first, written in collaboration with Woon Sun Hong, was entitled *Beginnings in Speech,* published by the Omungak Publishing Company, in Seoul, in 1961. The second book written by Mr. Chung, entitled *Speech for the New Age,* was published in Seoul by Athene Press. Mr. Chung's third speech book is his translation of the third edition of Alan H. Monroe's *Principles and Types of Speech.* Two other speech textbooks have also been written and published in Seoul, both by Yong-woo Chun. The first, *An Introduction to Speech,* was published in 1964 by the Munhaksa Company; and the second, *The Principles of Speech,* was published in 1966 by the Kyoyuk Chulpansa Company.

General textbooks used in the secondary schools virtually ignore speech. In the 1963 general revision of the national educational curriculum, lip service was paid to the need for educating students in their ability to use their own language orally with greater effectiveness; but in reality very little opportunity is provided the students for development of their speaking skills. For junior and senior high schools there are national language textbooks dealing with grammar, composition, and the Chinese classics, but nothing in speech. In the junior high school language textbooks, approximately 19 per cent of the content deals with speaking and listening abilities. In the senior high school composition textbooks, some 13 per cent of the content deals directly or indirectly with speaking and listening problems and methods. Not more than one-fifth of the assignments incorporate any consideration of problems of oral communication. Only one assignment relates directly to speech education. Any teachers who might desire to enhance the oral ability of their students must devise their own teaching materials and assignments; and, as has been indicated earlier, they are seriously inhibited from doing this by the fact that their success is judged wholly in terms of how well their students will do in the standardized examinations—in which speech is ignored.

There is in Seoul an oratorical academy sponsored by an association that was founded in 1947, and which is headed now (1970) by Hoojin Park. It not only offers courses in speech but also publishes a monthly speech journal, sponsors oratorical contests, and maintains agents who travel around the country encouraging wider participation in oratorical contests. Unfortunately, the emphasis is on posture, gesture, and an oratory of display, with virtually no considerations of principles of general oral effectiveness or of the uses of speech in ordinary discourse.

THE FUTURE–NEEDS AND OPPORTUNITIES

On the basis of this survey it may be predicted confidently that the future of speech education in Korea will manifest considerable improvement. One reason is that sound beginnings have been made as focal points around which improvements and expansions are sure to develop. The academic atmosphere, so far as speech is concerned, resembles extremely cloudy and inclement weather, in which tiny evidences of sunshine are just beginning to appear. The political and social circumstances of Korea, meanwhile, offer sound encouragement to those who seek to develop speech education.

The beginnings, which have been discussed in the preceding section, are not dissimilar from those which have occurred in other countries. There is some enthusiasm in limited circles, surrounded by general indifference. Some of the enthusiasm is misdirected. Some of the speech work that is being done is done so badly that observers are prone to be fortified in their objections to speech as an academic subject. Nevertheless, the principle is being implanted that just as students need to improve their abilities in reading and writing, so do they in speaking and listening. The point is being made that most human communication is through speech, rather than through print. Once the problem is posed for consideration, like Banquo's ghost it will not go away.

The academic climate of indifference and even of hostility has some notable alleviations. These are most notable, perhaps, in the elementary schools. These classrooms are overcrowded and under-equipped. Partly for these reasons the teachers must encourage the students to contribute to their own learning by taking field trips, by bringing to class exhibits of plants, artifacts, and other subjects, and by telling their classmates about them. Especially during the harsh years of the Korean War and immediately afterward, many Korean schools were conducted out-of-doors, or in partially ruined buildings, with few books, no blackboards, and few other teaching aids. Teachers and students had to use their ingenuity. Under these circumstances education was largely oral. Unfortunately, this was distinctly a "hardship" situation, and the gradual return to conditions under which students could be held under silent duress while listening to lectures or reading or taking written tests has been interpreted perhaps too stringently as an "improvement." But a few Korean teachers are being exposed in studies either abroad or at home to what speech education can and should mean; and in time, like yeast in dough, this influence will be felt.

Undoubtedly the most important circumstance affecting the future development of speech education in Korea is the ferment of democratic change in the social, economic, and political conditions of Korea. Under Japanese control, Korea was definitely a "closed society," in which freedom of speech was unthinkable and skill in oral discourse was of little use. After liberation, Korea became only partially an "open society," hampered by Communist terrorism, then by the years of war and invasion, and after that by the awesome tasks of rebuilding a smashed country. In recent years, however, and most notably since the military coup of 1961, Korean society has undergone a vast infusion of liberalism.

Social, business and professional clubs flourish, with widespread membership and with regular weekly meetings devoted to discussion of current topics. Youth is fully involved in this new socialization, through membership in the Boy Scouts, Girl Scouts, Four-H Clubs, and many similar organizations. Women are emerging into political, business, professional, and social activities to a far greater extent than ever before.[21] In the realm of politics, not only are election campaigns hard fought in the public forums but political issues and the conduct of political offices are under constant scrutiny, criticism, and discussion. Meanwhile, Korean commerce and industry are increasing at the enormous rate of from 10 to 15 per cent annually, with greatly accelerated demand for new managerial personnel. All these factors tend to bring into ever sharper focus the reality of the need for skill in oral communication.

At the same time, Korea is sharing fully in the world-wide development of radio, television, and motion pictures.[22] As Marshall McLuhan has vividly declaimed, the "revolution of print," which was inaugurated by the invention of metal movable type (in Europe in the sixteenth century, and in China and Korea perhaps two hundred years earlier), is now being superseded by the renewal of the age-old supremacy of speech. Face-to-face discourse is without doubt far more extensive today because of the vast improvements in transportation and a consequent increase in social mobility. The telephone brings to millions of people opportunities never before known for exchange of thoughts and sentiments in direct discourse. And radio, television, and the motion picture screen are rivals of the newspaper-magazine print medium for providing information and relaxed entertainment.

More and more educators of every stamp, in every field, are stressing that we live even more vitally in a "semantic environment" than we do in our "physical environment." As Susanne Langer points out in her book, *Philosophy in a New Key*, words are the "transformational symbols" by means of which mankind is able to interact with our environment. And it is readily observable that we speak a hundred words for every one we write, while we listen to perhaps two or three times as much total wordage as we read. These are cardinal facts of the life of our time; and in Korea as elsewhere these are facts that will bring speech education into the core curriculum of the schools of the future.

FOOTNOTES

[1]Key P. Yang and Gregory Henderson, "An Outline History of Korean Confucianism," *Journal of Asian Studies*, XVIII (November, 1958):81.

[2]Han Yong Lim, "A Short History of Korean Education," *Korean Report*, I (October, 1961):15 and *passim*. Cf. also, Chongsun Kim, "Hwarang and the First Unification of Korea"(Master's thesis, University of Washington, 1961); and Richard Rutt, "The Flower Boys of Silla: Hwarang," *Transactions of the Korean Branch, Royal Asiatic Society*, XXXVIII (October, 1961):1-66.

[3]Yang and Henderson, *op. cit.*, p. 83.

[4]B. H. Hazard *et al*, *Korean Studies Guide* (Berkeley: University of California Press, 1954), pp. 164-165.

[5]*The Analects of Confucius*, trans. Pyun Yung Tai [Korean scholar and statesman] (Seoul: Minjungsugwan, n.d.). The passages quoted are taken from the *Analects* in the following order: VI, 15; XIII, 3; XII, 8; XIX, 25.

[6]Han Yong Lim, *op. cit.*, p. 17.

[7]Yang and Henderson, *op. cit.*, p. 93.

[8]Korean proverbs may be found in Joseph Raymond, "Korean Folklore, II: Common Sayings," *Korean Survey*, III (December, 1954):10-12; Joseph Raymond, "Current Korean Proverbs," *Western Folklore*, X (July, 1951):237-244; Robert T. Oliver, *Why War Came in Korea* (New York: Fordham University Press and the Declan X. McMullen Co., 1950), pp. 88-90; and Sa-Yop Kim, "Korea's Proverbs," *Korean Report*, II (July, 1962):29-31.

[9]For an account of the development of fiction in Korea, see Peter H. Lee, *Korean Literature: Topics and Themes*, published for the Association for Asian Studies, Tucson: University of Arizona Press, 1965, particularly pp. 65-81.

[10]Chungil Y. Roe, "The True Function of Education in Social Adjustment" (Thesis, University of Nebraska, 1927).

[11]Chong-Sik Lee, *The Politics of Korean Nationalism* (Berkeley: University of California Press, 1963), p. 19.

[12]*Ibid.*, p. 33.

[13]Isabella Bird Bishop, *Korea and Her Neighbors* (New York: Fleming H. Revell, 1898), pp. 439-440.

[14]Clarence N. Weems, Jr., "The Korean Reform and Independence Movement, 1881-1898" (Doctoral thesis, Columbia University, 1954).

[15]Channing Liem, *America's Finest Gift to Korea: The Life of Philip Jaisohn* (New York: William Frederick Press, 1952), p. 50.

[16]This account of the Independence Club follows closely the interpretation by Chong-Sik Lee, who has carefully collated and scrutinized the extant sources, as presented in his *Politics of Korean Nationalism, op. cit.,* pp. 55-69.

[17]These passages from Rhee's book were translated by Kyung-ho Lee for inclusion in Robert T. Oliver's *Syngman Rhee: The Man Behind the Myth* (New York: Dodd, Mead, 1954, 1960), pp. 57-58. Oliver's account of the Independence Club movement and the arrest and imprisonment of Rhee, pp. 24-68, is based largely on discussions with Rhee himself and with Hugh Heung-woo Cynn, who was a fellow member of the club and who shared imprisonment with him.

[18]A chronicle of such public speaking as took place during the Japanese occupation of Korea is being prepared by Miss Myoung-Ja Chung as an M.A. thesis, for the Department of Speech, The Pennsylvania State University.

[19]Cf., for example: Yung Tai Pyun, *Korea My Country;* Younghill Kang, *The Grass Roof;* Kyung Cho Chung, *Korea Tomorrow;* Fred Harvey Harrington, *God, Memmon and the Japanese;* Homer B. Hulbert, *The Passing of Korea;* Cornelius Osgood, *The Koreans and Their Culture;* and Robert T. Oliver, *Verdict in Korea* and *Korea: Forgotten Nation.*

[20]In 1910, a phonetics text was published: *Sounds of Speech,* by Si-Kyoog Chu.

[21]Some of the evidence is assembled by Hwang-Kyung Ko, "Korean Women and Education," *Korean Report,* IV (April-June, 1964):28-31. Cf. also the editorial report, "Korean Women's Status Elevated in Two Decades," *Korean Report,* V (July-September, 1965):12-13.

[22]Representative data on the growth of these three mass communications industries are found in *Korea: Radio and Television* (Korean Information Service, Inc., n.d.); *Korean Report,* II (March, 1962):15-16; and *Korea at a Glance* (ROK Ministry of Public Information, 1962), pp. 18-20.

SPEECH EDUCATION IN LEBANON

John Collins
Nabil Dajani

INTRODUCTION

The history of speech and speech education in Lebanon may best be understood by viewing the cultural values attached to the art of speech by the Lebanese and the Arabic-speaking people in general. To an Arabic-speaking person, the mastery of the art of speech is highly esteemed and is considered an important characteristic of leaders and of cultured men. Since the early history of the Arab world, oratory—or *Khataba,* as the term is known in Arabic—has been a cherished value.

Oratory and poetry during the pre-Islamic period had a prominent place in the life of the predominantly illiterate Arabs. The most popular events during the pre-Islamic period *(Jahiliah)* were those "markets" during which poets and orators met to recite poetry and prose. Oratory was one means of defending one's tribe and a way of praising the glories of the tribe's achievements, as well as a means of guiding the tribesmen. It was also one of the determining factors in the selection of a leader for the tribe.

During the early Islamic period, oratory became even more important since it was an essential means for spreading the faith of Islam. The Prophet Mohammed himself was an orator and his *hadith* (speeches) are among the cherished Islamic classics. Whole speeches of prominent Arab orators such as al-Hajaj bin Yousef,[1] are usually memorized by most high-school students all over the Arab world. In the high school attended by one of the authors, not only were the students requested to memorize whole speeches, but they were also requested to recite the speeches accompanied with appropriate movements and gestures.

Oratory reached its peak during the Omayyad period, and then began to degenerate during the Abbasid period. It remained a dormant art until the Arab renaissance of the nineteenth century when it found fertile ground and became more diversified. However,

152

at the time of this renaissance the classical Arabic language was weakened by the development of colloquial dialects—dialects which emerged as a result of various cultural influences and the division of the Arab world by political differences.

The weakening of the classical Arabic language and the development of colloquial dialects did not weaken the general value attached to the art of speech. Recitals of colloquial poetry *(zajal)* are still one of the most popular community events for the Lebanese. Almost every social gathering in the Lebanese villages—usually held by the *baydar,* where the summer harvest is kept—is brightened by the recital of *zajal.*

The development of the colloquial dialects did, however, weaken classical Arabic as the language of instruction and consequently affected speech education. Thus, while Westerners speak and write the same language, the Lebanese speak one language and write and read another. This means that the study of speech at the elementary- and high-school levels is basically carried out in the classical Arabic. Although English and French are also languages of instruction in Lebanon, they are generally not used in formal programs of speech education.

THE EDUCATIONAL SYSTEM

To understand the methods of speech education in Lebanon one must briefly summarize the important features of the total educational system in this country.

The modern educational system of Lebanon is based completely on the French system. Having been under the French mandate for some thirty years, Lebanon patterned most of its modern institutions after the French when it gained its independence in 1943. Thus, on September 30, 1946, the Lebanese Minister of Education and Fine Arts, Mr. Philip Takla, submitted to the Prime Minister drafts of decrees establishing the system of education in Lebanon. These drafts were officially adopted and issued in six separate decrees on October 1, 1946.

The decrees divide the Lebanese educational programs into three stages: (1) an elementary stage which extends over a period of five years and leads to the Lebanese *certificat* degree; (2) a higher elementary or preparatory stage that extends over a period of four years and leads to the Lebanese *brevet* degree; and (3) a secondary stage that extends over a period of seven years and leads to the Lebanese *baccalaureate* degree, which the government equates with the sophomore degree in the American university system.

The educational decrees of 1946 give a detailed description of the curricula of the different stages of this educational system. These curricula suggest that although speech is not viewed as a separate subject of instruction, it is given prominent attention in the teaching of the Arabic language as well as in the teaching of the additional foreign language (French or English), which is obligatory even in the first year of the elementary school.

In its description of the aims of the Arabic-language curriculum in the elementary education stage, one of the decrees states: "The teaching of the language aims at achieving two basic goals: understanding and expression. The teacher should be aware of these two goals in teaching his students the principles of grammar and their application in exercise of grammatical analysis, dictation, and composition, as well as in reading and speech."[2] The same decree adds further: "The child feels the need for expression and speech, and he should be helped to exercise. . . .The teacher should not forget that we face in Lebanon a special problem due to the duality of our language. The daily language of speech at home and in the market is different from that of writing and reading."

The teaching of Arabic in the Lebanese system of education is divided into separate departments within the general field. Speech education thus falls mainly in the departments of recitation and memory and grammar. According to the decree, recitation and memory includes "a selected poem that should be recited in a form of acting." Grammar, on the other hand, includes "exercises in the proper pronunciation of the letters and words."

Speech education in either French or English is aimed, according to the decree, at the "informal introduction to the language through hearing and conversation." The decree itemizes some specific pedagogical techniques which may be employed to achieve this aim:

1. Vocabulary concentrating on objects and activities in the classroom.

2. Drill on English sounds, especially those new to the pupil.

3. Formation of the letters.

4. Simple songs and poems to be learned by ear.

Teaching methods also employ dramatized reading as well as oral and silent reading from the texts, and the answering of simple questions on the text. The emphasis in conversation is upon correct pronunciation and the use of words in simple but correct sentence structure.

Perhaps a brief description of the subjects taught in the Lebanese primary and secondary schools will help in the development of an overall frame of reference necessary for understanding the nature of speech education in Lebanon.

During the first year in the primary level a student has a twenty-seven hour schedule. These hours are divided among the following subjects: Arabic language, including reading and recitation (6 hours); religious education (1 hour); moral and civic education (1½ hours); general science and conversation (2 hours); mathematics (5 hours); drawing and handicraft (2 hours); music and singing (2 hours); physical education (2½ hours); and foreign language, either English or French, (5 hours).

During the second and third years, more emphasis is given to Arabic reading, recitation, composition, grammar, and dictation. These are divided into separate subjects during the last two years of the primary level, the fourth and fifth elementary classes.

Speech education during this period is restricted, for the first year, to correct pronunciation of words and syllables, construction of sentences, and reproduction of certain words and passages. Recitation is restricted to selections of poetry of clear meaning and syntax.

The second, third, and fourth elementary classes emphasize correct reading of texts and comprehension. Selected pieces of clearly understood poetry are memorized and reproduced with the proper tone inflection, movement, and gesture. During the fifth year, careful reading of passages, syntax, meaning, and comprehension are emphasized. Recitation during this year includes poetry and prose.

On the secondary level, the first and second years stress correct reading, syntax, and pronunciation. Works by contemporary writers and poets are taught, and recitation includes prose, poetry, and proverbs. The third year stresses the same subjects, except that the passages selected include ancient as well as contemporary writers. The fourth year stresses the explication of passages by writers and poets of all periods.

During the fifth and sixth secondary years, speech education becomes quite complex. The fifth year includes the study of the historical and aesthetic development of literature. It also includes the study of the fundamentals of rhetoric and the appreciation of literature. The context of prose is studied according to the literary arts. Stories, narration, plays, and dialogues are studied. Famous literary figures and works such as *A Thousand and One Nights,* the poems of Antar bin Shaddad, and proverbs and passages from Ali bin Abi Talib and Abdullah ibn al-Moukaffa' are studied during this year. The sixth year stresses prose and oratory *(khatabah)*. It deals with the qualifications of the good orator, methods of speech writing, and close examination of the different kinds of speeches—social, political, religious, and military. The importance of speech, not only in the past but in the present, is also considered.

SPEECH EDUCATION

A closer look at the curriculum of one of the schools in Beirut, the International College, may give an example of this Lebanese educational system at work. The college is divided into two sections, French and English. It grants both the Lebanese baccalaureate (a thirteen-year program following the French pattern) and the high school diploma (a twelve-year program following the American system).

The English department, within which are to be found the elements of a speech education, has a three-fold function:
1. to teach English for the elementary school (K through 6)
2. to teach English as a third language in the French section
3. to teach English as a second language—and as the language of instruction—in the English section

Speech education in the lower classes of the college includes oral work. This involves practice in oral English: the student tells a story, and gives a description. In the middle classes (III-IV secondary) oral composition is stressed. Given a topic, the student is required to deliver a talk. The students are concerned primarily, however, with practice in oral English. Although some particulars of speech technique are taught, the major focus in these classes is generally in the transfer of a standard written composition to oral delivery.

In addition to formal classroom training in speech and the history of Arabic oratory, many schools have extracurricular activities related to speech education. For instance, the stated aims of the Arabic Club, sponsored by the English section of International College, include several speech activities and represent the range of such activities to be found in many other schools. These aims include:
1. Strengthening the Arabic language in the school
2. organizing competitions in composition writing (writing for style) and in oratory
3. presenting plays (acting and drama)
4. presenting lectures and speeches by prominent literary figures

5. hearing poetry read by prominent Arab poets
6. sponsoring debating groups on literature, journalism, novels, history, etc.
7. inviting some educators to speak to students
8. inviting specialists on the baccalaureate program to speak to the students
9. creating a cooperative and friendly spirit between I.C. and other sister schools
10. nourishing the Arabic magazine *Sawt al-Shabab* with good literary and social subjects
11. organizing intelligence-knowledge contests on various subjects—science, literature, sociology, history, etc.
12. creating a spirit of cooperation, understanding, and friendship among the students as well as training them in parliamentary procedures in their speech, oratory, discussion, and elections

Membership in the Arabic Society at the International College is restricted to the upper secondary classes (grades IV-VII) but is not required. In 1968, there were 257 members. The group sponsors an annual oratorical contest.

SPEECH IN HIGHER EDUCATION

The general features of the educational system in the elementary and secondary levels in Lebanon are determined to a large extent by the national system outlined by the decrees of 1946. This system is patterned after the one introduced to Lebanon by the French during their mandate period over this country. However, since the majority of the Lebanese schools are private institutions, mostly missionary schools established by either French, British, or American missionaries, these schools offer programs that are a blend of the national and the Latin-French or the Anglo-American systems.

The system of higher education in Lebanon is less influenced by the national system since only in the last few decades did Lebanon have its own higher educational organizations set up. Prior to that the only existing universities were the American University of Beirut, which was established by American missionaries, and the St. Joseph University, established by the French Jesuit missionaries.

At present Lebanon has six institutions of higher learning. These are, in the order of their founding, The American University of Beirut; St. Joseph University; Beirut College for Women; the Lebanese University; Haigazian College; and the Arab University of Beirut.

The Lebanese University, which is the national institute, the St. Joseph University, and the Arab University of Beirut, a branch of U.A.R.'s Alexandria University, represent the Latin-French system. Speech education, as such, is not a part of their curriculum, although such organizations as debating societies do exist. In colleges following the Anglo-American pattern, however, public speaking courses are offered.

The Beirut College for Women was established in 1835 as the American School for Girls. In 1924, it became a junior college and in 1949 began offering a full four-year college program. It is chartered by the New York State Board of Regents and awards both the bachelor of arts and the bachelor of science degrees. A required course in fundamentals of speech is offered each semester. The syllabus presented to the students explains the major objectives of the course:

1. To aid each student to become a more effective and responsible speaker. To this end, each of you will be asked to take part in a series of directed experiences in speaking. Through preparing and presenting speeches, readings and discussions; through listening to and criticizing the speaking of your classmates; and from the comments of the instructor and your classmates you should be able to achieve some measurable increase in speaking skill.

2. To aid each student to acquire reliable knowledge about speech processes. Speech is viewed as man's most distinctive behavior, and reliable knowledge concerning the processes and forms of speech should be a part of the knowledge of every educated person. Such knowledge should help you to understand better your own behavior, and that of your associates; it should enable you to conduct yourself with greater efficiency and discrimination in the variety of communication situations which you constantly confront; it should aid you to make better use of whatever measure of wisdom or skill you may possess. In order to acquire knowledge about speech, you will be asked to observe reflectively the events of the class, to write analyses of speech events, to participate in class discussions of speech events, and to study carefully the text for this course.

(The text, incidentally, is currently Monroe and Ehninger's *Principles and Types of Speech.)*

Students are expected to attend at least three speech events outside the class and to present a written report on each one. In addition, bibliographies, speech outlines, and criticisms of in-class speeches are required. The students are also informed about the standards of speech performance:

We recognize that many of you take speech because of certain speaking problems which you recognize. For example, some of you are fearful, or ill at ease while speaking, and you may know that speech courses serve as one of the established ways of overcoming such problems. We shall be mindful of such individual problems, and work with you to meet them.

At the same time, we do not wish any of you to lose sight of the fact that average achievement in a speaking performance (a grade of C) must represent very thorough preparation on your part, regardless of whatever body of speech skills you may have acquired up to this point. That is to say, we think of a "C" performance as one worthy of a person who has gained admission to the College and who aspires to achieve the ends of higher education.

Special notice is given in the syllabus to the problem of originality and the use of resource materials, a point which perhaps had not been emphasized in the student's primary and secondary rhetorical training.

During the first semester of the 1968-69 academic year, there were four sections of Fundamentals of Speech scheduled, with from twenty to twenty-five students in each section, taught by three instructors. A fourth instructor, Miss Irene Faffler, the head of the department at B.C.W. (there is no separate speech department in any of the three institutions mentioned in this chapter), had returned to the United States to complete requirements for her Ph.D.

The second institution in Beirut which generally follows the Anglo-American pattern is Haigazian College, founded in 1955. There is presently one instructor of speech, Miss Anais Ohanessian, who teaches English 202 (Public Speaking), a required course for all English majors. Miss Ohanessian is a graduate of the American University at Cairo; she received her teaching diploma in drama from The Guildhall School of Music and Drama, London.

English 202 follows a sequence of speech assignments found in many American colleges and universities. The course begins with some preliminary instruction in voice production and exercises in breathing control. Exercises in pronunciation are also provided, although emphasis is not placed on perfect English because most of the students are using English as a second, if not third, language. The general focus is on form, delivery, and audience adaptation. A series of seven speeches is assigned during the course of the semester. The first assignment—an action talk—emphasizes posture, movement, gesture. This speech is followed by four assignments which concentrate on problems of audience adaptation. For the first, the students are asked to assume that they are addressing an audience of their own choice, and in the second, they are asked to assume that they are involved in an occasion of a formal or ceremonial nature. This is followed by an extemporary after-dinner speech. The final speech of this series requires the student to attend an outside event of some sort—a concert, speech, play, art exhibit—and then to present a critique to an audience assumed to have a special interest in such an activity.

The fifth assignment in the program concentrates on research and organization. The students are required to deliver a biography of a famous person, in which they develop a main idea, restricted to the main contributions of the subject. As a change of pace, the students, for their next assignment, are asked to draw a slip of paper which indicates the nature of the speaking situation (they have just been elected president of a society, for instance); they are then required to deliver an appropriate impromptu speech. The final speech is one of their own choice and generally takes from fifteen to twenty minutes. The only requirement is that they use an audio-visual aid of some sort. In line with the general emphasis on audience adaptation, outsiders are invited to attend all speeches and are particularly urged to attend the final speeches. The first speech in the series of audience interest speeches is taped, and then, at the end of the semester re-taped, so that the students are able to compare performances. According to Miss Ohanessian, they are generally impressed with their own improvement.

The response to the course has been enthusiastic. The course is required for all English majors and is restricted to fifteen students per semester, to give adequate time for student and instructor criticism. There are usually twice that number of requests, however, and the open invitation to attend the speeches generally fills the hall in which the class is held.

The American University of Beirut was founded in 1866 as the Syrian Protestant College. In addition to the school of arts and sciences, which began in 1866 with a class of eighteen students, it is comprised of schools of medicine, pharmacy, nursing, engineering and architecture, agriculture, and public health. It is chartered by the State of New York Board of Regents, and has offices in New York City, headquarters for its Board of Trustees. The enrollment in 1968 numbered 3,550 students, coming from a total of sixty-six different countries.

A.U.B. does not offer a separate speech course. Instruction in speech is, however, a part of the required three-semester Communication Skills Program. This program emphasizes language study, reading comprehension, and rhetoric—including oral as well as written discourse. The first semester concentrates on basic grammar review, reading comprehension, and the rhetoric of short units of composition. But at least one unit is devoted to speech work. Since the semester emphasis is on descriptive and narrative discourse, the speeches follow the same pattern.

Instruction in rhetoric during the second semester emphasizes expository discourse. At least two units of the program are devoted to oral communication. The students are asked to develop a working bibliography and a series of annotated note cards as a part of their general training in research techniques, but they are then required to make an oral report on their findings. The final unit of the program is devoted to an informative speech in keeping with the general focus on expository discourse. Students receive basic training in speech techniques and in adapting material to a face-to-face speaking situation.

The third semester of the sequence concentrates on argumentative and persuasive discourse, and again the students are required to deliver at least one speech. Many instructors also make use of group discussion techniques as a means of exploring the more complex novels which have been assigned as a part of the continuing practice in reading comprehension.

There were, during the first semester of the 1968-69 academic year, nineteen instructors and over 700 students in the Communication Skills Program. Because of the diverse language background of the students, there are three different tracks within the program: a remedial level, the regular three-semester program, and a two-semester honors course. In addition, there is a remedial course offered at the graduate level. For most of the students, English is the second or third language, although the language of instruction at A.U.B. is English. Thus, there is a real need for giving students the opportunity to become comfortable in the oral use of the language as well as giving instruction in written composition. Consequently, instructors frequently encourage student participation through informal class discussion—a pedagogical technique which is relatively unfamiliar to many students. Thus, while training in formal public speaking is not emphasized in the A.U.B. Communication Skills Program, informal oral communication is.

During the spring of 1968, there was an attempt—in large part the result of the SAA's interest in international speech education—to bring together, for the first time, all those who were teaching speech (or who were interested in developing a program of speech education) in the Beirut area. Planning was begun by those who attended the initial meeting to have a working conference at the A.U.B. campus during the 1968-69 academic year. Questionnaires have been sent to schools throughout Lebanon to begin gathering information on the types of speech education programs now being offered, the numbers of students involved in the programs, the materials, facilities, and equipment available, and the types of research projects which may be underway. The initial response for this project has been encouraging, and plans for a spring conference continue.

Those who were involved in the organizational meeting or who have indicated an interest in such a project are:

Clair Cowan	American Community School
William Blakemore	American Community School
Albert Miller	International College
Bruce Howell	Brummana High School
Irene Faffler	Beirut College for Women
Leonard Lee	Near East School of Theology
Anais Ohanessian	Haigazian College
Richard Yorkey	American University of Beirut
Thomas Buckingham	American University of Beirut
Nabil Dajani	American University of Beirut
John Collins	American University of Beirut

FOOTNOTES

[1]al-Hajaj bin Yousef was an Arab leader of outstanding power of oratory. Among his famous orations is the one he delivered in Baghdad on his arrival there. He had been sent by the Caliph to bring the country back into line, and he was faced with a very hostile, stone-throwing crowd. One speech gave him complete control over the people.

[2]Decree No. 6998.

SPEECH EDUCATION IN NEW ZEALAND

John Nicolls Thomson

INTRODUCTION

The Dominion of New Zealand is an independent and self-governing member of the British Commonwealth. Situated in the South Pacific Ocean, some 1,400 miles east of Australia and 6,500 miles southwest of California, it consists of three main islands totalling some 103,000 square miles in area and over 1,000 miles in length. It includes various island territories nearer to the tropics (notably the Cook Islands, Niue, and the Tokelau Islands in Polynesia).

Although New Zealand had been discovered in 1652 by the Dutch navigator Abel Tasman, rediscovered in 1769 by the Royal Navy explorer Captain James Cook, and visited by whalers, sealers, and traders in the early nineteenth century, it was not until 1840 that Britain formally proclaimed sovereignty over the country, granting it self-government in 1852. It was still heavily populated by tribes of Maoris and Polynesian people (believed to be originally of Asiatic origin), who had migrated to New Zealand mainly in the fourteenth century.

The present population of approximately two and three-quarter million people is primarily of British stock, about 10 per cent being Polynesian. This tenth of the population is dominantly Maori, but in recent years there has been a continuing influx of Polynesians from Fiji, Samoa, Tonga, the Cook Islands, Tokelau, and other Pacific islands.

To the Islanders now living in New Zealand, English is a second language; this fact presents special speech problems in some Auckland schools.

THE EDUCATION SYSTEM

It is customary to describe education in New Zealand as free, secular, and compulsory. It is free in the sense that children may

163

enroll at free kindergartens between the ages of three and five; they may attend school at five; and they must attend between the ages of five and fifteen. Education continues to be free up to the age of nineteen, and thereafter, students may attend university without cost, provided that they attain the required academic standards each year.[1]

Primary education is offered at primary schools (primer classes and Standards I to IV) and intermediate schools (Forms I and II), although some primary schools incorporate intermediate departments. All these schools are controlled by the (Government) Department of Education operating through district education boards.

Secondary education begins at twelve or thirteen years of age when children attend secondary schools, which are controlled by independent Boards of Governors and are variously known as grammar schools, colleges, high schools, or, in country areas, district high schools. These provide third- fourth- and fifth-form education leading to the school certificate examination and sixth-form studies (including second-year sixth form) at university entrance, bursary, and scholarship levels. The schools have choice in the arrangement of their curricula, but must meet requirements defined by the Department of Education, and are subject to departmental inspection.

In addition to the state schools, there are a number of private schools (at both primary and secondary levels), most of which are controlled by the churches, but which follow the departmental requirements of curricula and receive limited government financial assistance. Some follow the basic traditions of English public schools. All are visited by departmental inspectors and provide education for approximately one-eighth of the children in the country.

Post-secondary, or tertiary, education is offered by several technical institutes which hold day and evening classes in trade-training, as well as in many commercial and business subjects. There are also four teacher training colleges in Auckland, and others at Hamilton, Palmerston North, Wellington, Christchurch, and Dunedin. Universities are also established in these six cities.

THE CHARACTERISTICS OF
NEW ZEALAND SPEECH

New Zealanders are themselves generally conscious of certain traits of speech commonly referred to as the New Zealand or "kiwi" accent. These were first recorded by McBurney, who visited New Zealand in 1887.

While some authorities believe, as McBurney did, that New Zealanders share with Australia some recognizable features of London (Cockney) speech, it must be observed that the New Zealand accent varies markedly throughout the country. There is scope for much research, but thorough examination presumably must wait for the establishment of a phonetics laboratory and research personnel. Certainly, regional differences are observable, but more obvious are the extremely varying degrees in which individual speakers employ the national accent.

Professional men, business executives and their families, tend to have a mild accent. People who make extended visits to the British Isles are inclined to modify their speech. There also seems to be a growing opinion among many people that a strong accent is something of a disadvantage, that "good speech," in the sense of the absence of an accent and near approximation to educated southern English, is important and socially desirable. On the other hand, among some New Zealanders there is a marked suspicion of speech, in people who are native born and bred, which is unduly imitative of southern English. This is commonly referred to as an "affected accent." It should be noted that the remote sheep farmer may have very little accent, possibly being a graduate of a university school of agriculture, and the graduate professional man may have a strong accent.

In brief terms the New Zealand accent, in its most marked forms is characterized by:

1. tendency toward harsh voice and nasal vowels
2. modification of diphthongs and long vowels (go, stay, how, high, who, far)
3. lengthening of nonstressed initial syllables (receive, deny), and nonstressed final syllables (lovely, babies, Thursday)
4. modification of vowels before *l* (milk, goal)
5. modification of short vowels (it, just, cat)
6. a generally heavy rhythm
7. a lack of free use of intonation and vocal range
8. slurred diction

Some critics of New Zealand speech, both New Zealanders and visitors, deplore these characteristics.

There are also local pronunciations, local usages, and indigenous words; some aspects of all these categories are common to Australian accent.

SPEECH IN EDUCATION

Definition of Terms

Unfortunately terms relating to speech are not used consistently, either in this country or overseas (a fact reflected recently in England by the introduction of the word "oracy," meaning fluency in oral expression). For the purposes of this essay, therefore, it will be endeavored to use the following terms with the meanings indicated:

Speech: Either the basic skills (or techniques) when discussing accent or clarity of utterance, or the whole range of speech processes including techniques as well as what is said and how it is expressed.

Oral expression: The communication of original material as in conversation, discussion, creative drama, talks, and speeches.

Speech training: The conscious educational processes of teaching and learning speech.

Formal speech training: Speech training which is concerned mainly with basic skills.

Some Background Matters

Present attitudes toward speech in education are best understood in the light of policy developed some forty years ago when, in the late 1920s and 1930s, educational authorities encouraged speech in schools and particularly emphasized formal speech training.

Teachers were required to spend time on vowel and consonant drills and were encouraged to do much choral speaking. But as they themselves, for the most part, were not trained, lessons were often dull, unrelated to everyday speech needs, and conducted without knowledge, interest, or enthusiasm. The scheme was consequently regarded as a failure, without the reasons for its lack of success being understood. It was rejected, therefore, and replaced by the beliefs that formal speech exercises were largely without value, and that if children were sufficiently encouraged to speak, their doing so would of itself result in improvement. So was born the theory of indirect instruction—a theory still widely held today.

But speech is not a natural process. It is imitative and learned, and therefore can be both consciously taught and consciously learned—and learned the more proficiently under competent instruction. This factor appears to have been largely ignored.

Moreover, another factor probably had some influence on the situation. Many New Zealanders, with growing pride in their country's development (and possibly with some resentment of the rather cold, impersonal style of B.B.C. announcers), together with a dislike of the older elocutionary style of speech training, expressed strong dislike for what has been, and still is, called an "affected, or Oxford accent"—meaning a local imitation of the cultured, upper-class English speech. This was, and sometimes still is, equated, in many people's minds, with speech training. It is possible, or even probable, that former generations of speech teachers contributed to this opinion by failing to recognize that the New Zealand accent was not automatically "a bad thing."

Be that as it may, there is certainly a strong apprehension in the minds of many teachers that formal speech training must result in affected speech and is not related to the needs of children. That this attitude still exists is evident in quotations included later in this essay.

Believing that there have been woeful inadequacies with respect to speech in education, the New Zealand Association of Teachers of Speech and Drama, *(q.v.),* has made several representations to the Department of Education and in 1961 made a submission to a government commission (of enquiry) on education in New Zealand. The specific submissions of the Council of the Association are reprinted here. (The commission made no recommendations to the government concerning them.)

This Association makes the following recommendations:

1. *Appointment of Speech Supervisor:* That a Speech Supervisor, with an adequate administrative staff, be appointed. The Supervisor should be fully trained as a specialist in the work and should be required to define a completely revised policy on speech in education. He should also be responsible for implementing the following further recommendations:

2. *Universities:* That there be established at Universities, Departments of Speech where all aspects of the subject may be studied to Degree level.

3. *Teacher Training:* That in selecting trainees for Teachers' Colleges, the standard of speech of candidates be given due consideration.

   That the following dual policy be implemented:

   A. That all teachers be given adequate instruction in voice production and other aspects of speech training.

   B. That teachers be trained to teach speech to the following levels:

      (a) *All primary and intermediate teachers:* ability to teach the subject to a satisfactory standard as defined from time to time,

      (b) *Teachers of English in secondary schools:* more advanced training in specific aspects, and ability to teach to the level of the Spoken English requirements in our suggested School Certificate and University Entrance examinations,

(c) *Specialist teachers of speech and drama in schools:* extended training in all aspects.

These requirements presuppose the appointment of an adequate number of fully trained teachers of speech to the staffs of Teachers' Colleges as part of the implementation of the Speech Supervisor's policy. It is recommended that a separate Speech and Drama Department be established at Teachers' Colleges, allied to, but not under the control of the English Departments.

4. *Secondary Schools:* That Speech be included as a formally recognized compulsory subject, and that Speech be permitted as an optional subject in University Entrance and School Certificate examinations.

5. *Intermediate and Primary Schools:* That Speech be included as a formally recognized compulsory subject.

It is recognized that the foregoing is a progressive programme and that it cannot be implemented in all its aspects simultaneously.

Despite the failure of the Commission on Education to make any recommendations arising from these suggestions, the situation concerning speech in education has changed in some respects in the last years, and this change appears to be a continuing process.

SPEECH EDUCATION IN THE UNIVERSITIES

Unlike the situation in the United States and in a few of the English universities, speech is not a subject of detailed study in New Zealand. There are neither departments of speech nor lectures in speech or speech education. Speaking privately, some professors and lecturers have expressed the opinion that students would benefit from such studies. The need is evident from the fact that, as one professor has said in conversation, "Certainly a number of our students contribute well in discussion, but I believe that the greater number are ill-equipped to do so upon entering the university." Another has stated, also in conversation, "My tutorial sessions fail miserably as such, I feel, because students won't contribute; this means that I have to do most of the talking."

Nevertheless, tutorial discussion and seminar methods are frequently employed in the universities, especially on the higher academic levels, and many students do go through a natural process of speech education in such activities. Group dynamics are part of the M.A. studies in educational psychology in departments of education, and law students are required to participate in a certain number of practice moots.

Although no phonetics laboratory exists in New Zealand, and, apparently, no pure phoneticians are at work, English language departments do teach phonetics as an integral part of their courses, the subject being a necessary study for students of language. Consequent upon the nonacceptance of speech as an academic subject, research in speech is rarely undertaken, although a few theses on regional aspects of speech and the development of speech in children have been presented. At the present time Professor L. F. Brosmahan, professor of English language at the Victoria University of Wellington, and Mrs. Helen Wylie are involved in research leading to a pronouncing dictionary of New Zealand English, and Professor F. S. Scott of Auckland University is making pilot explorations concerning speech in Auckland.

In nonacademic areas, students have opportunity for participation in voluntary speech activities. University student associations sponsor debating, public speaking and drama societies, and informal forums for open discussion are popular. There are annual interuniversity debating contests and oratory contests, but these do not arouse interest or receive the same support as similar activities at most American universities.

English-speaking foreign students attending New Zealand universities present some special problems, which are referred to later in this article.

SPEECH EDUCATION IN TEACHER COLLEGES

Students training to be teachers generally follow one of two courses. If they are to teach in secondary schools they take a university degree first and then attend one of two secondary teacher colleges. If they are to be teachers in primary and intermediate schools, they normally attend one of the eight (primary) teacher colleges (at which the courses were formerly for two years but which are now being extended to three years). They may, in addition, take university studies if they wish.

Considerable autonomy being given to the principal of a teachers' college, it may be observed that the nature and extent of speech training differs among the colleges. In the past, appointment of full-time lecturers, fully trained as specialists in speech, has been rare. However, some lecturers in English with special qualifications in speech and drama have been appointed, and some part-time appointments of specialists in speech and/or drama have been made.

The situation appears to be improving, though the writer is of the strong opinion that there should be three or four full-time lecturers in speech and drama at every teachers' college. He justifies this on the grounds that every student should receive continuous training, not only in basic skills, interpretation, and oral expression, but also in the teaching of these subjects as appropriate to his intended career.

This is not to say that the colleges ignore speech training, or to deny integrity or honesty of purpose in colleges. The speech of applicants for entry to teachers' colleges is considered, and student speech is under constant criticism by lecturers in all subjects while supervising teaching practice. Lecturers in English are most concerned with student speech, and work is carried out in oral expression, and, increasingly, in creative drama. In one college, where a full-time specialist lecturer in speech is employed, there is considerable class and individual attention given to the subject, and in all colleges it is usual for some work to be done in interpretation. Remedial assistance is also generally offered to students who have particular problems, and music departments give tuition in voice production. It is common for student- or staff-produced plays to be publicly performed, although the number of plays presented may be limited to one or two a year. Discussion methods are commonly featured in the colleges, and these are often related to liberal studies as well as to the main subjects of the curriculum.

SPEECH EDUCATION IN SECONDARY SCHOOLS

The Department of Education, among its regulations, issues "Notes on the Syllabus of Instruction and Details of courses to be followed." The following quotations pertaining to speech are from the 1968 document.

> The primary aim of teaching English is to develop:
> (a) The power of expression in speech and writing;
> (b) The ability to understand the spoken and written thoughts of others.
>
>   Oral work should be strongly emphasized. Pupils should be encouraged to speak naturally, clearly, and with confidence. Artificiality and affected correctness are not wanted; indeed, the need is not so much for

speech training as for more opportunity for speech. The most potent influences can be brought to bear, first, through good example on the part of all teachers, and, secondly, through singing and dramatic work. Debates at the secondary stage are not recommended as they are apt to be artificial and to encourage fluent insincerity. Much more valuable both as oral exercises and as a means of intellectual and social education are, for example:

(a) talks given by children on subjects of their own choice, with questions by the class and free discussion;

(b) panel discussions on subjects close to the pupils' interest;

(c) practice in committee procedure and in reaching decisions through group discussion. In such ways the schools may help to re-establish the tradition of humane discussion.

This syllabus, without being highly definitive, both requires and gives ample scope for a considerable amount of work in speech. It implies that speech training is an integral part of the English syllabus. Indeed, as exceedingly few state schools employ teachers trained as specialists in speech, the work must be carried out primarily by English teachers (reinforced by teachers of other subjects), or it may not be done to any extent at all.

Speech training in the teacher colleges, however, has been carried out only on a limited scale in the past, for the teacher colleges themselves have, for the most part, lacked trained teachers of speech.

The teachers of English in secondary schools, therefore, may be said to start with the initial disadvantage that they themselves have been trained neither in basic skills and interpretation nor in the teaching of these subjects.

Speaking in October, 1967, at the Annual Conference of Teachers of Speech and Drama, which was concerned with speech in education, J. K. Bedrook, Acting Senior District Inspector for Secondary Schools, Auckland, made reference to the subject:

The conference theme, it seems to me, is both a statement and also a question: "Speech in Education." It is no doubt intended to be a challenge, both to those who are teaching in the classroom, and to those who are concerned with curriculum development; and whilst there is an implied suggestion here that speech already plays a vital role in education (both children and of adults), I think there is also the implication that it is not contributing as much as it should or could to the development of the personality of children and adolescents. I don't think that teachers would take issue with you on this particular point.

I must admit that there are few secondary schools where there is any formal speech training. There are very good courses at one Auckland school, but this is not general. Perhaps this is wrong. You may wish to make a statement about this during the course of your conference.

At the same conference, Ivan Moses, head of the general studies department of the Auckland Technical Institute, discussing students after two, three, or four years of secondary schooling (while admitting that they were not the most able, linguistically, of those who go to secondary school), stated that the Institute "enrolls, at some stage in their education, about 40 per cent of Auckland's secondary school population. Whether we blame the home, the debasing influence of the advertiser, the inadequacy of the education system, or the affluent society we have known, it seems to me that we must squarely face the fact that, after twelve or thirteen years at school, too many of our pupils are unable to express themselves clearly when they speak or write." He stated also that "The Technicians Certification Authority has been so unimpressed with the ability of the majority of these young men and women, throughout our country, to speak and write, that they have insisted that every student who hopes to qualify for a New Zealand technician's certificate shall take English at a technical institute, no matter what English has been studied before."

This is a severe indictment of the extent to which the syllabus in English is actually carried out. (Mr. Moses and his colleagues are tackling the problems involved "using the technique of group discussion to establish a context in which the use of appropriate language can be taught, enquiry can be stimulated, and confidence in speech developed." Tentative conclusions are to the effect that lecturers "have been able to achieve a higher standard of spoken and written work than we have ever managed to achieve before.")

While considering these comments, it should also be noted that in many secondary schools it is quite customary for students to be asked to give talks, to read aloud plays which are under literary and dramatic study, to read poetry aloud, and to participate in discussions on literature and other classroom subjects. But written examinations, teacher shortages, and larger classes than are considered desirable are added factors which, no doubt, also contribute to less oral work being done than many teachers would prefer. One senior English master, for instance, speaking conversationally, recently remarked, "I would prefer to spend half of all my English periods in oral work, but I simply cannot afford the time to do so."

SPEECH EDUCATION IN PRIMARY SCHOOLS

Speech training in the primary and intermediate schools is much influenced by *Suggestions for Teaching English in the Primary School*—a series of three bulletins issued by the Department of Education in the first half of the current decade and republished in book form in 1966.

All quotations in this section are from these bulletins, which "contain notes and articles by teachers and inspectors which attempt to show . . . how the new syllabus in language might be carried into effect . . . they are not to be regarded as authoritative statements of procedure to be followed by all teachers." Emphasis is placed on the principle that "teaching is a personal art . . ."

In general terms, formal speech training is neither considered necessary or desirable by some of the writers: ". . .there is a place for exercises and practices only for the children who need them, who know they need them, and who will later practise them on their own and of their own accord. Whenever conversation, discussion, or argument is going on in the classroom the children are learning how to use the organs of speech for effective communication. First aid is required when communication breaks down. Attention needs to be paid to the mechanics of speech only when first aid is necessary . . . . If a teacher has had special training, of course, and is able to interest children in improving their speech, he should use this skill to the full in his teaching just as he would use any other special ability."

Some head teachers in schools assume more responsibility than others in determining the detailed syllabuses of the work to be carried out in classrooms, so that where a head teacher is enthusiastic about speech it tends to be featured throughout the school if the staff feel competent to handle it—though not all teachers do; and it is a common experience for students and new staff members to be warmly welcomed if they have studied speech privately and can employ their knowledge in classrooms.

Similarly, where teachers are given more freedom to devise the details of their own syllabuses and are speech enthusiasts, speech training, including formal work, will be carried out. A number of head teachers are enthusiastic, but it appears that in numerous classrooms little or no formal speech training is done.

Emphasis is placed on the teacher's personal example, the importance of reading to children, and of freedom for discussion. ". . .children should have plenty of opportunity for their own personal and imaginative expression, and also plenty of opportunity to read and hear good stories, poems, and other literary material. As a general rule the teacher should every day read to the children . . ." Class meetings are common.

In recent years there has been an evident increase of interest in creative dramatic activity, and this is common in primary and intermediate schools. It is often allied to other subjects in the curriculum, especially creative writing and social studies.

To summarize, it is probably reasonable to say that much attention is given in many classrooms to oral expression although this is less true of reading aloud and formal speech training; there appears to be, however, a growing body of teachers who are anxious to carry out more effective speech work and are seeking the means of doing so.

SCHOOL SPEECH PRIZE CONTESTS

One valuable incentive toward interest and improvement in speech is through speech contests; these give, in some cases, an interesting sidelight on the attitude towards the importance of, and emphasis placed upon, various aspects of speech in a school. It is observable that secondary schools differ quite a lot in the matter. Primary schools do not all offer such prizes.

Some secondary schools hold contests in oratory, some in public speaking, some in speech, and some in reading aloud. Quite a general pattern is for prizes to be offered for the senior school (Forms V and VI), and for the lower school (Forms III and IV); although some schools offer a prize only for the school as a whole, and a minority offer a prize for each of the academic levels.

It is quite common for English teachers to select the best speakers from each class to participate in the final contests. Sometimes this actively involves every pupil in a school; in other cases, however, class selection is made only from those who volunteer to speak. A third system involves only those pupils who volunteer to enter the contest. For example, in one prominent school of 1,200 pupils, a recent contest drew some ten entries only, the finalists speaking to an audience of about twenty. More usual, however, is the contest in which delivery of finalists' speeches takes place before a crowded school hall.

Standards as well as requirements differ markedly from school to school, and this also appears to be a significant factor, sometimes reflecting the lack of speech work in teacher training. For instance, in one school contest all candidates but one read their speeches from full texts—the candidate who had evidently prepared and practised her work most thoroughly and referred to brief notes only a few times was chided for lack of preparation.

Sometimes speakers memorize their speeches and deliver them as painfully obvious recitations. The visiting judge has little difficulty in discerning whether there is tuition and classroom experience offered in a school.

Undoubtedly the most stimulating and valuable speech contests are those which require the entrants to be involved in several speech situations, including a direct confrontation with audience questions. Unfortunately this type of contest seems to be most rare. King's School in Auckland, a private preparatory, or primary, school, offers an admirable example of a broad and stimulating test. The requirements (quoted by permission of R. G. Pengelly, headmaster), are

(a) *A Prepared Speech*

(I) The subject shall be any topic, event, development or person of personal interest to the speaker. (Encyclopaedic or book knowledge is not required—rather that speakers talk about personal experiences or interests, or offer knowledge or opinions which are related to their own lives and activities.

(II) Talks should neither be memorized nor read, but speakers may, if they wish, use brief notes.

(III) Speakers may use diagrams or show any objects which would add interest or meaning to their talks.

(IV) The time limit for this speech shall be 4 minutes.

(V) Marks will be allotted:

1. For the Subject Matter 40%—its general interest, arrangement, and the use of imagination.

2. For the Presentation 60%—the choice of language; the various aspects of firm voice and clear, lively speech; the ability to be interesting, alert and convincing; and for general bearing.

(b) *Speaking from Memory*

To speak from memory, for about one minute, any prose extract, poem or part of a poem, or lines from a Shakespearean play. These are to be selected by competitor.

Finalists only will be required also:

(a) To answer questions or reply to comments (for not more than 3 minutes), which may be offered by any member of the audience or the judge. Such questions and com-

ments to be concerned with what the speaker has said in his talk.

Marks will be awarded as in section (v) above, and for the direct readiness of the speaker to respond to what is said to him.

(b) To make a few appropriate remarks—Competitors will be given a slip of paper bearing the title of a talk such as a person may be called upon to deliver at a social, family, business, or educational gathering. The topic will be given to speakers 2-3 minutes before they are required to speak. Notes may not be used.

ENGLISH AS A SECOND LANGUAGE
A PARTICULAR PROBLEM

Foreign Students

Under the Colombo Plan, a number of students from Asian countries attend universities in New Zealand. They come from countries as dispersed as Ceylon, Nepal, Korea, Viet Nam, and Indonesia.

Many such students have a limited knowledge of English, if any, and the Victoria University of Wellington has established The English Language Institute (H. B. George, director) to assist students in this problem and in the teaching of English as a second language. Since its establishment in 1961, the Institute has had a total of 763 students. It offers two courses a year: (1) an ordinary academic course for teachers who will be teaching English as a second language (although most students attending this course are under the Colombo Plan, it is also open to New Zealanders, and course numbers total sixty); (2) a pre-university summer course for Asian students who will attend the universities at the opening of the academic year in the following March.

Maori and Polynesian Children

Although a great number of Maoris speak English, some children have problems of vocabulary (its extent and usage), grammar, and fluency. The department makes provision for this problem and authorizes increased staff numbers in some schools, so that more personal attention may be given. Similar difficulties arise with children of immigrants from the Polynesian Islands. Concerning these, Mrs. Carole Babcock, a teacher in the Mount Albert Primary School, writes:

The problems, among the growing numbers of Polynesian children in New Zealand preschool, primary, and secondary educational institutions, are gaining more consideration in educational circles. Problems of integrating the races also exist, and are being examined by various committees. For instance, the Committee on Education Training and Research states:

The educational gap stems in large part from a severe language deficiency at the point of entry to school. Where this deficiency in verbal fluency is not overcome—and this failure is extremely common—the entire educational career of the child is handicapped.

It is with this problem of language in mind that increasing numbers of experimental and transitional classes are being set up in the metropolitan areas (especially Auckland, which is the principal point of immigration for the migrants from the islands of Niue, Western Samoa, Cook, Fiji, and the Tokelaus). These classes are Polynesian-orientated and concentrate initially on the oral aspects of learning.

The children may be bilingual or may speak only Polynesian. In these stages mime and movement help tremendously to give them some means of communication without frustration. English words, and even whole concepts, can be conveyed with mime and movement. The classrooms lavish music, books, and oral discussion on the children, who are mainly from homes where, if English is spoken, it may be quite inaccurate. The syllabus is carefully planned to ensure that the children's interest is maintained, and oral discussion is a primary factor in designing a timetable.

Polynesians have a natural feeling for rhythm and resonance in speech, and these can be cultivated in chants and choral speech. Improvisation in mime and movement (later with dialogue) around a central theme is most successful. The children are warm and quite uninhibited. Because of different language structures, intonation and stress have to be carefully taught by example. Grammar for a six-year-old Polynesian is "hit and miss"; plurals, tenses, and gender are all hopelessly muddled, and during the initial stages, communication is limited to timid monosyllables progressing to a conglomeration of omitted verbs, male "females," and vice versa. Speech generally is jerky; for example, ". . . I big boy." Vowels (long and short), consonants (voiced and unvoiced, lam*b*, *k*night), must be clarified, since all are bewildering to the children.

When the children in the transitional class have reached a satisfactory standard in oral expression, they move into ordinary classes, where they can communicate and compete with the indigenous New Zealanders.

SPEECH THERAPY

The New Zealand government has long recognized a responsibility to children who suffer from marked defects of speech, and a speech therapy service is well established and operates in over a hundred clinics. The majority of them are school speech clinics, although others are attached to cerebral palsy units and crippled children's homes. The general hospitals also maintain speech therapy clinics.

The national training center, directed by Dr. Jean Seabrook, is attached to the Christchurch Teachers College, and students are required to have attended at least one year of ordinary teacher training before continuing with the two-year, full-time therapy course. There are also some practicing therapists who have been trained in England, or who have gone overseas for additional training and refresher courses after working for some years in New Zealand clinics. Children who are in need of therapy attend without cost.

An important factor related to speech therapy is that the standard of plastic surgery in New Zealand is such that there is relatively little need for post operative treatment in a speech clinic for cleft-lip or cleft-palate cases. Incidence of these two disorders (and of hearing loss) is higher among the Maori population than might be expected.

SPEECH EDUCATION FOR THE DEAF

Another field in which the State accepts responsibility and, in fact, has done so since 1880, is the education of deaf children, for whom there are at present two main centers—in Auckland and Christchurch. These are residential schools for country children, but those whose homes are near attend by the day. There are also day centers in several other cities, and the number is shortly expected to increase, since the total number of children receiving tuition is approximately five hundred at the present time.

These children are taught by trained teachers, drawn either directly from teachers' colleges upon completion of their training or from among practising teachers in schools. All trainees then attend a further year's course in teaching the deaf at the training center also attached to the Christchurch Teachers College. This course was established in 1942.

Two other aspects of interest are that New Zealand is one of the relatively few countries in the world which started work with the deaf on the oral system of education (this system being still followed), and that there is a preschool training system organized on a national basis. This is unique because advisers on deaf education visit all homes concerned and recommend to parents the most helpful action they can adopt prior to a child's entry into a school for the deaf.

PUBLIC EXAMINATIONS IN SPEECH

For over forty years Trinity College of Music in London, England, has sent examiners to New Zealand, as to other countries, to examine candidates in music and speech. Prior to 1950, examiners were usually involved in both subjects, but in recent years speech examiners have been specialists in their own subject. So increased an interest has developed in these examinations that two examiners now visit the country annually and are fully occupied from June to December, sometimes being supplemented for a few weeks by a third.

The examinations are primarily taken by school children, young adults, school teachers, and would-be teachers of speech. They are defined in eight grades leading to teacher diplomas of associate and licentiate of the college, and to the highest qualification of fellowship. Trinity College has now revised its syllabuses, and beginning in 1969, the teacher diplomas are wider in scope and of a higher standard than was formerly the case. This change has been welcomed by New Zealand speech teachers. Examinations are held in speech and drama, effective speaking, spoken English (for students to whom English is a second language), and public speaking. Speech choirs may also be examined. In addition to the practical tests which demand the presentation of dramatic extracts, the oral interpretation of prose and poetry, the delivery of a speech, and the answering of questions relating to basic skills, communication, drama, literature, and teaching, diploma students are required to sit for written papers.

Over the years Trinity College of Music has been an important factor in the setting of standards, especially in performance work, but many speech teachers have long felt the need for an indigenous examining body. To this end the New Zealand Speech Board was established several years ago and is now also examining in many parts of the country. It works in close liaison with the New Zealand Association of Teachers of Speech and Drama and its diploma examination is recognized by the education department as a teacher's qualification. As the examination must be taken in two sections, a year apart, and a licentiate diploma in speech is a prerequisite, the implication is that a candidate will have been a speech student for at least three years. The Speech Board also offers graded examinations and, for adults, examinations for associateship of the Board. The grade examinations reflect awareness of the work of the English Speaking Board in England, and of the spoken English examinations now being offered for the certificate of secondary education newly introduced in that country. Perhaps here too, in time, speech will be offered as a school certificate and university entrance subject. It would seem to be a highly valuable and desirable extension of the present system of examining English only in written form.

The secretary of the New Zealand Speech Board, from whom examination syllabuses may be obtained, is Mrs. S. F. Futter, 8 Cressy Street, Lower Hutter, New Zealand.

THE NEW ZEALAND ASSOCIATION OF TEACHERS OF SPEECH AND DRAMA (THE N.Z.A.T.S.D.)

This Association, with 530 members, was established in 1953 by practising teachers of speech and drama to further the interests of the arts of speech and theater, as well as for the professional welfare and advancement of its members.

Membership is in five categories: fellows of the association (at present two), honorary members, members, student members, and associates. Full membership is open to all practising teachers of speech, drama, and public speaking who hold professional qualifications of diploma standard and who have taught for not less than two years; associate membership is available to any person who is interested in the objects and activities of the Association.

Members are dispersed throughout the country; there are branches in seven cities. These groups hold several meetings, and sometimes one-day or weekend schools, each year. In addition to lectures, discussions, demonstrations, and classes, branches sometimes hold speech festivals and contests.

The Association as a whole has its Annual Conference and General Meeting over the three days of Labor Weekend, which is the last weekend in October. Overseas visitors would be most welcome to attend these conferences, which are generally held in one of the main cities and which are sometimes residential. The 1969 conference was held in Wellington. On these occasions attendance varies from between forty to eighty members, according to the place of venue, although the 1967 meeting, which was on the theme of "Speech in Education" and was open to all interested persons, drew 160 participants.

Although statistics are not available, it is reasonable to state that the majority of the active teaching members teach individual students and classes in private studios or in their own homes. Some are employed full or part time in schools and colleges, while others are school teachers or teacher-college lecturers for whom speech is an added qualification. The number of men fully employed in this work is probably less than twenty.

Several times a year, the Association publishes a sixteen-page journal which features varied articles concerned with aspects of teaching, literature, and theater.[3] It also includes book reviews as well as reports of conferences, meetings, and other allied activities. The Council of the Association also collaborates with the Department of Education and with similar associations having allied interests, and it is now seeking affiliation and collaboration with similar bodies overseas.

The training of teachers of speech and drama in New Zealand presents special problems in that there is no public institution providing a full-time course in these subjects. Some teachers have attended courses of three years' duration or less in England, but the majority have studied over a period of years by taking lessons and classes with private teachers and attending conferences, summer, and weekend schools. Many are trained school teachers who have turned to this work as an additional or alternative subject and have been active in dramatic societies of various sorts.

There is a continuing and increasing public demand for private tuition in speech. People are prepared to buy, for themselves and their children, what is not yet fully available under the education system. While students are often concerned with improving their basic skills in speech, many speech teachers have found that their practice in recent years has swung markedly toward the communicative aspects. Another fact evident in the last year or so is that where there was formerly a greater demand for tuition for girls than for boys, this is no longer the case—a significant pointer in changing public attitudes.

The present secretary of the Association is Mrs. Nerissa Moore, 6 Hillary Street, Tawa, Wellington, New Zealand.

SUMMARY

Having looked at some aspects of speech in education in New Zealand, what conclusions may we draw?

It is evident, first, that there is public interest in speech and speech standards (and this is reflected in frequent references in the press). Although this is often related to accent (the absence or presence of marked accent being sometimes thought of as the test of good or bad speech), there is educational concern that speech training be carried out, related to child development in the widest sense, and that oral expression in particular be much encouraged as part of the process of fitting children to understand and take place in the society and the world in which they live. Speech training has been very clearly defined as part of English studies, and there are grounds for some excitement in the most recent explorations through informal drama and liberal or social education studies.

Nevertheless, there are no moves yet apparent toward establishing speech as an academic discipline or considering speech for acceptance as an examinable subject, either in schools or in the national school certificate or university entrance examinations.

Finally, it seems that there are important questions yet to be asked and answered:

Are the education department's precepts regarding speech actually being carried out effectively?

Is it possible that there is an unwillingness to accept the principle that what is learned may be best learned under competently trained guidance?

Does ample talking, of itself, necessarily result in improving speech in all desired directions?

Can we have the most efficient form of speech education, in its widest sense, until there is full provision for the supply of teachers, thoroughly trained in all aspects of the subject?[4]

FOOTNOTES

[1]Quotations in the text of this chapter are made by permission of the Acting Director-General of Education, from the following publications issued by the New Zealand Department of Education:

"Suggestions for Teaching English in the Primary Schools," Parts I, II and III, reprinted 1966.

"Social Education," Curriculum Development Unit Bulletin No. 10.

"Liberal Studies," Curriculum Development Unit Bulletin No. 13.

"Notes on the Syllabus of Instruction and Details of Courses to Be Followed," The Education (Secondary Instruction) Regulations, 1968.

The following publications are of allied interest:

J. L. Ewing, "Curriculum Development in New Zealand." *Education* (published by the Department of Education) XVII, No. 3 (April, 1968).

M. W. Hancock and W. K. McIlroy, "Family Life, Education and Social Studies," *Education,* XVII, No. 2 (March, 1968).

[2]The official organ of the New Zealand Speech Therapists' Association is *The New Zealand Speech Therapists' Journal.* (Christchurch: The Speech Clinic, Cranmer Square.) Twice yearly.

[3]*Journal of the New Zealand Association of Teachers of Speech and Drama.* Editor: Mrs. N. E. Russell, 76 Victoria Street, Hawera, New Zealand. Quarterly.

[4]Books relating to New Zealand Speech:

Arch. Acker. *New Zild and How to Speak It* [a gently amusing paperback purporting to show how English is actually spoken in New Zealand]. (Wellington: A. H. and A. W. Reed. 1966.)

Sidney J. Baker. *New Zealand Slang.* (Christchurch: Whitcombe & Tombs. 1940.)

The Right Honorable, the Viscount Cobham. *Lord Cobham's Speeches,* ed. O.S. Hintz. (Auckland: Wilson & Horton Ltd. 1965.)

Hilton M. Power, William G. Kerslake and Maurice A. Harris. *Aids to Democratic Leadership in Voluntary Organizations.* (The New Zealand Junior Chamber of Commerce.)

G. W. Turner. *The English Language in Australia and New Zealand.* (Longmans. 1966.)

SPEECH EDUCATION IN THE PHILIPPINES

Nobleza Asuncion-Lande

INTRODUCTION

Although speech as an academic discipline is a fairly new development in Philippine educational history, its beginnings can be traced to the early 1900s, with the establishment of the Philippine public school system during the first years of the American colonial regime.

The United States occupied the Philippines for about five decades (counting the brief interlude of Japanese occupation of the islands 1942-1945), from August 13, 1898 to July 4, 1946. Within that length of time, the Americans were able to bring into successful fruition their unique experiment in colonialism to train the Filipino youth toward democratic self-government and to unite them as a nation through the use of a common language.

The primary objective of the United States government in the Philippines, as enunciated by President McKinley's Philippine policy, was (1) to give every inhabitant of the Philippines a primary but thoroughly modern education; (2) to fit the race for participation in the act of self-government and for every sphere of activity offered by the life of the Far East; (3) to supplant the Spanish language by making English the *lingua franca* of the Far East, the basic language of instruction and the medium of communication.[1]

On January 21, 1901, Act No. 74 of the United States Commission for the Philippines created the Department of Public Instruction. Upon its inception, it took over the supervision of all the public schools that were established by the United States military government after Manila was occupied on August 13, 1898. A general superintendent of schools was appointed to administer and supervise the program.

Act No. 74 was amended by Act No. 477, which instituted the Bureau of Education. This agency was given direct control over the public schools under the Department of Public Instruction. Under this act, the public school system became subjected to a high degree of centralized government control which still prevails. It provided for a complete education, with free elementary instruction for all Filipinos regardless of social status, and laid the foundation for a compulsory education in the lower levels of instruction.

A primary objective of education during the American regime was "to train the Filipinos in the art and exercise of self government."[2] Political socialization—in this case, the deliberate inculcation of values appropriate for the citizens of a democracy, became a manifest aim of the educational system.[3] Considerable stress was placed upon citizenship training, and the design for instruction was to encourage social mobility, national unity, and training for political participation. The dignity of the human being, his responsibilities and duties under a regime of law, and the need for purposeful cooperative living was emphasized.

More opportunities for Filipinos to participate in public affairs opened up. Every citizen, whether rich or poor, was encouraged to participate in government. With increased participation came opportunities for self expression. For the first time in every Filipino's life, the full impact of "freedom of speech" was beginning to be felt.

Formal courses in speech-making and discussion-techniques were unknown at that time, but the occasions for public speaking, argumentation and debate, and persuasion increased tremendously. It was a new and exciting experience for the natives. In almost all of their history, they had been governed autocratically by rulers who did the talking and the planning, especially in public affairs. The laws and decrees for the colonies were issued by the King of Spain for the people to obey. The decrees were promulgated from the Peninsula or from Mexico without the knowledge, much less the consent, of the people for whom they were intended. The clergy or their delegated representatives were responsible for the implementation of the laws. The native was expected to accept without question what he was told to do. When the American regime took over the Philippines, a new orientation began.

The teachers, during this exciting period of the Filipino's development, were for the most part Americans. They presented every opportunity and encouraged their students to speak out openly and to express themselves creatively both in and out of the classroom.

Another far-reaching decision made by the American educational authorities, insofar as the Filipino's training for self-expression is concerned, was to give all instruction in the English language. The basic reason given for the use of the language was that "in teaching a people democracy, it was wise to use the language to which most great democratic principles were native."[4] The ordinary Filipino would no longer feel isolated from the elite of Philippine society; a common bond was being established between the two groups—a common language. It is generally acknowledged that the use of English was probably the greatest single factor of unification during the American regime, and the fact that "the child of a laborer or a peasant could learn the language of the courts and of the government in the public schools carried the Filipinos another long step forward on the road toward self respect which had been denied them for years."[5]

Education for democracy and freedom in the Philippines was an American innovation. Education before the American period had a different orientation.

In pre-Spanish Philippines, the emphasis was on training in the "art of warfare" for the boys, and the "art of wifehood and motherhood" for the girls. It was a mixture of academic and vocational training because the children were also taught reading, writing, arithmetic, religion, music, and customs. Vocational training consisted of farming, fishing, sailing, boat building, mining, and smithery for the boys; and for the girls, it was sewing, weaving, cooking, stock-raising, and other household arts. Education was largely informal for the children studied in their own homes under their parents or in the houses of some tribal *turos* ("teachers").[6]

The purposes of education during the Spanish period were the propagation of Christianity and the Spanish culture. The objectives were largely determined by the "aristocratic ideals of the function of society," which were for social refinement and distinction.[7] Education was for the elite, not for the masses. The Spanish authorities felt sorely the need of training young men, particularly the sons of the *conquistadores* ("conquerors") for the service of the king and the church. As a result, formal education started with higher institutions. Schools of higher learning were established under the supervision of the clergy. The medium of instruction was Spanish. Admission was limited and selective.

Some form of instruction was provided for the natives, but the principal purposes were to convert them to Christianity and "to make them obedient subjects of the Spanish king."[8] Men, women, and children were taught the catechism with some reading, writing, arithmetic, and sacred songs. Spanish was first used by the missionaries to convert the natives, but shortly thereafter, the local dialects supplanted the former. The missionaries considered it more practical and easier to use the native languages, so they learned the Philippine languages and proceeded to use them. While the intentions of the clergy in using the native languages to instruct the Filipinos were sincere, they were fostering and perpetuating class distinctions. The effect of making Spanish the "dominant" language and the language used by the elite, while the diverse Philippine languages became the "lower languages" used by the natives, was to widen the gap between the two societies.

The last forty years of Spanish occupation in the Philippines saw some changes in the educational system. This was in large part the result of a growing demand by the emerging Filipino intellectuals, a group of upper-class Filipinos who had been to Europe to study, and who had absorbed some of the "progressive" ideas current in Europe at that time. A royal decree in 1863 provided for a system of primary schools and for the establishment of a normal school for men to serve as a "source supply for religious, moral and educated teachers to take charge of native schools or of primary instruction." The prescribed courses included principles of teaching, theory and practice of good citizenship, elements of pedagogy, sacred history and religion, arithmetic, Spanish language, practical agriculture, vocal and organ music, and theory and practice of writing.[9]

The revolutionary period of the Philippines brought about some changes in educational philosophy. The purpose of instruction was to imbue in the Filipino a feeling of nationalism. It was to be free from church control, progressive in method, and free for everyone.[10] Spanish continued to be the language of instruction, but Tagalog (the basis of the national language of the Philippines and the native tongue spoken in the nation's capital) was introduced as a compulsary subject.

The First Philippine Republic (1898) continued the educational system enunciated during the revolutionary period. It recognized the "right of any Filipino to set up a school in conformity with the laws of the land." Freedom and equality of all religions and the separation of church and state were also declared. The serious intent of the leaders in regard to education is underscored by the fact that the "budget for public education was about one-half of the total appropriations for local expenditures."[11]

It was a short-lived Philippine Republic, for not long after, the American Army occupied the Philippines. A new regime was soon to take over which was to modify the Filipino way of life and usher in new concepts of government and of education.

DEVELOPMENT OF THE SPEECH CURRICULUM

The establishment of the public school system during the American occupation set in motion the revision of the school curriculum.

The primary curriculum, formulated in 1903 and prescribed in 1904, provided for two aspects of development—body training and mental training. The former comprised singing, drawing, handicrafts, and physical exercises; the latter included reading, writing, conversation, phonetics, spelling, nature study, and arithmetic. Geography and civics were added later to the curriculum of the upper grades.

The aims of the primary curriculum were to enable the pupil to understand, read, and write simple English; to provide him with general information; and to prepare him to earn a livelihood in later years. Although some changes have been made in the curriculum to keep abreast with the country's needs, the primary objectives have not basically changed.

The intermediate curriculum was at first patterned after the grammar grades in the United States. It was intended to complete elementary instruction and to give the child an actual fitness for life, to equip him for new duties and responsibilities, and to cultivate in him qualities of honor and unselfishness.[12] From 1908 to 1935, language arts (reading and phonics, language and spelling, in English) occupied the longest school period. From 1945 to 1951, the time allotment was reduced for the subject, but it still occupied one of the longest school periods, with the same length of time as vocational education. Currently, the instruction time for language arts in English is the same as for Tagalog, the national language. Instruction is still focused on the mastery of oral and written English.

The secondary curriculum is still designed to furnish the background for college work as well as to prepare the student for a definite profession. Opportunities for practice in the speech arts occur in cocurricular activities. Activities include dramatic presentations of plays in English, elocution and oratorical contests, poetry readings, and public speaking. Student government activities provide the students opportunities to use persuasive speaking in their campaigns for the various school offices. Winners of oratorical and declamation contests compete in the national contests sponsored by private industry or civic organizations. There are dramatic clubs and debating societies in the various high schools, and contests are regularly scheduled between them.

The curricula in both the public and the private precollege instruction offer the same basic courses. This is true because the control and administration of the entire school system is under a central office, the Department of Education.

The Philippine school curriculum has been one continuous adaptation to the needs of the country. During the pre-Spanish period, virtually nothing is known about the role of the ordinary individual in government. The island chain was sparsely populated, with a wide variety of small settlements whose leaders exercised varying degrees of control. A look at the school curriculum, however, indicates that a major preoccupation was protection of their settlements from outsiders since it was necessary to teach the young the art of warfare.

The American regime made the Filipino a participant involved in the conduct of public affairs. Long accustomed to a less active role, he abruptly found himself having a voice in the formulation of policies that would affect his life. He was encouraged to express his own opinions on things that he deemed important. Never before had he enjoyed real freedom of speech!

Conversation and phonetics were introduced at an early stage in the curriculum developed during the American regime. They were first taught by American teachers and gradually by Filipino teachers, until Filipinization of the system became complete.

The pattern of evolution from colonial dependency to complete statehood and finally to membership in the family of nations is reflected in the curriculum changes through the years. This evolution, in turn, reflects the development of speech instruction in the Philippines.

SPEECH AS AN ACADEMIC DISCIPLINE

Historically, speech instruction commenced when the Americans started teaching the Filipinos about democratic principles and when English became the language of instruction in the Philippines.

Among the first schools in higher education which began to offer formal speech training were the University of the Philippines, the major state university, and the Ateneo de Manila University, a Jesuit institution.

In the early 1920s, the Ateneo de Manila had a course in the English department entitled Rhetoric. This course was designed for "students to discover rules that underlie effective expression of ideas, and skill in applying these rules, particularly to argumentation and debate." Another course was added later, Latin Oratory, which is described as "eloquence or the art of persuasion through the study of Cicero's speeches." American Jesuit priests taught the courses. A debating society was organized and weekly debates were conducted among and before its members. Its purpose was "to give the students practice in clear and persuasive exposition (in English) and exercise of control under the stress of argumentation."[13]

Rhetoric and Latin Oratory, labelled as English courses, are current offerings on the undergraduate level at the Ateneo. The school does not offer a specialization in speech. The speech-oriented English courses are required of all students who are candidates for B.A. and B.S. degrees.

The Ateneo Debaters, which is the name of the debating society, has participated in intercollegiate debating since 1953. The members write their own pieces and deliver them. In this way they put into practical application what they learn from Rhetoric and Latin Oratory, as well as practice their English speech.

The Graduate School of the Ateneo de Manila currently offers two courses in speech improvement and speech education: Oral English I, which is identified as Linguistics 103, and Oral English II, which is Linguistics 104. Both are offered in the Institute of Languages and Linguistics. Oral English I provides intensive drill in spoken English. It is designed to perfect the pronunciation of the teacher. Extensive use of tapes and the speech laboratory are required for all students of English literature and languages and linguistics. Oral English II is a continuation of Oral English I. It is designed to help the student deal with spoken literature and prepare him for written literature. Extensive use of tapes and the speech laboratory is also required.[14] Most of the students are public and private school English teachers who want to improve their English proficiency, particularly in speech. While most of the students work toward a master's degree in English or linguistics, many of them just take the courses for self-improvement.

The University of the Philippines is the major state university of the country. Because of its unique position in the educational system, it has a nation-wide influence in setting standards and developing trends. The university was organized in 1908 to enable gifted Filipinos to be trained for leadership.

The university began its program of speech training under the Department of English. Four courses were offered, all labeled English: Oral English, which was actually public speaking, Argumentation and Debate, Elementary Stagecraft, and Acting and Directing.

In the school year 1953-1954, the program was expanded.[15] An English major could now have a concentration in speech. Eighteen credit hours of speech out of the forty-five credit hours of English, which were required of all English majors, could be taken. In addition to the four courses that were then being offered, Elements of Oral Interpretation, Forms of Public Address, Group Discussion and Conference Leadership, and Directed Speech Activities were added to the curriculum. The Oral English title was changed to Fundamentals of Speech and the course content was revised. These courses were, however, still labelled English. That year also marked the first time that faculty members with speech degrees from American universities were hired at the University of the Philippines. These were two Filipinos.

The Department of Speech at the University of the Philippines came into existence in the school year 1958-1959. All of the speech courses under the Department of English were given speech numbers. These formed the nucleus of the offerings of the new department. New courses were added to the eight then being taught. Currently the offerings include the eight original courses plus Voice and Diction, Bases of Speech, Oral Interpretation of Children's Literature, Oral Interpretation of Drama, Playwriting, Art History of the Theater, Principles of Speech Correction, Teaching of Speech, Basic Radio Procedures, Radio Writing, Radio Speech, Program Building, Radio Production, Station Management, Audio-Visual Communication, and Research in Speech.

The areas covered are speech fundamentals, oral interpretation, speech education, speech correction, public address, and group communication, radio, theater and drama, and research. The university maintains a radio station which is used as a laboratory by the radio majors.

The principal textbooks are generally American speech texts. Representative speeches by Filipino leaders, Philippine short stories, poems and plays, and local and national issues are used as enrichment materials. All of these are in English.

The department provides other services to the university curricular offerings. Speech I (Fundamentals of Speech) is required of all degree candidates regardless of majors. Some courses are suggested cognates in various curricular programs. Oral Interpretation of Literature is a required subject, and Directed Speech Activities is a suggested course for graduate students in the College of Education who are majoring in second-language teaching. Six credit hours of speech may partially fulfill the requirements in English for B.S. premedicine students.

During the last three years, the department has conducted a debate workshop and a drama workshop. These are noncredit courses whose purpose is to provide opportunity for nonspeech majors to have instruction in debate and drama. The speech department is usually invited by the College of Education of the University of the Philippines to conduct seminars in speech for the faculty and for the practice teachers.

The extracurricular activities that are sponsored by the department include the annual speech festival and the invitational.speech contests. The former involves a week-long activity of speech consisting of public speaking, oral interpretation, dramatic presentations, exhibition debates, impromptu speech contests, and special radio programs over the university station. The invitational speech contests are in oratory and debate, extemporaneous and impromptu speeches, and oral interpretation.

The clubs that are sponsored and supervised by the speech department are the University of the Philippines Speech Association, an organization of the speech majors, and the University of the Philippines Dramatic Club, which is open to all students regardless of their majors. The Speech Association presents speech programs during the year. The members provide the talent, production staff, and crew for the departmental productions. The Dramatic Club presents one major production each semester.

The degrees offered in the department are a B.A. in speech, with a concentration in general speech, and another in radio. A major must have at least forty-five credit hours of speech.

During the last five years, the number of students who have majored in speech averages about seventy a year, distributed in the areas of general speech and speech education, oral interpretation and theater, and radio. Nonmajors average approximately fifty each semester. The department has graduated about one hundred speech majors since its inception. This includes those who had B.A.'s in English with concentration in speech. Within the last two years, it has had about fifteen graduates yearly. These graduates readily find employment in schools, government, and industry.

The underlying philosophy of speech instruction at the University of the Philippines is the concept of speech as communication. The emphasis is "on communication in a democratic society, with speech as a requisite for participation and leadership in human affairs." The specific objectives are to provide theoretical orientation and practical experience in the different areas of speech and to develop interest in research in the field of speech.

The largest private university, and one of good reputation in the Philippines, is Far Eastern University. It has a well-developed speech program. The Department of Speech and Drama offers specializations in general speech, speech arts and drama, or drama and radio, with a degree leading to a bachelor of arts. Like the University of the Philippines, it has followed the current trends in Philippine education. The department enunciates its underlying philosophy by viewing speech as a "tool of self-expression; mode of fulfillment; means of social control; and measure of social progress."[16]

There are three general divisions within the department: speech, radio-television, and drama. The speech courses that are offered are Voice and Speech Improvement (beginning and advanced), Beginning and Advanced Interpretation, Public Speaking, Argumentation and Debate, Group Discussion, Conference Leadership, Forms of Public Address, Phonetics, Psychology of Speech, and Introduction to Speech Correction.

The courses in radio and television are Announcing for Radio and Television, Radio and Television Production, Radio and Television Management, Radio and Television Advertising, Radio and Television Drama, and Radio and Television Writing.

In the drama division, the course offerings are History of Drama and Theater, Beginning Acting, Advanced Acting, Drama Production, Beginning Direction, Advanced Direction, Costuming, Light Designing, Scenic Design, Drama Laboratory A and B (actual execution and practical application of theories in drama), Children's Theater and Summer Workshop.

A bachelor of arts degree candidate who elects speech as his major field of concentration must finish at least thirty-six credit hours from the department for graduation. Speech I and II are required courses for all students who enroll under the general B.A. and pre-law B.A. programs. The pre-law B.A. student can major in speech and/or drama or a combination of both, with at least thirty-six credit hours of work done in the department. Speech I is a required course for students who enroll under a B.S. program. An English major desiring to take more speech courses outside of the required core can do so. Some of the courses in the speech department are cross-listed with the English department.

The principal textbooks are generally the same books that are used in American universities. Laboratory manuals for speech improvement are, however, specially designed for the Filipino students. They are based on research findings in contrastive analysis between a Philippine language and English. Enrichment materials provide the Philippine cultural orientation. Representative works of Filipino writers, such as plays, short stories, poems, and speeches, are utilized. Works of representative Asian writers are also studied.

Far Eastern University maintains a junior and senior language laboratory, recording and listening booths, a theater complex, and a radio station for its students.

The Department of Speech and Drama conducts in-service training courses for the university faculty, speech improvement for foreign students, tutorial sessions for articulatory disorders, lecture demonstrations on new methods of language teaching, national tours to introduce new theater forms, and a consultation and training service for speech tournaments.

Workshops for body movement and speech for theater and plays, plus seminars and conferences on local and foreign aspects of communication in radio, television, stage, and other speech arts are conducted by visiting and local experts in the communications field.

The activities sponsored by the department include impromptu speaking contests, oratorical and declamation contests, debates, poetry recitals, concert readings, choreographed interpretations, commercial modeling, guest-shot appearances on local radio and television shows, drama coaching, directing, judging, and producing drama presentations.

The organizations supervised and administered by the speech staff include the Chamber Theater Group, The Far Eastern University Dramatic Guild and the Far Eastern University Speech Club. Membership is open to any student enrolled at the university. The two debating clubs, one for day students and one for night students of the university, hold annual debates. Oratorical contests are held regularly, and the winners represent the university in national interuniversity tilts.

Siliman University, one of the highly respected private universities and the leading Protestant institution of the country, has a variety of speech courses. There is no speech department, so the courses are listed under the English department.

At the present time, the university offers no major field of concentration in speech.[17] However, a bachelor of arts or a bachelor of science in education degree candidate can minor in it. English 55, which is Public Speaking, is a general education course and is required of all who enroll at the university who work toward a degree. English I and II (Basic Communication), with emphasis on oral and written English, is required of all English majors and minors.

Other courses in speech which are listed as English courses are Voice and Diction, Advanced Public Speaking, Discussion and Conference, and Argumentation and Debate.

The university maintains a radio station, which is often used as a laboratory by students who enroll in Radio Announcing and Radio Drama. The course offerings in drama include Stage Technology, Fundamentals of Acting, Contemporary Drama, and Development of Drama.

Activities by the students include oratorical and debate contests, impromptu and extemporaneous speaking. Plays are presented regularly on radio and on stage. Supervision and direction of such activities are by the English staff teaching the speech courses. There are no specific speech clubs, although there is a dramatic club, and a debate team. The underlying philosophy of instruction appears to be ability to express oneself clearly and effectively.

The Philippine Women's University is a progressive institution "dedicated for the education of Filipino women."[18]

The curricular offerings in speech are integrated in their speech education program. Its objective is effective communication and the learning of English as a second language.[19] The courses of a general speech nature are in the Department of English, and the speech-improvement course falls under the jurisdiction of the Institute of Filipino Culture and Foreign Languages.

Under the English program the courses are Voice and Diction, Fundamentals of Speech, Public Speaking, Argumentation and Debate, Speech Correction I and II, Dramatics, Children's Drama, and Children's Literature.

The Institute of Filipino Culture and Foreign Languages administers the speech clinic and the speech-improvement program. This program concentrates on improving the English speech of the non-native speaker of the language. There are not enough courses for a student who wants to specialize in the field of speech. But all of the speech courses are required of students who major in English on the B.A. or the B.S. education programs.

In the graduate division of the university, a course in speech improvement is required of an M.A. candidate in English; and a course in speech correction is required of a student who specializes in special education under the M.A. in education program.

Textbooks in speech are mostly by American authors, and the tapes used in speech improvement are done by native speakers of English in the United States. Supplementary materials consist of books written by local authors. For the speech-improvement course, the readings are compilations of research findings about second-language problems that are unique to the Filipinos in their English speech and language tapes that incorporate the results of research activities. Most of these materials are joint efforts of American and Filipino specialists.

The facilities available for the students at the Philippine Women's University include a speech clinic for the "shy and nervous" students who need counselling and a language laboratory for the students who want to improve their English proficiency.

The English faculty and the staff of the Institute of Filipino Culture and Foreign Languages conduct research on Philippine languages contrasted with English for a systematic inventory of the learning problems of Filipino speakers of English.

The speech curriculum at the university was introduced in 1957, after a report of a survey conducted by American language specialists on the state of English language instruction in the Philippines.[20] Among their recommendations was that "the teaching of English in the Philippines should be upgraded."

The pioneer teacher-training institution, and the college which sets the trends in the training of elementary-school teachers and administrators is the Philippine Normal College. It has led the country in the area of arena theater production. It also has an outstanding speech program in the Department of English, which integrates the areas of general speech and teacher training in the language arts.

The Arena Theater was established in 1953 at the Philippine Normal College. It was conceived as a "major community project of the College to help in the development of the Filipino drama, because the theater is one of the most effective values in mass communication, and because it is a dynamic instrument in influencing the thinking and the feeling of our people."[21]

Its founder and director is Dr. Severino Montano, who obtained his training at Yale University (M.F.A.) and at American University (Ph.D.). Since the inception of the Arena Theater, it has accomplished the following: (1) the organization of forty-five branches in the Philippines, producing Filipino plays written by local talents and mounted by public school teachers and officials; (2) the penetration of the villages by the various units presenting these plays in the vernacular; (3) the training of a group of Filipino playwrights who are now writing plays not only for the Arena Theater in Manila but also for the provincial branches and other theater groups as well; (4) the training of other theater technicians who are now directing, designing, acting and organizing work for the community theaters; the persons who have received training number over a thousand; (5) the enrichment of community life wherever the Arena Theater is in operation.[22]

Arena Theater also conducts an annual playwriting contesting for both one-act and full-length plays to encourage Filipino artists and to insure a continuous supply of good plays to produce.

The drama program of the college is offered in both the undergraduate and graduate levels. On the undergraduate level, students who are in their second year may take up additional courses outside of their regular program for a bachelor of science in elementary education degree. This is the specialization curriculum, which is open only to students who maintain a high grade-point average in their regular program. Upon finishing 75 per cent of the eighteen credit hours that are required in the specialization curriculum, the student qualifies for a certificate of specialization, which is awarded to him in addition to his diploma when he graduates from the college.

One of the areas for specialization is drama. The courses under this program include Voice, Diction, Body Control and Interpretation, Elements of Play Production, Acting and Directing, History of the Theater and Dramatic Criticism, Theater Organization and Management, and Playwriting.

The graduate level program in dramatic and theater arts is incorporated in the program for a master of arts in education. Of the thirty credit hours that are required for the graduate degree, ten credit hours should be taken in drama and two credit hours in interpersonal and mass communications. The graduate drama courses are Aesthetics, Fundamentals of Dramatic Speech, Fundamentals of Play Production, Advanced Acting and Directing, Playwriting Workshop, and Interpretive Reading of Shakespearean Tragedies.

The graduate student who enrolls for a certificate in language teaching must take four credit hours of drama courses out of a total of twenty-four hours of academic work. The student who majors in supervision and administration can elect to take the course Fundamentals of Play Production.

The general-speech, speech-education curriculum was introduced in 1954. This was in response to a directive by the Department of Education to all Philippine educational institutions "to upgrade the teaching of English in the Philippines."

The courses that are offered in this general area are classified as English courses in the Department of English. English 101, which is "to help the student establish a level of competence in the oral language," is required of all incoming freshmen.[23] The course averages about 1,500 students annually. The basic materials are local and American books. Study tapes of the English language recorded by native speakers of the language, educational films distributed by the United States Information Service and also by The Philippine Normal College Philippine Center for Language Studies are also utilized. Speech Arts (English 305) is an elective in the junior year. This course involves the "application of oral skills in different situations as in the oral interpretation of literature, public speaking, interviews and the speech choir." An average number of 225 students enroll in the course each year.

The speech faculty in the English department of the college conduct workshops in speech care for teachers who want to improve their English proficiency, and who want to augment their training in the speech arts.

Other courses in the English department of the Philippine Normal College which relate to speech are Problems in Conversational English, Phonology, Children's Literature and Story Telling, and Laboratory Experiences in English Communication.

The college has a speech laboratory, which is used as a regular classroom, and a laboratory for English speech improvement and for language learning. The speech clinic and recording room provide facilities for carrying out the remedial function of the speech laboratory program. Students who have problems in pronunciation due to dialectal influences, and those who manifest shy or nervous behavior in speaking in front of an audience, are referred to the clinic for assistance.

Cocurricular activities are an integral part of the college program at P.N.C. At least four semester noncredit hours of cocurricular activities are required for graduation. Students should participate in any of the activities of the Senior Arena Theater, Junior Arena Theater, Children's Theater, or the Theater at the Grass Roots. The Tributary Theater, the Speech Choir, and the Speech Club are listed among other clubs and societies on the campus. These clubs provide activities intended "to enrich classroom instruction and to contribute to the education of their respective members."

Another unique program at the Philippine Normal College and at other leading institutions in which there has been an effective combination of speech education and applied linguistics techniques, is the program for learning a second language. A pervading objective of Philippine education has been "to learn how to speak English correctly so that it will be an effective tool for communication within the country and with other countries." Ever since the publication of the survey report on the status of English in the Philippines,[24] the government, through the Department of Education, has directed that there should be a reexamination of the methods of teaching the English language in the Philippines, and a revision of the curriculum if it is indicated.

The Department of Education, which is the central governing body in charge of education in the Philippines, in line with the recommendations made in the survey, issued a directive to upgrade the teaching of the English language in the country. A great number of the schools of higher learning responded to the directive by setting up speech-improvement courses and language laboratories for such purposes. Joint research efforts by Philippine and American scholars resulted in curriculum revisions, materials development, teacher training, and experimental classes on the levels of education. A good number of language teachers and prospective teachers were sent, and are still being sent, to the United States to specialize in second language teaching methods and in speech improvement techniques.

A joint Philippine-American undertaking that sprang up as a result of the survey report is the Philippine Center for Language Studies, which is currently affiliated with the Philippine Normal Colleges. Its primary objective is research on languages and on particular second language techniques that would be applicable to the peculiar problems concerning English language learning in the Philippines. This project is underwritten jointly by the Ford and Rockefeller Foundations.

The United States Educational Foundation in the Philippines, the Asia Foundation, and the Philippine government, in the form of scholarships and travel grants, fellowships, assistantships and/or scholarships from American universities have made it possible for qualified and promising Filipinos to come to the United States to specialize in the field of second language teaching.

In addition to financial aid from these agencies, the individual institutions of higher learning in the Philippines also have some forms of assistance for their respective faculty members in the form of study leaves with pay, or "salaries-in-training," to make it possible for them to further their professional training, particularly in the United States.

SUMMARY

As can be seen from the above discussion, the concept of speech education held in the Philippines is somewhat different from that held in the United States. The principles of applied linguistics and of applied speech correction have been integrated in a unique manner, which can only be interpreted in the Philippine educational setting.

The institutions of higher learning that have been mentioned in this article are only a representative selection of the universities and colleges that list speech courses in their curriculum. The speech curriculums vary from two or three service courses under the general education program to a sufficient number to allow for specialization in the area. The privately controlled universities that have speech courses include the University of the East, Adamson University, Lyceum of the Philippines, University of Manila, and Manila Central University. The Catholic institutions include the University of Santo Tomas and the colleges run by the different missionary orders for young men and young women. These schools are all located in and around Manila. Institutions of higher learning outside Manila are the University of the Philippines College of Agriculture in Los Banos, Laguna, Mindanao State University in Lanao del Sur, the University of San Carlos in Cebu City, and the Central Philippine University in Iloilo City, to mention a few.

About 20 per cent of the current speech faculty in the Philippines who have graduate degrees or specializations in this area are graduates of American universities and colleges. The others are locally trained.

A review of the current speech programs in the Philippines indicates the heavy emphasis on English speech improvement. The speech education program is concerned primarily with the training of teachers to be effective speakers and teachers of English.

Drama and theater courses appear to be the most developed in the speech and drama curriculum. Such courses even antedate the speech improvement and the general speech curricular offerings. This may be a reflection of the Filipino's propensity for the "great show" and his flair for the dramatic.

PROSPECTS FOR THE FUTURE

The speech area which needs to be expanded rapidly is speech pathology. There is an urgent need for clinicians to work in special programs for defectives.

Television courses should also be expanded, now that the Philippines is utilizing the medium increasingly as an entertainment medium, as a communication medium for government and industry, and as a teaching tool.

Facilities, though adequate in some instances, need to be increased and improved to keep abreast of current needs and technological advances.

The concept of speech as communication should be emphasized more in curriculum change and development.

Opportunities for research in all areas of speech in the Philippines are wide open. There is a pressing need for more materials that would reflect the Philippine cultural setting and the Filipino personality.

There is a great demand for graduates who are speech majors. Speech teachers are needed at all levels of instruction. Government and industry need personnel trained in the communication arts. The schools in the Philippines cannot turn out enough graduates to supply the demand.

American institutions of higher learning can share in this exciting phase of development by extending forms of assistance such as fellowships, assistantships, or scholarships to promising graduates of Philippine speech programs; by enabling some of their outstanding speech faculty to go as visiting professors to help develop graduate programs, and by joint cooperative cross-cultural research in the communication arts.

There is no national speech organization in the Philippines comparable to the Speech Association of America. Individual schools have their own speech clubs in which memberships are limited to students and staff of the respective institutions. There is a need for such kind of organization in the islands to serve as a clearing house for the exchange of new ideas and research activities, and as a way of bringing together the experts and the amateurs so the latter can learn from the former in less "forbidding" circumstances.

The future of speech as an academic discipline is optimistic. The tendency to regard speech as a useful tool in the country's efforts to insure the survival of its democratic institutions is a healthy sign.[25]

FOOTNOTES

[1]Unesco-Philippine Educational Foundation, *Fifty Years of Education for Freedom, 1901-1951* (Manila: National Printing Company, Inc., 1953), p. 99.

[2]*Ibid.,* p. 24.

[3]Carl H. Lande, "The Philippines," in *Education and Political Development,* ed. James S. Coleman (Princeton: Princeton University Press, 1965), p. 314.

[4]*Ibid.,* p. 144.

[5]*Ibid.,* p. 144.

[6]*Ibid.,* p. 73.

[7]*Ibid.,* p. 68.

[8]*Ibid.,* p. 313.

[9]Eufronio M. Alip, *Philippine History,* p. 89, as quoted in Carl H. Lande, "The Philippines," in *Education for Political Development,* ed. James S. Coleman (Princeton: Princeton University Press, 1965) p. 69.

[10]Unesco-Philippine Educational Foundation, *Fifty Years of Education for Freedom, 1901-1951* (Manila: National Printing Co., 1953), p. 70.

[11]*Ibid.,* p. 71.

[12]*Ibid.,* p. 100.

[13]*Bulletin of Information* (1965-1966), Ateneo de Manila University.

[14]*Information Bulletin of the Graduate School* (1966), Ateneo de Manila. Additional information about the program was supplied by Rev. John McCarron, S.J., who was former head of the Institute of Languages and Linguistics, Ateneo de Manila University in an interview with him by the author in Washington, D.C., September, 1968.

[15]Information about the speech program at the University of the Philippines was supplied by Dr. Alejandro Casambre, chairman, Department of Speech, University of Philippines, in response to a questionnaire survey sent by the author.

[16]*Bulletin of Information* for the Department of Speech and Drama (1965-1966), Far Eastern University.

[17]*Bulletin of Information* (1964-1965), Siliman University. Other information came from informal conversations with former faculty members.

[18]*Bulletin of Information* (1965-1966), Philippine Women's University.

[19]Information of the P.W.U.'s speech program is from Mrs. Yolanda Yumol-Veloso, who responded to a questionnaire sent by the author, and who was also interviewed by Mrs. Josefa C. Asuncion in Manila.

[20]The survey mentioned here by Mrs. Y. Y. Veloso was conducted by Swanson and Monroe on the teaching of English in the Philippines.

[21]*Bulletin of Information* (1966), Philippine Normal College.

[22]*Ibid.* Additional information about the activities of the organization was also obtained by Mrs. Josefa C. Asuncion in interviews she conducted with some members of the Arena Theater at the Philippine Normal College in Manila.

[23]Information about the general speech education curriculum was furnished by Mrs. Alice Tarampi of the Philippine Normal College in response to a questionnaire sent out by the author, and also in an interview with her conducted by Mrs. Josefa C. Asuncion in Manila.

[24]Clifford Prator, *Language Teaching in the Philippines* (1950). In this report, he comments that "The success of the almost all Philippine education depends at present on the degree of the pupil's command of English, the medium of instruction; and yet that command which by the very nature of things it would be impossible to develop too highly seems to have deteriorated rapidly in recent years," p. 41.

[25]Resource persons for this paper include the following:

Dr. Alejandro Casambre, Chairman, Department of Speech, University of the Philippines, Quezon City, Philippines

Mrs. Alice S. Tirampi, Teacher-in-charge, Speech Laboratory Philippine Normal College, Taft Avenue, Manila, Philippines

Mrs. Yolanda Yumol-Veloso, Acting Director, Institute of Filipino Culture & Foreign Languages, Philippine Women's University, Taft Avenue, Manila, Philippines

Rev. John A. McCarron, Institute of Languages and Linguistics, Ateneo de Manila University, Loyola Heights, Quezon City, Philippines

Mrs. Josefa C. Asuncion, Teacher of English, 2400 Parkway, Cheverly, Maryland

Mr. Florentino G. Ayson, Institute of Arts and Sciences, Far Eastern University, Quezon Boulevard, Manila, Philippines

Mr. Jose Mordeno, Department of Speech, University of Hawaii, Honolulu, Hawaii

Mrs. Arabella Bengson, Department of Speech, University of Hawaii, Honolulu, Hawaii

SPEECH EDUCATION IN SWEDEN

Carol S. Ramsey

INTRODUCTION

The present study views speech education in Sweden from a Swedish perspective, and within that context recognizes the importance of the progress that has been made in the past few years.[1]

SPEECH AND ADULT EDUCATION PROGRAMS: A HISTORIC OVERVIEW

Speech has gained its strongest foothold in the adult schools of Sweden, and since speech education grew out of the development of adult education in Sweden, I shall briefly sketch the significant points in the history of both. Interest in developing adult-education programs reached its zenith during the popular movements at the early part of this century when large groups that did not have the right of suffrage began to seek outlets for their energy and new ways to exert influence on their society. The popular organizations, and the programs they developed to enlighten the uneducated masses of people, form an integral part of Sweden's history. They not only grew with, but also influenced, the industrial, economic, and cultural revolution which led to Sweden's rapid and smooth transition from an agrarian to an industrial society.[2]

The educational programs sponsored by popular groups representing the labor, temperance, and various religious movements took the form of study groups, or *studiecirkel*. The first study group, resembling those currently in existence, was established by the International Order of Good Templars (IOGT) in 1902. Each group consisted of ten or twelve persons who met and discussed social problems, religious and ethical questions, philosophy, history, literature, etc. The study groups were designed to give members of the working classes the greater self-confidence and knowledge they needed to take responsibility in the different activities in the society. This form of adult education played a major role in the development of Sweden's present form of democracy from the hierarchical society that existed then into the early twentieth century.[3] Today the study groups are not limited to the working classes but have their roots in them.

A few years after the establishment of the study groups, special study departments *(studieförbund)* were established within the various groups of the popular movement. The first, and still the greatest, was the Workers' Educational Association, more commonly known as ABF *(Arbetarnas Bildningsförbund).*[4] The Templars, the Christians, and the agricultural movements also founded study departments between 1920 and 1940. Today there are a total of twelve departments in Sweden. In 1947, the State began to contribute to the activities of the study departments, thus making it possible for them to increase the number of study groups, to prepare study materials, to train leaders, and to organize lectures throughout sparsely-populated Sweden.

The first study groups in speech can be traced back to around 1920, when two-week courses were given at Brunnsviks Folkhögskola for leaders of study groups in speech. Public speaking and discussion techniques were taught, but there were no textbooks or written materials available on the subject at that time. As an adjunct to the study groups, and a medium through which more adequate course materials could be provided, the study departments developed correspondence schools. There are two such schools operated by popular organizations: Brevskolan, or the "Letter School," owned by the labor organizations; and Lantbruksförbundets Korrespondensskola, LTK, owned by the agricultural movement.

The first correspondence course in speech was offered in 1929. It utilized a series of study plans incorporating instructions, suggested exercises, and questions for each meeting of the study group. Following each meeting, the group leader sent the students' answers and an evaluative summary of the session to the correspondence school. After several days, these materials were returned to the leader with corrected answers and comments. This method is still used in many study groups, especially where professional teachers and leaders are not available. In this way, a member of the group can function as the leader with the aid of the constantly updated materials provided by the correspondence school. In some study groups, professional teachers utilize correspondence school materials independently from the central school.

All study departments conduct study groups in speech regularly or sporadically, with the course content varying between an emphasis upon voice and diction or public speaking, depending upon the qualifications of the leader. Rektor Sven-Arne Stahre, director of ABF, describes the function of the study groups in speech as "to train the participants' ability to participate in conversations, discussions, and conferences in clubs and organizations, including exercises in how to group one's material during the course of discussion, and how to factually and effectively put forth one's arguments."[5] Most study organizations are interested in making study groups in speech available to as many persons as possible, and for convenience, weekend courses are offered in many different parts of the country. During the study seasons from 1964 through 1967, ABF alone offered 199 study groups in speech in which more than 2,000 persons participated.

Within the temperance movement, especially, there has been a great deal of interest in speech education, and in the 1930s the movement sponsored the first summer courses in speech taught by the wellknown educator, Carl Cederblad. His lectures from the summer courses were published as a book entitled "The Living Word,"[6] the first popular handbook giving practical instruction in the art of speaking to appear in Sweden. During the fifties more speech handbooks and correspondence courses were developed and adapted to modern needs and newer study methods. In 1949, Mrs. Gundel Rende wrote *Tala Bättre!*, or "Speak Better!", the textbook most resembling those used in basic speech courses in the United States. Unable to find other materials, Mrs. Rende wrote the book primarily for her own use in teaching speech classes for ABF and other study departments. Now going into its seventh edition, *Tala Bättre!* has been in use since 1950 in the various types of schools in Sweden, and for many years it has been the most popular speech textbook in the country. In 1956, Brevskolan produced a new correspondence course entitled "The Modern Speaker" *(Den Moderna Talaren)* written by the leader of ABF, Sven-Arne Stahre. The course is still widely used in study groups throughout Sweden.

A survey of adult education in Sweden could not omit the *folkhögskolor,* literally "folk high schools," born in Denmark, which have for more than a century augmented the regular school system and formed a part of the very active free and voluntary popular education movement in Sweden. The *folkhögskola* fulfilled a vital role well into the first half of this century, when a majority of the people received only six years of schooling. Its most important function has been to instruct young people from the countryside in general citizenship, social science, Swedish, mathematics, and leadership.

The *folkhögskolor* limit enrollment to those eighteen years of age and older; there are even some courses exclusively for pensioners. The majority operate as boarding schools and are supported jointly by the State and the various popular groups. One of the most famous *folkhögskolor* is Brunnsvik, which is operated by the labor movement organizations and is the school where many of Sweden's leading politicians in the Social Democratic Party received their education and inspiration. The schools offer two- or three-year courses that are considered essentially nonacademic in nature. The schools are not bound by a national education code, so their offerings are varied. Many schools have specialities such as: theater, music, leadership training, etc. Speech classes are offered sporadically in the folk high schools. However, since literature is usually not included in the study of Swedish, as much as one-third of the time in Swedish classes may be devoted to speech training.

A medium of popular education developed in more recent years is the State-owned Swedish Broadcasting Corporation, which devotes one of its three radio frequencies to educational programming. The first radio course in speech for adults was conducted in 1951, consisting of a series of six weekly broadcasts accompanied by the small textbook entitled *Tala,* or simply "Speak." This first course was written and recorded by pioneer speech educators Stig Hedén, Sven Björklund, and Gundel Rende. A second ten-part radio course was developed in 1963 by Gundel Rende, entitled "Can You Speak?" which included a textbook with the same name.[7] The course was designed primarily for participants in study groups throughout the country and was supported by the study departments, which subsequently bought the recorded programs for use in speech study groups. The course textbook sold approximately 12,000 copies and was recorded on tape for organizations of the blind. The course was regarded as a success, and in the spring of 1964, it was rebroadcast.

Popular education has played a dominant role in Sweden's social development unparalleled in most other countries, and its importance has continued into the present. Each year, it is estimated, 800,000 persons participate in study groups, folk high school courses, and other adult educational activities.[8] The heritage of speech education in Sweden can be found in such programs, for popular organizations recognized early the need for speech training and have incorporated it in their educational programs for more than three decades.

SPEECH IN PUBLIC EDUCATION

Officials of the regular State-owned school system are only beginning to recognize the need for speech training, although Bengt Kinnander, lecturer in Scandinavian languages at Uppsala University, pointed out in an interview that "for twenty years schoolmen have been conscious of the lack of speech education." In these past twenty years, three articles worthy of note have appeared in various editions of the "Association of Teachers of Swedish Yearbook" in an attempt to make administrators and curriculum planners aware of this deficiency. The first of these articles was written in 1949 by Mrs. Rende and entitled "En Svensk Tiger."[9] Employing the ambivalence of the word *tiger,* which in Swedish means "silence" as well as the orange and black feline, the author expressed the need for taming an enemy which was stalking the hallowed academic halls, by including speech training in the public schools. Mrs. Rende's suggestions were followed up by two progressive educators who undertook two experiments and reported their results in subsequent editions of the same journal: Bengt Holmberg, who wrote about his experience with "Public Speaking in the High School."[10] and Erik Yrgard, writing about "A Year's Speech Training,"[11] a program which he undertook in an Uppsala high school *(gymnasium).*

Despite the efforts of these and other educators interested in furthering speech-education programs in the schools, progress has been extremely slow. Research revealed, and several educators I interviewed concurred, that there are three inherent elements hampering the inclusion of speech in Swedish public school curricula on all levels.[12]

Public schools, particularly the basic compulsory schools, place a great deal of emphasis upon learning foreign languages. This has the effect of limiting the number of elective courses a pupil may include in his course of study. Swedish is a language spoken by slightly more than ten million people and has little use outside of Scandinavia, with virtually no significance in world-wide communications. The Swedish people, who travel widely and who are extremely interested in world affairs, must necessarily speak more than one language. For this reason, every pupil compulsorily studies four years of English, and the majority study it for six years. Pupils commonly elect to take a second and third foreign language as well. Most of the university students the writer encountered in Sweden were fluent in two and three languages in addition to their own, and several students spoke five foreign languages.

A second factor hampering speech education in the public schools and universities of Sweden has been their traditional orientation to the so-called academic, or theoretical, studies. Where physical education, art, music, or drama are offered in the comprehensive and high schools, these subjects have received little emphasis and are not elected by many pupils. The universities offer virtually no subjects that could be called "practical." The history and traditions behind European education are partly responsible for this phenomenon: the five Swedish universities are still rather rigidly divided along the lines of the four traditional faculties of medicine, law, philosophy, and theology,[13] and the notion that the university exists solely for the purpose of educating scholars still prevails.

A third, and very practical consideration, is the lack of teachers trained in speech. The national education codes prescribe that the oral as well as the written expression of Swedish should be taught in all grades, yet most teachers have had very limited speaking experience themselves. At best, a teacher may have received a total of eight hours of instruction in public speaking during his or her semester of study at a teachers college.

These three elements have for many years inhibited the inclusion of speech in the curricula of Swedish schools. However, some inroads have been made. Let us turn, then, to a general survey of education in Sweden,[14] focusing upon signs of progress, or potential progress, in introducing speech into the schools of Sweden.

A SURVEY OF EDUCATION IN SWEDEN

The majority of students in Sweden—more than 1,200,000—are enrolled in the free public schools consisting of the *grundskola, gymnasium,* and *fackskola.* The regular school system is supported on the state level and is centrally controlled by the Ministry of Education and Ecclesiastical Affairs through the National Board of Education *(Skolöverstyrelsen).*[15] This agency publishes education codes, or *läroplaner,* for each of the three types of public schools referred to in the chapter. Over the past decade the *Riksdag* (parliament) has approved a great number of changes which have subsequently been introduced into the public schools of Sweden in the interest of modernization and greater flexibility. The present *gymnasium* and *fackskola* are radical reorganizations of those in existence only three years ago. All children now receive nine years of compulsory education, which is incorporated into the modern *grundskola*, introduced in its present form in 1962. The emphasis in reorganization has been upon breaking down the rigid specialization at early levels of schooling which tended prematurely to classify pupils according to long-range educational and vocational goals.

The compulsory *grundskola*, or comprehensive school, offers nine years of education and is divided into three levels: the junior stage (Grades 1-3), the intermediate stage (Grades 4-6), and the senior stage (Grades 7-9). Pupils begin the first stage at seven years of age. During the first six years of *grundskolan*, children are taught all subjects by one class teacher. At the senior stage instruction is given by subject-teachers. At this level all pupils study common subjects for a certain number of weekly periods: thirty and twenty-eight for seventh- and eighth-grade pupils respectively. From five to seven hours are allotted for a group of subjects elected by the individual pupil. These groups of subjects, or "streams" as they are called, consist of courses in a second foreign language or in purely practical subjects such as handicrafts. Considerably more than one-half of the pupils elect to study a second foreign language.[16] In the ninth year, studies are organized entirely by streams. There are nine streams, five theoretical and four practical, as follows:

9 g (theoretical)	is a year of preparation for the gymnasium. The pupils take three foreign languages.
9 h (theoretical)	is mainly a humanistic line, giving a good general education.
9 pr (practical)	is a practical line, offering workshop practice, domestic science, and office and shop practice.
9 t (theoretical)	offers an introduction to technology with the emphasis on mechanical and electrical engineering.
9 tp (practical)	gives a more specialized education than 9 t and aims at prevocational training.
9 m (theoretical)	is a general commercial course with a broad general content.

9 ha (practical)	offers a more specialized commercial training.
9 s (theoretical)	is a line offering social and domestic subjects as a preparation for careers as social workers, nurses, etc.
9 ht (practical)	gives a specialized education in the same field as 9 s but with a rather strong emphasis on work in the home.[17]

Before pupils choose the stream they wish to follow, they are given a thorough orientation by the school authorities in the various courses of study and professions open to them. In addition, it is compulsory for all pupils during their eighth year to have three weeks of practical work experience. Besides helping pupils to choose which stream they will follow in the ninth year, it is felt that this working experience is of great pedagogical value. School authorities have found that pupils, almost without exception, are highly enthusiastic about this experience.[18]

An estimated 25 to 30 per cent of the pupils enter *gymnasium* upon graduation from the *grundskola* for an additional three years of voluntary schooling. The old *gymnasium,* in existence until June 1968, was divided into three types: general, technical, and commercial. The general *gymnasium,* like the last year of *grundskolan,* was organized into streams and terminated with the *studentexam,* the qualifying examination for university entrance. More than 80 per cent of the pupils proceeded to a university or professional school. The technical gymnasium consisted of a four-year course offering seven different curricula, with mechanical engineering, electrical engineering, and building being the most popular. Upon completing his studies, the student received the certificate of *gymnasium* engineer, which had the same value as the *studentexam* but did not qualify him to enter a university. The commercial *gymnasium* offered a specialized course along four lines, and again the pupil received a certificate of completion which did not qualify him to enter a university. The old *gymnasium* was highly specialized. Once a student began his studies in one of its three branches, he could not change to another branch without starting from the beginning. It was this prohibitive specialization and inflexibility that prompted the introduction of Sweden's new *gymnasium* in 1965. However, it was not until May, 1968, when the last *studentexam* was given, marking the end of that 200-year-old tradition, that the transition from old to new *gymnasium* was complete.

The new *gymnasium* offers five general lines of study: arts, political science, science, economics, and technology. The course requires three years to complete, with technology students having the option to continue their studies for a fourth year. With the dissolution of rigid divisions of subjects, students now have a greater choice of courses and the possibility of changing lines of study without being severely penalized. In the new *gymnasium* all students receive the equivalent of a diploma upon completion of their studies, and entrance to the universities will be determined by courses studied and academic achievement.

For graduates of the *grundskolor* not wishing to go to the *gymnasium* but desiring a few years of further education, an entirely new kind of school called *fackskolan,* or continuation school, was added in 1965. The course of study lasts for two years and is intended to provide training on the so-called intermediate level. It is expected that when the *fackskola* is fully operative in 1970, it will absorb 20 per cent or more of the students leaving *grundskolan* each year.[19]

The *fackskolor* are of three types. The social and economic continuation schools provide a general theoretical course of study. The economic school has four separate divisions; however, training here is so little specialized that pupils are able to go on to other more advanced training, or they can, after certain supplementation, enter the *gymnasium.* The technical school also has four divisions: mechanical engineering, electrical engineering, building, and industrial chemistry. The training a pupil receives here is intended to qualify him for the lower types of engineering work. A requirement for completing training in the technical *fackskola* is that the pupil shall have completed at least one year's working experience, which may be served before entering the school or between the first and second school years. Pupils of the technical continuation school also have the option to pass on to *gymnasium.*

SPEECH INSTRUCTION IN
SWEDISH SCHOOLS

With the recent revision of the entire Swedish regular school system, course offerings and pedagogical methods are under close scrutiny and, in some cases, important alterations have already been made. However, speech is not currently taught as a separate subject, nor is it likely to be taught as such for many years to come, in light of the three factors mentioned earlier: (1) the emphasis upon learning foreign languages, which restricts the number of elective subjects a pupil may study; (2) the orientation to the so-called academic and theoretical subjects; and (3) the lack of teachers trained in speech.

The national education codes, or *läroplaner,* for the *grund-skola,*[20] *gymnasium,*[21] and *fackskola*[22] now include subsections on speech under the title devoted to teaching Swedish. Some indication that progress is being made to include speech education in the schools is evidenced by the fact that the section on speech in the 1965 edition of the *Läroplan för Gymnasiet* now covers nearly five pages, compared with only two and a half in the 1960 edition.[23] The *läroplaner* for all three levels of schools prescribe topics and suggest methods for teaching the oral expression of Swedish. For example, the *Läroplan för Grundskola* recognizes "that it is of great importance to the individual to be able to express his thoughts through a relaxed, coherent oral presentation" (p. 141), and suggests simple exercises for teaching oral proficiency in the first six grades similar to those found in elementary schools in the United States. For the first year of instruction the code suggests the following activities (p. 142, G. Rende, trans.):

> Free conversation about the children's experiences and findings, actual happenings, and reading.
>
> Opportunities for every child to tell the class about his own experiences, a dear toy, etc., and show things, for example drawings of his own, together with the speech.
>
> Training in handling everyday speech situations, for example, speaking over the telephone, at the dinner table, in the shops, or on the train.
>
> Simple improvised dramatic expression where children act out what they have read, been told, or invented themselves.
>
> Training in listening to stories, tales, or instructions.
>
> Individual speech correction *(tal- och röstvard).*

In the intermediate grades instruction is broadened to include training and practice in giving short narrative, descriptive, and demonstration speeches; note-taking; simple discussion exercises; interviews; and dramatic improvisations.

On the senior stage of *grundskolan,* and in the *gymnasium* and *fackskolan,* the pupils are taught by subject teachers, and speech instruction is included in Swedish classes. The education code for *grundskolan* prescribes generally that "the teacher should try to take advantage of the natural speech occasions that the daily schoolwork presents, or which can be created by easy means so as to prepare the students for different kinds of presentations." (p. 142) The *gymnasium* code adds:

> Class discussions and conversations in connection with the presentation of the course materials of the different subjects are the best forms of practice in speech. With freer and more independent work forms (group work, study circles), the opportunities to practice the oral proficiency should become even more plentiful. Besides this, however, long-term plans for practice in oral exposition, diction, and speech are needed. (p. 86)

All three *läroplaner* place a great deal of emphasis upon utilization of the natural classroom activities for speech training.

A very comprehensive, if somewhat ambitious, list of speech forms to be covered in teaching the oral expression of Swedish is included in the *läroplaner.* Interpretative reading, expository and argumentative speaking, discussion, interviewing, parliamentary procedure, voice and diction, and speech criticism are all mentioned as areas in which pupils are to receive instruction during the three years of Swedish taught in the senior stage of *grundskolan* and *gymnasium,* or the two years in the *fackskolor.* Many of these areas are dealt with in some length in the *läroplaner,* and specific assignments or instructions are often included. The following paragraph on group discussion is from the *Läroplan för Fackskolan:*

> Discussion practice gives the students a habit of participating in a controlled discussion. If the students have no experience in discussion techniques, it is suitable, for a start, to let a debate be led by two individuals or a group, with the class as listeners in general. The topic of the discussion practice should be of a pressing nature, controversial, and so decisively formulated that the different contributors are able to reach a clear point of view. The regular forms of meeting should be used. The teacher in Swedish should, when needed, make clear the importance of following the rules for a polite exchange of opinions. These are: differentiate between person and object, wait until it is your turn to speak, accommodate yourself to the speaker. The discussion in a class can sometimes degenerate, partly because a couple of students dominate and take most of the time allowed, partly because too many do not want to speak. To get the quiet to speak, or at least give them an opportunity to voice their opinions, the teacher should from time to time initiate the form of discussion which probably is familiar to many from basic school, known as "the beehive." Minutes should be taken at all discussion practices. (p. 85)

Not all forms of speech receive as much attention in the education codes as is given to discussion in the above section. However, in format, the sections on oral expression in the *läroplaner* resemble a much-abbreviated fundamentals of speech textbook.

The emphasis actually given to speech training in Swedish classes reflects the varying natures of the *grundskola, gymnasium,* and *fackskola.* In *grundskola,* the stream in which the student is enrolled will affect the amount of speech training he receives. Literature and writing receive considerably more emphasis in *gymnasium,* which prepares the majority of its students for higher education, than in the *fackskola,* where "a theoretical training in preparation for a practical life"[24] is provided. There is usually greater flexibility in planning the course content for Swedish classes in the *fackskola,* thus allowing more time to be devoted to speech education. All textbooks currently used in Swedish classes in all three public schools include a section on public speaking. Much depends upon each teacher's interest and ability to carry out the intentions of the *läroplaner,* and for the pupils in the schools of Sweden it is largely a matter of chance whether they receive any speech training or not. Many victims of this arbitrary system are recognizing the need for improvement. Mrs. Rende has observed during her years of teaching:

> Most of the students at the universities and teachers' colleges regret that they so seldom during all their previous years in school have received a fundamental training in speech, which would have enabled them to take part in discussions and other activities without feeling inferiority and insecurity. If speech would have been recognized as a separate subject, it would have guaranteed a certain amount of training.

The younger generation of teachers now studying at the teachers' colleges are getting more qualified instruction in handling the oral expression of Swedish as outlined in the *läroplaner,* and, Mrs. Rende has noted, they are, on the whole, more open to the field than were the teachers of the generation before.

SPEECH EDUCATION AT SWEDISH UNIVERSITIES

Approximately one-quarter of the pupils who complete *grundskolan* eventually find their way into one of the institutions of higher education in Sweden. These institutions fall into four categories: universities, technical colleges,[25] teachers' colleges, and arts academies.

There are five universities in Sweden; the oldest one is Uppsala University, which was established in 1477. The universities are organized into faculties, and the majority of the students are enrolled in those faculties offering a liberal arts course similar to that offered by colleges of letters and sciences at major universities in the United States. The degrees offered by this division of study are *Filosofie kandidatexamen (Fil. kand.)*, which is of a higher standard than the American B.A. or B.S. degree;[26] *Filosofie licentiatexamen,* roughly equivalent to the American Ph.D.; and *Filosofie doktorsgrad,* equivalent to post-doctoral work in the United States. University degrees are awarded on a system of points, or *betygs,* each one of which equals at least one semester's work in a prescribed series of courses terminating in a final comprehensive examination. A student officially studies in only one institution, or major-subject department, at a time, although students commonly study other subjects simultaneously to pass comprehensive examinations from institutions in which they were previously enrolled. Students have three chances to take and pass the exams, and there is no time restriction as to when they must complete a *betyg.*

The first degree, the *Fil. Kand.,* requires the completion of six points in at least two subjects with a minimum of two points in each subject, or three points in one of the subjects. These six points may be taken in any combination of subjects as long as they are within the institutions of the college of letters and sciences. For example, a student may have one point each in botany and Finnish and two points each in sociology and history. Beginning in 1969, however, a series of changes which will "Americanize" the Swedish universities will be introduced which will allow only certain combinations of subjects for the *Fil. Kand.* degree.[27]

For those students wishing to become teachers on the senior stage in the *grundskola,* or in *gymnasium* or *fackskola,* a variation of the first degree called *filosofisk ämbetsexamen,* or *Fil. mag.,* must be completed. The *Fil. mag.* also requires six *betygs.* However, two or more of the subjects elected by the student must belong to one of the specified groups of subjects taught in the schools, e.g., English and German, Swedish and history, mathematics and physics, etc. In audition, a course in education *(pedagogik)* is required for the degree of *Fil. mag.*

Very little attention is given to speech education on the university level. There are, however, a few scattered examples that deserve attention. The institutions of Scandinavian languages *(nord-*

iska språk) are where we can find the greatest emphasis on speech training. In the Universities of Stockholm, Goteborg, and Umea there is one speech teacher in the institution, who gives from four to six lectures on voice and diction and works with students of the institution in groups of from ten to fifteen on voice improvement and oral expression. The group work amounts to twelve hours for future teachers of Swedish and slightly less for other students. Sweden's two largest universities, Uppsala and Lund, have a university-wide speech therapist who gives lectures on voice and speech production to students of Scandinavian languages and theology. The therapist makes a voice analysis of each of these students, as well as of other students in the university who feel they require help, and works with those having speech problems. At Lund, study groups in public speaking are also arranged from time to time by the university speech therapist.

As a part of the one-*betyg* course in Scandinavian languages, a class entitled Oral and Written Expression, or stylistics, is required. Here language problems are discussed, with the difference between oral and written Swedish, and aspects of the spoken language as subjects commonly receiving attention. Oral reports are given in class by the students, affording them some opportunity to speak in front of others, even if this is not the main purpose of the course. At Uppsala University, Docent Bengt Kinnander requires each student to give at least one speech in his stylistics course. These speeches are recorded and later criticized and discussed by the class. Although Docent Kinnander and others readily admit the inadequacy of this course for training students in speech, he has to admit that it is the best, if not the only, speech education available to liberal-arts students at Uppsala University. Moreover, only 200 students out of the total of 22,000 in the university are able to take this course each year.

There exists in the universities another institution where a specialized program of speech education, in the very broad sense, is offered. At the universities of Uppsala, Lund, and Stockholm, students can study for *betygs* in an institution of phonetics *(fonetiska institutionen)*. Here, as in all other departments of the universities, the courses are strictly theoretical in nature; no instruction in speech correction is given. Many students, however, enroll in a speech therapy or speech correction course outside the university after completing a *Fil. kand.* with several *betygs* in phonetics. At Uppsala University approximately one hundred students are enrolled in the *Fonetiska Institutionen* per semester.

Brief courses in public speaking are offered in the phonetics departments at Lund and Stockholm. At Stockholm, the chairman of the *Fonetiska Institutionen* is to be credited with requiring all students of the institute to take what is possibly the only course in the schools and universities of Sweden that is devoted entirely to speech, as Americans understand the meaning of the word. Seven sections of this course are taught each semester by Gundel Rende, with each section having an average enrollment of twelve. The course meets for a total of only four hourly sessions, and not every student has the chance to give a speech. There is hope that the length of the course may be extended in the future, but, for the moment, this limited amount of time is rationalized with the well-worn cliche: "It is better than nothing."

Leading educators in Sweden's universities recognize the need for more speech education at the university level. Margita Liljefors, speech therapist of Uppsala University and currently president of the Swedish Association for Teachers of Singing and Speech, stated her conviction, which is more radical than most, in an interview: "A student ought to be able to take a degree in speech as in Greek or *Nordiska språk* ['Scandinavian languages'] ." Mrs. Liljefors has tried single-handedly to induce Uppsala University to sponsor a speech course for potential teachers of Swedish in their last semester of study in Scandinavian languages and a speech institution for teachers with credentials. The latter aim has been partially fulfilled by a university extension course in speech pedagogy, offered at night in Stockholm. So far this one year's course has been completed by two groups of seven students.

In the spring of 1968, a group of professors and instructors, representing the departments of Scandinavian languages, phonetics, and linguistics at four of Sweden's universities, joined the fight for more speech education. The group sent a two-page petition to the University-wide Committee on Courses presenting their rationale for greater emphasis being given to speech in the *Nordiska Språk* institutions. It proposed that one-half of the class hours in one semester be devoted to the following:

Theory
1. Anatomy and physiology of the voice and speech organs.
2. Serious voice and speech defects.
3. Phonology and Swedish pronunciation.
4. Prosody, meter, and style.
5. General speech theory and speech psychology.

Practical
1. Voice and speech improvement; speaking methods.
2. Oral interpretation. Methods.
3. Analysis of tape-recorded material: the standard language in its regional nuances, dialect.
4. Public speaking and dramatics.
5. Seminar practices on selected speech problems and stylistic, semantic, or speech psychology questions.[28]

This petition represents the first united appeal by university educators for speech education. The gears of progress have been engaged, and with the overhaul of the university system currently in progress, the chances for more comprehensive speech education being included in higher education are better than ever before.

THE PREPARATION OF SPEECH THERAPISTS

As mentioned earlier, training for speech therapists, or *logopeds,* is given outside the universities at a type of technical college which holds classes in the phoniatric clinics of two hospitals in Stockholm—Karolinska Sjukhuset and Sabbatsbergs Sjukhus. In order to qualify for the course in speech pathology, which lasts for three semesters, students must have completed a minimum of three *betygs* in phonetics and/or education at one of the universities. Because only twelve students are accepted into the program each semester, competition for places is quite keen. However, due to the great need for speech therapists and the large number of applicants for the program, it is likely that more courses offered at shorter intervals will be started in the next few years. Speech correctionists for the speech clinics in the public school system receive two semesters of training in a course offered each year at the teachers' college in Stockholm. The students are certified teachers from the low and middle stages of *grundskolan.* After completing the course, speech correctionists work with pupils from all three types of public schools.

SPEECH EDUCATION AT TEACHER
TRAINING INSTITUTIONS

The major function of the teachers' colleges *(lärarhögskolor)* is to train subject teachers for the high level of *grundskola* and for *gymnasium* and *fackskolan*. As of the fall, 1968, there were six teachers' colleges in Sweden, located in Stockholm, Uppsala, Malmö, Göteborg, Umea, and Linköping. Students who have received the *Fil. mag.* degree in the subjects they plan to teach spend one semester at the college studying theory and receiving practical teacher training. Under the new study plan that went into effect in the fall of 1968, every prospective teacher is required to have a voice analysis at the beginning of the semester and to attend lectures on voice and diction from a specialist in this area. If necessary, students can follow up the analysis and receive help from the speech correctionist. For the average 250 students enrolled in the teachers' college, the speech correctionist is employed for 600 teaching hours per semester, with part of that time devoted to observing student teachers in the schools. The earlier maximum hours of teaching was 410.

It is now required that public speaking be taught in the teachers' colleges, whereas before it was offered only sporadically. The law states that every student shall receive eight hours of instruction in public speaking, which is to be divided between two hours of lecture and six hours of study in groups of eight students so that they have the opportunity to give short speeches. The speeches given by the students should be based on hypothetical teaching situations, e.g., lecturing to pupils on different school levels, speaking to parents' groups, and leading extracurricular activities. At Stockholm, where there are 250 students attending the teachers' college each semester, the speech teacher has 250 class hours at his disposal. The same proportion is employed at the five other teachers' colleges in Sweden.

SPEECH EDUCATION IN OTHER INSTITUTIONS

Also worth briefly mentioning is the emphasis given to speech in the State-owned academies of music and drama. The Royal Drama School in Stockholm, with only forty-eight students, employs three full-time speech teachers, and the students of the Royal Academy of Music receive voice and diction training for three semesters. The counterparts of these academies in Lund, Örebrö, and Göteborg put similar stress on speech training in their programs. The Swedish Broadcasting Corporation *(Sveriges Radio och Television)* training school in Stockholm also employs a speech teacher.

Summer courses are given in speech each year at *Klosters Röstskola* (Kloster's Voice School), a private school founded in 1914 by Karl Nygren Kloster, which is now operated by members of the Nygren family. Over the years the school has become quite famous as a center for people who want to train their voices and improve their speech and singing. Near midsummer, three or four courses, each of from ten to twelve days' duration, are offered in southern Sweden at a seaside resort, where participants combine voice studies with swimming and other recreation. During the summers of 1967 and 1968, one of the summer sessions was given in Finland for the Swedish-speaking population there. Participants in the courses come from many different professions. The teachers, including the Nygrens themselves, are specialists in the different fields of speech and singing. At the present time Klosters Röstskola provides the only speech courses that are offered consistently and are open to everyone.

PROFESSIONAL ORGANIZATIONS

There are three professional organizations related to speech education in Sweden: Swedish Association for Phoniatrics and Logopedics, The Swedish Association for Speech Therapists, and The Swedish Association for Teachers of Singing and Speech. The first two organizations include members of the various phonetics institutions in Sweden. However, the group that has been the most influential and involved directly with the issue of speech education in Sweden has been the third group, Svenska Sang- och Talpedagog-förbundet, which was formed in 1959, when speech teachers were invited to join the twenty-five-year-old Swedish Singing Teachers' Association. The purpose of the organization is to raise the standards of the arts of speaking and singing and to furnish the schools with qualified teachers. Requirements for membership in the Association are quite strict, and only members have the privilege to use the title "authorized" speech (or singing) teacher. In May 1968, the Association had a membership of fifty-five speech teachers. The majority of these members specialize in voice and diction *(röst- och talvård)* with only sixteen names indicated in the Association's directory as being qualified to instruct groups in public speaking. The Swedish Association for Teachers of Singing and Speech is attempting to make educational authorities aware of the need for a state school to train speech teachers, and it has submitted a proposal for such an institute to the Ministry of Education. At present the Association is the only formally organized group working with the goal of including more speech education at all levels of education in Sweden.[29]

CONCLUSIONS

While the majority of the examples of speech education I have discussed are scattered, and often isolated,it must be emphasized that the number of these incidences is increasing, and they are likely to develop more consistency as existing ideals are put into effect. Movements are now being started by individuals to make educational authorities more aware of the need for speech education in the schools, to the extent that languages will no longer prohibit a pupil from having a chance to receive speech training. Nor will the traditional orientation to the so-called academic subjects exclude speech from Sweden's schools. There has been much progress in the last five years, and in the face of more changes in the Swedish school systems, more progress is likely to be made in the field of speech education. Docent Claes Elert, chairman of the Phonetics Institute at the University of Stockholm, has observed the following about the prospects for speech education in Sweden:

> The ability to express one's self in speech is an important personal asset for every individual. For society in general, it is important that this proficiency be trained and developed. With the ever-increasing educational level, the demand to express and clarify the nuances of an expanded thought-content also grows.
>
> A marked change in the attitude towards this important problem is noticeable in the newer curricula for the schools, where speech is beginning to receive a more prominent place. One looks forward to a broadening of the teachers' education in regard to the teaching of speech, so that the aims of the curricula are put into practice in a satisfying way.

In short, Gundel Runde's Swedish "tiger" is being tamed.

For further information, the following organizations and persons interested in speech may be contacted.

Svenska Sång- och Talpedagogförbundet
(Swedish Singing and Speech Teachers' Association)
Storgatan 44, 114 55 STOCKHOLM Ö

Mrs. Margita Liljefors, President
Brunkebergsgatan 10, 111 52 STOCKHOLM

Svensk Förening för Foniatri och Logopedi
(Swedish Association for Phoniatrics and Logopedics)
Dr. Sören Fox
Foniatriska Kliniken, Allmänna Sjukhuset, MALMÖ

Svenska Logoped Förbundet
(Swedish Association for Speech Therapists)
Logoped Ingrid Westerlund
Foniatriska Kliniken
Sabbatsbergs Sjukhus, Dalagatan 9-11, 113 24 STOCKHOLM

Gunner Bjuggren (medical superintendent) Foniatriska Avdelningen, Sabbatsbergs Sjukhus, STOCKHOLM

Claes C. Elert (chairman) Fonetiska Institutionen, Stockholm Universitet, Hagagatan 23A, 113 47 STOCKHOLM

Stig B. Hedén, Hagagatan 22, 113 48 STOCKHOLM

Bengt Holmberg (university lecturer) Institutionen för Nordiska Språk, Göteborg Universitet, GÖTEBORG: Aschebergsgatan 5, 411 27 GÖTEBORG

Margita Liljefors (speech therapist of the University) Uppsala Universitet, Institutionen för Nordiska Språk, Philologicum, Thunbergsvägen 3C, 752 38 UPPSALA: Brunkebergsgatan 10, 111 52 STOCKHOLM

Marianne Mörner (instructor in speech) Folkuniversitet, STOCKHOLM: Valhallavägen 51, 114 22 STOCKHOLM

Lennart Norman (speech therapist of the University) Lund Universitet, Fonetiska Institutionen, Kävlingevägen 20, 222 40 LUND: Rabyvägen 32A, 223 57 LUND

Åke Nygren (director) Klosters Röstskola, Bergstigen 12, 182 74 STOCKSUND

Ruth Agneta Öslöf (assistant speech therapist of the University) Uppsala Universitet, Övre Slottsgatan 1 nb, 752 20 UPPSALA: Sibyllegatan 30, 114 43 STOCKHOLM

Gundel Rende (instructor in speech) Fonetiska Institutionen, Stockholms Universitet, Hagagatan 23A, 113 47 STOCKHOLM: Gubbkärrsvägen 29/13, 161 51 BROMMA

Hervor Rosén (instructor in speech) Lärarhögskolan, Seminariengatan 1, 752 28 UPPSALA

Kerstin Wibom-Lönnqvist (speech instructor for the Swedish Broadcasting Corporation's Training Program) Besmansvagen 6, 161 43 BROMMA

Claes R. Witting (associate professor phonetics) Fonetiska Institutionen, Uppsala Universitet, Philologicum, Thunbergsvägen 3D, 752 38 UPPSALA; Sturegatan 20B, 752 23 UPPSALA

Erik M. Yrgård (instructor in Swedish) Lärarhögskolan, Seminariegatan 1, 752 23 UPPSALA: Österplan 13, 753 31 UPPSALA

SELECTIVE LIST OF SPEECH-RELATED PUBLICATIONS

Studiecirkel ("study groups")
Hedén, Stig B. *Tala Bra med Egna Ord.* Stockholm: Gebers, 1968.
Rende, Gundel. *Tala Bättre! En Handbok i Muntlig Framställning* 6th rev. ed. Stockholm: Bonniers, 1967.
Stahre, Sven-Arne. *Den Moderna Talaren.* Stockholm: Brevskolan, 1956.

Folkhögskolor ("folk high schools")
Kämpe, Yngve. *Talaren.* Stockholm: LTs Förlag, 1951 (used for reference only).
Rende. *Tala Bättre!*

Gymnasium and *Fackskolor*
Brodow, B., S. G. Edqvist, C. Kavaleff, and G. Öh. *Svenska för Gymnasiet.* 3 eds. Stockholm: Biblioteksförlaget, 1966, 1967, 1969 (most popular Swedish textbook for *gymnasium*)
Holmberg, Bengt and Verner Ekenvall. *Svenskan i Tal och Skrift.* 3 eds. Stockholm: Svenska Bokförlaget-Norstedts, 1966, 1967, 1968.

Nordiska Sprak Institutionen, Uppsala Universitet
Hedén, Stig G. *Att Tala med Framgang.* 2nd ed. Stockholm: Tullbergs, 1957 (currently out of print).
Holmberg, Bengt and Margita Liljefors. *Att Läsa Högt.* Stockholm: Svenska Bokförlaget-Norstedts, 1963.
Rende. *Tala Bättre!*

Fonetiska Institutionen, Stockholms Universitet
Holmberg, Bengt and Margita Liljefors. *Talvard.* 5th ed. Stockholm: Svenska Bokförlaget-Norstedts, 1966.
Rende. *Tala Bättre!*

Periodical Publications
Modersmalslärarnas Förening. Arsskrift. (Yearly publication of the Association of Teachers of Swedish.)

Nordisk Tidsskrift for Tale og Stemme. (Phoniatrics journal published in Denmark.)
Svenska Landsmal och Svenskt Folkliv. (Journal of linguistics, dialectology, and folklore established in 1878.)

FOOTNOTES

[1] The author was aided greatly in the preparation of this chapter by comments and information supplied by Mrs. Gundel Rende, instructor of speech for the Phonetics Institute of Stockholm University and the Stockholm Teachers College. Mrs. Rende attended the University of Kansas in 1947, where she spent one semester intensively studying speech. She is a leading authority on speech education in Sweden, and author of the textbook *Tala Battre!*

[2] See Ingvar Andersson, "Social Change and Industrialization," *Swedish History in Brief,* trans. Nils G. Sahlin and Marjorie Lundin (Stockholm, 1965), pp. 31-38.

[3] *Ibid.,* p. 34.

[4] During the nine-month study season, 1966-67, ABF conducted a total of 48,008 study groups with 447,091 participants. This represents a substantial increase over the 1964-65 total of 36,966 study groups and 347,015 participants.

[5] Kathy Shull, trans.

[6] Carl Cederblad, *Det Levande Ordet,* (5th ed. rev.; Stockholm, 1955.)

[7] Gundel Rende, *Kan Du Tala?* (Stockholm, 1963).

[8] Jonas Orring, *The School System of General Education in Sweden* (Stockholm, 1967), p. 13.

[9] Rende, "En Svensk Tiger: Några Synpuncter på Undervisningen i Muntlig Framstallning," *Modermalslärarnas Förening (Årsskrift,* 1949).

[10] Bengt Holmberg, "Muntlig Framställning på Gymnasiet" *(Årsskrift:* 1955-56).

[11] Erik Yrgard, "Ett Års Talarträning" *(Årsskrift,* 1957-58).

[12] Orring, *op. cit.,* p. 9.

[13] In recent years the faculty of philosophy has split to form the additional faculties of social sciences, natural sciences, and economics. The degrees awarded by the universities, however, retain the names of the traditional faculties, i.e., *Filosofie kandidatexamen, Juris kandidatexamen, Teologie kandidatexamen, Medicine kandidatexamen.*

[14] For a more detailed analysis of the public school system see Orring, *op. cit.,* available upon request from The Swedish Institute, Box 3306, 103 66 STOCKHOLM 3 Sweden.

[15] Current plans call for a transfer of responsibility for the entire school system, with the exception of special schools, progressively to the communes. Orring, *op. cit.,* p. 3.

[16] All pupils in *grundskola* are required to study English in grades 4 through 7; from 80 to 85 per cent voluntarily continue their study for two additional years.

[17] ERGO International, *The Intellectual Face of Sweden,* ed. Timo Kärnekull (Uppsala, 1964), p. 19; also Orring, *op. cit.,* p. 7.

[18] Orring, *op. cit.,* p. 8.

[19] *Ibid.,* p. 5.

[20] Skolöverstyrelsens Skriftserie 60, "Lyssna Se och Tala," *Läroplan för Grundskolan* trans. Kathy Shull (Stockholm, 1962), pp. 141-144.

[21] Skolöverstyrelsens Skriftserie 80, "Muntlig Framställning," *Läroplan för Gymnasiet* trans. Kathy Shull (Stockholm, 1965), pp. 86-90.

[22] Skolöverstyrelsens Skriftserie 81, "Muntlig Framställning," *Läroplan för Fackskolan* trans. Kathy Shull (Stockholm, 1965), pp. 83-86.

[23] Kungliga Skolöversstyrelsens Skriftserie 36, *Kursplaner och Metodiska Anvisningar för Gymnasiet* (Stockholm, 1960).

[24] Orring, *op. cit.,* p. 5.

[25] Fields of study requiring a primarily practical education, such as dentistry, economics, technology, pharmacology, agriculture, veterinary medicine, and forestry, are taught in technical colleges which are entirely separate from the universities.

[26] Swedish students enter the universities from the *gymnasium* where they receive a comprehensive liberal arts education roughly equivalent to that required in the United States for the associate of arts degree given by the junior colleges. Accordingly, the *kandidatexamen* degree of the universities, which takes a minimum of three years to complete, is valued as slightly higher than an American bachelor of arts or bachelor of sciences degree. For a more detailed account of university degrees in Sweden see ERGO International, p. 19.

[27] Thirty-four lines which combine two and three related subject fields, e.g., psychology, sociology, and education, are suggested in the tentative plans published by Universitetskanslersämbetet, 1968.

[28] C. Ramsey, trans.